QuickBoo

for the Restau

QuickBooks®
for the Restaurant

Stephanie Murphy

Alisa Robertson Neuneker

WILEY

John Wiley & Sons, Inc.

For general information on our other products and services, or technical support, please contact our Customer Care Department within the United States at 800-762-2974, outside the United States at 317-572-3993 or fax 317-572-4002.

Wiley also publishes its books in a variety of electronic formats. Some content that appears in print may not be available in electronic books.

For more information about Wiley products, visit our Web site at http://www.wiley.com.

Library of Congress Cataloging-in-Publication Data:

Murphy, Stephanie.
    Quickbooks for the restaurant/Stephanie Murphy, Alisa Robertson Neuneker.
      p. cm.
   Includes index.
    ISBN 978-0-470-08518-9 (paper/cd)
     1. Restaurants—Accounting. 2. QuickBooks. I. Neuneker, Alisa Robertson. II. Title.
  HF5686.H75M87 2010
  657'.8375028553—dc22
                                                      2008033317

Printed in the United States of America

10 9 8 7 6 5 4 3 2 1

Contents

Preface

Food and beverage operators perform and oversee multiple operational tasks, such as purchasing inventory and equipment; recruiting, hiring, and training staff; producing menu items; and servicing guests. Restaurant operators must also be mindful of many other challenges, including increased competition, controlling food and labor costs, building customer loyalty, consistently producing a quality product, and providing excellent service. Given the time required to perform these functions, monitoring the finances of the restaurant may not be a top priority. For financial success, it is important to efficiently track and record business transactions and to generate financial data on sales, variable and fixed expenses, and other data. Financial statements should be prepared on a timely basis so that the restaurant operator can analyze current data and make appropriate business decisions in a timely manner. Restaurant operators should have the necessary resources available to determine the financial position of the restaurant at any given point in time. Tracking past and present transactions will establish a financial history, an essential tool that will allow restaurant operators to plan and predict the future performance of the restaurant.

Using Accounting Software in the Food and Beverage Industry

QuickBooks Accounting Software is a cost-effective software solution that meets the needs of various types of industries, including restaurants. The software is easy to use and can be customized to meet the needs of individual restaurant operations. When used properly QuickBooks can assist management in producing real-time financial data that can help operators with day-to-day functions and enable them to make informed short- and long-term operational decisions. Much progress has been made over recent years in the development of new software and software integration. Integrating a point-of-sale system with accounting software (and inventory software, if not using QuickBooks inventory) enables managers to track their costs daily, monitor sales and inventory, produce financial reports, provide an up-to-date cash flow status, and fulfill a host of other necessary business functions. These tools can contribute to the overall financial and operational success of the restaurant in a highly competitive market.

Special Features

QuickBooks for the Restaurant takes a step-by-step, hands-on approach to instruct readers on how to record daily business transactions for a restaurant. For purposes of this book, we have created a table service restaurant named "Aroma Ristorante" to enable users to apply the skills and concepts to a realistic (albeit fictional) example. We have designed transactions to simulate daily operations similar to this type of restaurant.

Each chapter provides detailed instructions and immediate application of various QuickBooks functions. A comprehensive project, simulating one month of financial activity of a restaurant, is included at the end of the book. This project supports the key skills and concepts in the text.

The comprehensive project reinforces accounting principles and managerial decision making. Readers will generate transactions for Aroma Ristorante using QuickBooks software. You can choose between two options—either recording business transactions and generating and analyzing reports for the third month of an existing restaurant operation, or recording business transactions and generating and analyzing reports for your own start-up restaurant. Transactions are outlined on a weekly basis. After recording transactions in QuickBooks, you will prepare financial statements, analyze the statements, and make recommendations based on your findings.

In addition to demonstrating how to use an accounting software package, the hands-on comprehensive project can help facilitate student learning of accounting topics introduced in the classroom. This hands-on project will keep students actively engaged. By completing the comprehensive project, readers gain a better understanding of the entire accounting cycle.

Accounting Tips provide students with a review of accounting concepts and demonstrate their relevance to a particular QuickBooks feature.

Helpful Tips provide students with additional information as it relates to the material.

Industry Facts provide information on current industry trends and practices. Industry interviews with prominent industry professionals provide insight into the many advantages of using QuickBooks software in the industry.

Instructional Guides provide assistance with data entry.

QuickBooks Tips highlight certain functions of QuickBooks and identify additional software features, functions, and alternate methods of performing tasks.

This text is designed to be used in conjunction with QuickBooks chapter data files, which are included on QuickBooks Pro the CD-ROM that accompanies this book. These files are QuickBooks Pro 2008 and 2009 data files that should be used with QuickBooks software. These files will enable the reader to engage in hands-on activities that are designed to meet the objectives outlined in each chapter. Data files are available for each chapter of the text. These data files were created to reduce the amount of data entry required and to allow the individual to focus on the specific learning objectives within the chapter. They also allow flexibility for instructors to complete each chapter sequentially or to select individual chapters that are relevant to their individual course objectives.

When prompted at the beginning of each chapter, students should download the chapter data file and use the file to follow the step-by-step instructions. Practice problems are provided at the end of each chapter.

This text is designed to expose the user to QuickBooks functions that can be used in the operation of a table service restaurant. Readers will record transactions for a fictitious restaurant named Aroma Ristorante. All information, including vendor, employee, and customer names, addresses, and phone numbers, used in this text is QuickBooks Pro fictitious.

This text can be used with multiple versions of QuickBooks. The step-by-step instructions included in this book follow QuickBooks Pro 2008 and 2009. QuickBooks offers a new version of the software each year. The primary functions of the different versions of the software are fundamentally similar so other versions of QuickBooks can be used along with this text. Chapter data files provided along with this text are available for QuickBooks Pro 2008, 2009, and future versions of QuickBooks Pro. Updated chapter data files and instructions for using **QuickBooks for the Restaurant** with future versions of QuickBooks software will be available at this book's companion web site, *www.wiley.com/college/murphy.*

Audience

QuickBooks for the Restaurant can be used as a supplemental resource for a financial and managerial accounting course, computer course, or as a resource for a food and beverage professional. Individuals using this text should have a basic business background as well as an understanding of basic accounting concepts. Computer skills are also needed in order to achieve an optimal learning experience. This text reinforces previously learned accounting principles and financial statement analysis by exposing the reader to one of the most widely used accounting applications on the market today. Special emphasis has been placed on critical thinking and decision making, requisite traits of successful managers in the restaurant industry.

This book's unique approach to learning QuickBooks software and reinforcing accounting principles as they relate to a restaurant's operation can easily be incorporated into several different courses by using many of the resources provided with the text—in particular, the CD-ROM, which allows users to take full advantage of the step-by-step approach in the book. Readers enter business transactions into QuickBooks using the chapter data files provided on the CD.

Some of the culinary and hospitality courses where *QuickBooks for the Restaurant* could be used as a primary or supplemental textbook include:

- **Accounting lab:** *QuickBooks for the Restaurant* can reinforce classroom instruction in an accounting lab. Students can immediately apply the skills and concepts to a realistic restaurant operation during an accounting lab period.

- **Managerial or financial accounting:** *QuickBooks for the Restaurant* chapters can be used individually to introduce or reinforce accounting concepts. Hands-on activities can be used to enhance accounting topics covered in the course. This book can also be used as a comprehensive project at the end of the course. The project would assist with tying accounting principles together and reinforcing the objectives for an entire course.

- **Computer course or computer lab:** *QuickBooks for the Restaurant* can be used to assist in meeting objectives in a computer software application course.

QuickBooks for the Restaurant is a useful resource for restaurant owners and operators with limited accounting knowledge, resources, and time. This text provides easy-to-read, step-by-step instructions along with visuals on how to set up a restaurant, process business transactions, and generate financial reports.

Overview of This Book

Each chapter provides chapter objectives, step-by-step instructions, and end-of-chapter practice problems. The practice problems reinforce concepts covered in each chapter.

Chapter 1 provides an overview of QuickBooks, a profile of Aroma Ristorante which is used throughout the book, tips on how to use the QuickBooks Help feature, and instructions on how to use the chapter data files.

Chapter 2 creates a company file for a start-up restaurant by following the steps outlined in the Easy Step interview, backs up and restores QuickBooks files, establishes company preferences, and outlines the steps for setting up QuickBooks to manually process payroll.

Chapter 3 identifies and creates essential lists, such as a customer list, a vendor list, and the chart of accounts necessary for processing transactions for the restaurant.

Chapter 4 covers functions used to order, receive, and pay for goods and services. You learn how to track and adjust inventory items, prepare reports to assist in purchasing, and make payment decisions.

Chapter 5 covers functions used to record customer estimates, sales, and advance deposits; receive payment from customers; and manually or electronically transfer financial information from the point-of-sale software into QuickBooks.

Chapter 6 identifies various payroll options available to restaurant operators, provides information on how to use the software to create and manage employee records, and explains how to manually process payroll.

Chapter 7 identifies the steps in the accounting cycle and how to record the necessary adjustments at the end of the accounting period.

Chapter 8 generates financial reports such as the Profit & Loss Statement, the Balance Sheet, and the Statement of Cash Flows, and reviews useful methods and tools to assist in the analysis of financial data.

Chapter 9 provides an overview of an operating budget and how to create a budget and prepare budget reports.

Chapter 10 describes the year-end closing process and federal tax forms, such as Form 940: Employer's Annual Federal Unemployment Tax return; Form W-2: Wage and Tax Statement; and Form 1099 MISC: Miscellaneous Income.

Chapter 11 covers other restaurant operating functions, such as managing fixed assets, recording gift certificate transactions, and preparing bank reconciliations.

Chapter 12 contains a complete, hands-on project allowing learners to apply accounting and QuickBooks skills and concepts to a restaurant. The project also reinforces analytical skills necessary for successful business decisions.

Student Features

QuickBooks for the Restaurant provides step-by-step instructions on how to perform tasks in QuickBooks. This easy-to-read guide and CD provide users with multiple opportunities to practice QuickBooks functions through end-of-chapter practice problems and online problems.

In the comprehensive project, users are provided with weekly real-life restaurant-related transactions. These transactions reinforce the skills outlined in the book by requiring readers to record the transactions independently and at their own pace. Readers can see how seemingly independent day-to-day transactions result in financial statements and how to use these statements to make business decisions.

Supplementary Materials

An Instructor's Manual (ISBN 978-0-470-25730-2) is available to assist instructors in incorporating the text and comprehensive project into their courses. Instructors can incorporate a realistic, hospitality-related project that exposes their students to QuickBooks software, reinforces accounting principles, and incorporates critical thinking skills. The project can be the application component to accounting concepts.

The Instructor's Manual includes a sample syllabus, a complete data file for the entire book, solutions to chapter problems, a solutions guide to the comprehensive project, additional online problems, restaurant industry data, project tips, and other resources. These resources can also be accessed at the book's companion web site at *www.wiley.com/college/murphy.*

Acknowledgments

We offer a special note of thanks to our families, especially, Brant, Zach, Emma, Jeffery, Damone, and Janelle. Thank you for your support, patience, and understanding.

Without the insight and contributions from the following individuals, this book would not have been completed: Dr. David L. Robertson, William Oleksinski, Michael DeWeese, Susan Wysocki. Thank you for your assistance and suggestions.

We also appreciate Dr. Kathy Merget, Dr. Peter Rainsford, and Dr. Denise Bauer for providing us with time, resources, and encouragement throughout the writing of this book.

We would like to thank the reviewers who provided feedback on this book in its various stages of development:

Michael Petrillose, SUNY Delhi, NY

Gregory Charles, Western Culinary Institute, OR

Marsha Huber, Otterbein College, OH

Ronald Jordan, University of Houston, TX

Introduction

About This Book

QuickBooks for the Restaurant is a step-by-step guide written expressly for current and future food and beverage operators. It provides detailed instructions and immediate application of various QuickBooks functions. The book guides the reader through a series of activities, including setup of a restaurant's company file in QuickBooks; daily business transactions for a restaurant, including purchases, payables, sales, receivables, and payroll; and the preparation of financial statements. Practical, realistic, industry-specific scenarios are used throughout this book to reinforce the reader's understanding and application of the topics covered. Each chapter provides chapter objectives, step-by-step instructions, and end-of-chapter practice problems. Helpful Tips, QuickBooks Tips, Accounting Tips, and Food and Beverage Industry Facts are also included in many chapters. The practice problems reinforce concepts covered in each chapter. A comprehensive project, simulating one month of financial activity of a restaurant, is included at the end of the book. This project supports the key skills and concepts in the text. Individuals using this text should have a basic business background as well as an understanding of basic accounting concepts. Computer skills are also needed in order to achieve an optimal learning experience from the topics covered in the text. This text reinforces previously learned accounting principles and financial statement analysis while exposing the learner to one of the most widely used accounting applications on the market today. Special emphasis has been placed on critical thinking and decision making necessary for individuals to become successful managers in the restaurant industry.

This text is not a comprehensive guide of all the features and capabilities of the QuickBooks software. It is designed to expose the learner to QuickBooks functions most relevant to the operation of a modern restaurant.

Throughout this text, readers will "operate" a fictitious restaurant named Aroma Ristorante, which is located in Capital City, New York. Aroma Ristorante is a table service restaurant that operates as a privately held corporation. The restaurant provides a lunch and dinner menu, a full-service bar including wine selections, as well as off-site catering. Aroma Ristorante sells a variety of retail items, including cookbooks and specialty food items.

RESTAURANT PROFILE	
Name:	Aroma Ristorante, Inc.
Location:	Capital City, New York
Type:	Northern Italian
Hours of operation:	Lunch and Dinner Served Daily, Tuesday through Sunday, 11:00 AM –11:00 PM (Kitchen closes at 10:00 PM)
Number of seats:	122
Number of employees:	13
Projected check average:	Lunch $19.00 Dinner $32.00
Projected weekly covers:	550
Services provided:	Lunch and dinner menu, full-service bar, wine list, take out, off-site catering
Retail items sold:	Cookbooks, specialty food items, etc.
Projected food vs. beverage sales:	70%, 30%
Type of business organization:	Corporation (privately held)
Operating cycle:	Calendar year
Business start date:	January 1, 2008
Employee benefits:	Health and dental benefits start upon employment for full-time employees. Both the company and the employee contribute. No retirement benefits are offered. Sick and vacation paid time off begins at 90 days of employment for full-time employees. Payroll tax calculations include tip income, and tips are disbursed daily and are not included in employee paychecks.

While generally most restaurants outsource their payroll functions, this text provides readers with a comprehensive set of instructions to manually process payroll. Chapter 6 outlines the various levels of payroll services offered by Intuit, the company that provides software products including QuickBooks.

Numerous software solutions are available for food and beverage operators. These include front of house applications, such as point-of-sale systems, and back of house applications, including accounting and inventory management software. Many of these software solutions meet the needs of a variety of businesses, while others are industry-specific software. QuickBooks is used by many types of businesses and can be customized to meet the specific needs of each business. QuickBooks is a user-friendly, cost-effective option for computerized accounting. QuickBooks files can be customized to meet the needs of different types of food and beverage operations, including table service and quick service restaurants, bars, and catering operations.

QuickBooks Versions

Intuit offers Simple Start, Pro, Premier, Enterprise, and Online versions of QuickBooks software. See *www.intuit.com* for details on each version. This text uses QuickBooks Pro 2009. This version is suitable for restaurants with fewer than twenty employees and annual sales of less than $1 million. QuickBooks offers annual updates to each version of the software. These updates to the software are forward compatible. QuickBooks files can be upgraded to newer versions, but newer files cannot be used with older versions of QuickBooks. The primary functions of the different versions of the software are fundamentally similar. This text can still be used with other QuickBooks versions in addition to Pro 2009.

QuickBooks Data Files—Using Data Files Along with This Text

This text is designed to be used in conjunction with QuickBooks chapter data files. These files will enable the learner to engage in hands-on activities that are designed to meet the objectives outlined in each chapter. It is necessary for learners using this text to access the QuickBooks data files from the CD that accompanies this book or download the files from the web site. Data files are available for most chapters of the text. When prompted at the beginning of each chapter, you should download the chapter data file and use the file to follow the step-by-step instructions. These data files were created to reduce the amount of data entry required and allow the user to focus on the specific learning objectives within the chapter. Use of the data files allows flexibility by enabling you to focus on specific areas within the text. We strongly suggest that you use the data files and complete each chapter in sequential order.

Data files for certain versions are available online. Check *www.wiley.com/college/murphy* for additional data files.

Overview of QuickBooks Software

Open the QuickBooks software.

Click **Start.**

Click **All Programs.**

Click **QuickBooks.**

Click **QuickBooks Pro.**

In the No Company Open window, click the **Open or Restore an Existing Company** icon.

In the What Type of File Do You Want to Open or Restore? window, select **Open a Company File** and then click **Next.**

Navigate to the location where you saved the downloaded data file.

Select **AromaRistorante.QBW.**

Click **Open.**

QUICKBOOKS TIP

QuickBooks uses two types of file extensions, .QBW and .QBB:

- **QuickBooks Working File .QBW:** A QuickBooks company file.
- **QuickBooks Backup File .QBB:** An additional, compressed file that is created for use when a working QuickBooks file is compromised. Backup files should be stored in a location separate from the working file. Backup files must be restored using the QuickBooks application prior to use.

After opening the company file, the QuickBooks Home page is displayed on the desktop. This Home page displays an overview of the major components of the business cycle. These components are broken up into the following sections: Vendors, Customers, Employees, Company, and Banking (see Figure 1-1).

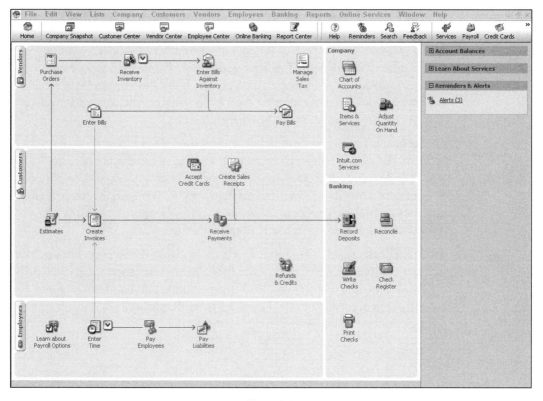

Figure 1-1.

Several of these sections display a flow chart showing the natural progression of the major tasks in each area. It is not necessary to perform these tasks in sequential order. They can be performed in the order most beneficial to the needs of the restaurant operator.

Explore the following sections by clicking the Customer Center, Vendor Center, Employee Center, and Report Center icons.

Customer Center

Information and transactions for all customers are located in the Customer Center, which can be accessed and edited by using the drop-down lists or by clicking specific tabs or icons. The Customers & Jobs tab displays a list of customers, customer information, and balances. The Transactions tab displays a history of customer transactions, such as estimates, invoices, and payments received. New customers and transactions are entered using the Customer Center. Various customer-related reports can be generated from the Reports Center.

Vendor Center

Information and transactions for all vendors are located in the Vendor Center, which can be accessed and edited by using the drop-down lists or by clicking specific tabs or icons. The Vendors tab displays a list of vendors, vendor information, and balances. The Transactions tab displays a history of vendor transactions, such as purchase orders, bills, and checks. New vendors and transactions are entered using the Vendor Center. Various vendor-related reports can be generated from the Reports Center.

Employee Center

Employee information is located in the Employee Center, which can be accessed and edited by using the drop-down lists or by clicking specific tabs or icons. The Employees tab displays a list of employees and employee information. The Transactions tab displays specific transactions for payroll activities such as paychecks and liability checks. Various employee-related reports can be generated from the Reports Center.

Report Center

All QuickBooks reports can be easily generated from the Reports Center. This includes company reports such as the Profit & Loss, Balance Sheet, Statement of Cash Flows, and Tax Reports. Customer, vendor, and employee reports can also be generated from the Reports Center. Reports can be customized to meet the unique needs of an individual restaurant.

Importance of the Accounting Process to the Restaurant Manager

What do aircraft manufacturers, accounting firms, used car dealerships, pizza parlors, and florists all have in common? They all share a common business language: the language of accounting. The foundation on which every business operates is the recording and reporting of its sales, expenses, and net profit or loss. When any business owner or manager responds to the question "How is your business doing?" the answer is most often expressed in financial terms: "Our sales are up," "Our new products have been well received in the market," "We are experiencing higher turnover this quarter," and so on. All of these responses are a direct reflection of the financial challenges and opportunities in every business. It is imperative for successful restaurant operators to understand financial reports, use the information to enable better management decisions, and take ownership of the financial performance of the operation.

Restaurant operators focus on menu items, controlling costs, customer attraction and retention, supplier relationships, and employee relations issues.

Each of these challenges, and a restaurant operator's response to them, is affected by or has an impact on the financial structure of the business. Menu items drive inventory costs; the location of the restaurant affects the rent or lease expenses of the operation; and turnover drives recruiting and training costs. The list of examples is endless.

Restaurant operators can be overwhelmed by the complexity and details of finance, and, as a result, they do not give this critical issue the time and attention it deserves and requires. Business operators may focus on things they know best and ignore things with which they are less familiar. In the case of accounting, a lack of attention can be fatal to any business. QuickBooks can provide the appropriate tools to allow a business operator to focus on customers, employees, and the local marketplace with the confidence that all the necessary and important financial data are being collected and reported in a timely fashion. Accurate and timely data allow a restaurant operator to adjust the business to the inevitable changes in the marketplace. This information allows a restaurant operator to make timely changes to better serve customers, maintain required compliance and tax data, and keep an accurate analysis of the performance of the operation. An easy to use, accurate, and current set of financial and operational reports from QuickBooks will enable a restaurant operator to confidently adopt the universal language of accounting. QuickBooks can turn the mystery and overwhelming process of accounting and financial reporting into the most valuable resource for the restaurant.

Obtaining QuickBooks Help

Several options are available to obtain help with QuickBooks. Some of these options are identified below.

QuickBooks Help Using Search

QuickBooks will search its database and return related topics. The returned data will include step-by-step instructions on how to perform a specific task or will give the user further details on a QuickBooks topic. You can print this information by clicking the Print Topic icon.

Accessing This Tool

Click the **Help** drop-down menu.

Click **QuickBooks Help** from the menu.

Click the **Search** tab.

Type in keywords related to your question and click the **Arrow** icon (see Figure 1-2).

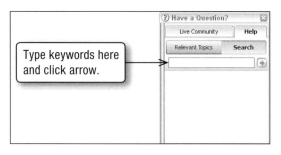

Figure 1-2.

Learning Center Tutorials (Audio and Internet Connection May Be Required)

Users can watch and listen while QuickBooks Tutorials communicate features and step-by-step instructions on how to perform tasks. Learning Center categories include: QuickBooks Installation, Update and Conversion, Working with a Data File, Journal Entries and Accounting Tasks, Paying Bills and Managing Vendors, and Receiving Money and Managing Customers. Each category includes several video tutorials related to the topic.

QuickBooks Coach (Audio and Internet Connection May Be Required)

QuickBooks Coach is a tool that walks a user through business transactions located on the Home page's flowchart. Coach communicates tips on how to use QuickBooks to meet individual business needs and provides tutorials to explain how to perform certain transactions.

QuickBooks Live Community

Users can find answers to questions by accessing the live community. Resources include QuickBooks forums, blogs, and a library.

Turning Coach and/or Live Community On/Off

Click the **Edit** drop-down menu.

Click **Preferences.**

Click **Desktop View** from the menu on the left side of the window.

Click the **My Preferences** tab.

Select (or clear) the **Show Coach window and features and/or Live Community** option.

Using Coach

Click either **View Tutorials** or **View Coach Tips** located on the top-right of the desktop. Tutorials provide information on how to use the features of QuickBooks and how to perform specific QuickBooks functions. The Coach Tips feature provides further detail and tips on how to use the business functions located on the Home page's flowchart.

Aroma Ristorante's Operating Processes and Activities

Each restaurant operator may use different features and functions of QuickBooks to best meet their individual needs. For users to fully understand how and why the software is used to meet the needs of Aroma Ristorante, it is important to identify the operating processes and activities of this restaurant. The following is an outline of Aroma Ristorante's operating processes and activities.

Aroma Ristorante's Purchases and Payables

Fixed Assets

Fixed assets (over $1000 value) must be added to the Fixed Asset Items list → Purchase Orders Created → Goods are Received and Recorded in Fixed Asset Account → Purchase Order turned into Bill → Bills are Paid

Food and Beverage

Items (including cost) must be added to the Items list as Inventory Parts → Purchase Orders Created → Goods are Received and Recorded in Inventory Account → Purchase Order turned into Bill → Bills are Paid

Retail Items

Items (including cost) must be added to the Items list as Inventory Parts → Purchase Orders Created → Goods are Received and Recorded in Inventory Account → Purchase Order turned into Bill → Bills are Paid

Other Purchases

Noninventory Items (such as floral arrangements or office supplies) are purchased by Entering Bill and Paying Bills or Writing Checks.

Aroma Ristorante's Sales and Receivables

Food and Beverage Sales

Sales transactions are recorded via a point-of-sale system. Using a point-of-sale report, data is recorded in QuickBooks using a journal entry. Inventory levels are adjusted at month end, and the related cost of goods sold is recorded by adjusting the quantity on hand

Retail Sales

Sales transactions are recorded via a point-of-sale system. Using a point-of-sale report, data is recorded in QuickBooks using a journal entry. Inventory levels are adjusted at month end, and the related cost of goods sold is recorded by adjusting the quantity on hand

Catering Sales

Catering food and beverage items (including selling price) are added to the Items list as service items → Catering customers must be added to the Customer list → Estimates can be created → Estimates can be turned into Customer Invoices or Customer Invoices can be created without Estimates → Customer Payments are received and recorded

Employees

QuickBooks must be set up to manually accept payroll → Payroll setup must be completed → Employee list must be created including payroll and compensation information → Hours worked and applicable deductions are entered → Paychecks are created

Setting Up Your Restaurant in QuickBooks

Chapter Outline

EasyStep Interview—Creating a New Company File

Backing Up and Restoring QuickBooks Files

Establishing Company Preferences

Setting Up an Additional Bank Account

Recording Opening Balances

Setting Up QuickBooks to Manually Accept Payroll

EasyStep Interview—Creating a New Company File

The purpose of the EasyStep Interview is to create and customize a QuickBooks working file. During the EasyStep Interview, various questions are asked about the business; QuickBooks customizes a company file based on the user's responses. Files can be further customized to meet an organization's needs by turning functions on or off using the Company Preferences Feature, which is discussed later in the chapter. Not all functions need to be established during the initial file setup; they can be set up or altered as needed. This book provides a step-by-step approach to the EasyStep Interview, utilizing the QuickBooks Pro 2009 format. Other QuickBooks versions may ask slightly different questions in a different order, but the critical questions covered in the interview are similar. QuickBooks provides default responses to questions based on the business type selected, and in most cases, the default responses to interview questions should be accepted. Keep in mind that they can be changed as needed.

The EasyStep Interview instructions that follow are for the Aroma Ristorante setup and are based on the profile given in Chapter 1. The answers and setup will vary depending on the organization's needs. Many answers to the questions in the EasyStep Interview can be changed by changing Company Preferences. See the section "Establishing Company Preferences" later in this chapter.

 Click **File** from the drop-down menu and select **New Company,** or click the **Create a New Company** icon from the No Company Open window.

Click the **Start Interview** icon.

In the Enter your company information window, enter the following information (see Figure 2-1):

Company name	Aroma Ristorante, Inc.
Legal name	Aroma Ristorante, Inc.
Tax ID	00-0000000
Street address	5000 Capital City Park
City	Capital City
State	New York
Zip	11100
Phone	555-555-5000
Fax	555-555-5100

HELPFUL TIP

The Tax ID number is a nine-digit federal employer identification number (EIN) or social security number. This number is used for various tax and government forms.

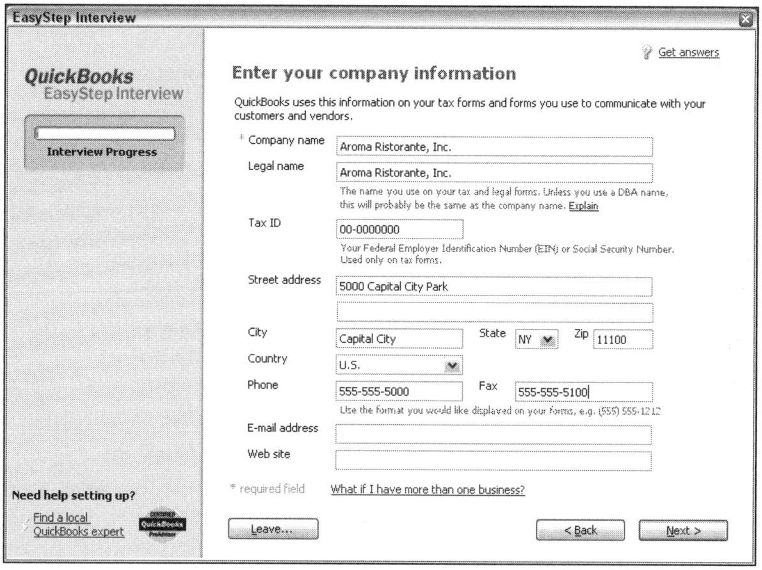

Figure 2-1.

Entering in company information allows QuickBooks to use this information to complete company forms, such as invoices and tax forms. The user will not have to reenter the company information every time a form is required. The company information can be changed at any time, and QuickBooks will use the new information on invoices and forms. To change the company information, click the Company drop-down menu and select Company Information.

The legal name of a company is the name that is connected with the federal employer identification number or social security number (Tax ID number). For a sole proprietorship, the company name and legal name can be the same or different. For example, the owner of the company is Mrs. Sally Shareholder who operates a restaurant named Aroma Ristorante (or doing business as Aroma Ristorante). In this case, the legal name is Mrs. Sally Shareholder and the company name is Aroma Ristorante.

Click **Next.**

To select your industry, select **Restaurant, Caterer,** or **Bar.**

QuickBooks can be used for various types of industries, such as advertising and public relations, agriculture, ranching or farming, lodging (hotel, motel), and legal services. These different industries have their own distinct set of needs. Selecting the correct industry will allow QuickBooks to establish company files that are appropriate for that particular business. It is important to select the appropriate industry during the EasyStep Interview. The industry type cannot be changed.

Click **Next.**

For Company Organization, select **Corporation.**

> The business type depends on the business and the personal objectives of the owner. QuickBooks associates income and expense accounts to specific lines on different tax forms. These tax forms are based on business type. QuickBooks will assign Form 1120 to a Corporation, whereas Form 1065 is assigned to a Partnership.
>
> QuickBooks offers the following business types:
>
> **Sole Proprietorship:** An unincorporated business with one owner (Form 1040).
>
> **Partnership or LLP:** An unincorporated business owned by two or more partners (Form 1065).
>
> **LLC:** A formal business entity that provides limited liability to its owners.
>
> **Corporation:** A formal business entity with one or more shareholders (Form 1120).
>
> **S Corporation:** A corporation that has elected to pass tax liability to its shareholders (Form 1120S).
>
> **Non-Profit:** A not-for-profit organization exempt from paying taxes (Form 990).
>
> For more information on business types, go to *www.irs.gov* or consult an accountant or an attorney.

Click **Next.**

For Fiscal Year, select **January.**

> A calendar year begins in January and ends in December, whereas a fiscal year is a 12-month period beginning with any other month. Using a calendar year, which is the same as the tax year, makes it easier to prepare the year-end tax forms. A fiscal year may be more appropriate for restaurants that have seasonal business.

Click **Next.**

> Passwords are a sequence of characters that are used to gain access to a computer system. This is an important feature for restaurants that have multiple individuals using a QuickBooks file. An individual can be set up as an administrator. Administrators have full access to all QuickBooks features and company information. Passwords should be created for multiple users of the same computer or a multi-user networked environment. Administrators can limit access to company data for individual users and track changes to the file by user. A user who forgets his or her password cannot access the QuickBooks file. Intuit will charge the user a fee to regain access to a file.

In the Set Up Your Administrator Password window, leave the password fields blank for Aroma Ristorante.

Click **Next** twice.

In the Create Your Company File window, click **Next.**

When prompted, select file location, file name, and file type.

Click **Save.**

Click **Next.**

Now QuickBooks will create a company file.

This process may take a couple of minutes.

In the Customizing QuickBooks for your business window, click **Next.**

In the What do you sell? window, select **both services and products.**

> QuickBooks offers the following options: Services, Products, and Both Services and Products. Selecting Both Services and Products enables the user to set up inventory accounts.

Click **Next.**

In the Do you sell products online? window, select **I don't sell online and I am not interested in doing so.**

> If a user selects the option **I sell online,** QuickBooks will offer information on additional QuickBooks services applicable to restaurants that sell items online.

Click **Next.**

In the Do you charge sales tax? window, click **Yes.**

> Click No if the restaurant is located in a state that is exempt from sales tax on food and beverages. If you select Yes, QuickBooks charges sales tax on invoices and creates a Sales Tax account.

Click **Next.**

In the Do you want to create estimates in QuickBooks? window, click **Yes.**

> Estimates are useful for catering businesses as well as restaurants that offer catering and banquet services. Managers can provide potential customers with QuickBooks Estimate Forms for specific catering jobs. Upon completion of the catering job, the estimate can be used to create an invoice.

Click **Next.**

In the Do you want to use sales receipts in QuickBooks? window, click **Yes.**

> Sales receipts are generated for customers who pay for a service or product. Sales receipts can be provided in lieu of a customer invoice. See page 110 for additional information.

Click **Next.**

In the Do you want to use billing statements in QuickBooks? window, click **No.**

> Billing statements are generated for customers who accrue charges and are billed on a regular basis. Restaurant operations may extend credit to regular customers and bill them on a monthly basis. Billing statements can also be used as reminders to pay outstanding invoices.

Click **Next.**

In the Do you want to use progress invoicing? window, click **No.**

> Progress invoices are used in businesses that bill customers based on progress, such as completion of a segment of a project. Progress invoicing is more appropriate for manufacturing and construction businesses.

Click **Next.**

In the Do you want to keep track of bills you owe? window, click **Yes.**

> QuickBooks allows a user to either pay bills when received or enter bills when received and pay at a later date. By choosing to pay at a later date, a restaurant manager can identify and prioritize the bills. A QuickBooks reminder can be set up to prompt a manager when the bill is due. This will assist in managing the restaurant's cash flow.

Click **Next.**

In the Do you print checks? window, select **I print checks.**

> Checks can be written by hand and recorded in the check register or printed from QuickBooks. Printing checks from QuickBooks offers time savings over writing checks by hand.

Click **Next.**

In the Do you want to track inventory in QuickBooks? window, click **Yes.**

> The inventory feature can help a business manage increases and decreases in inventory levels and remind the user when inventory needs to be reordered. In addition, restaurants can enable the inventory feature to allow the user to enter catering menu items into QuickBooks. In turn, invoices can be created for catering customers. The inventory feature can also be used to track retail items or cases of liquor or wine. A restaurant operation can also track inventory using an inventory management system designed specifically for the food and beverage industry.

Click **Next.**

In the Do you accept credit cards? window, select **I accept credit cards and debit cards.**

> If you select I accept credit cards and debit cards, QuickBooks will provide information about QuickBooks Merchant Services. Credit card transactions can be processed and recorded directly from QuickBooks. Restaurant point-of-sale systems use credit card software to process credit card transactions.

Click **Next.**

In the Do you want to track time in QuickBooks? window, click **Yes.**

> QuickBooks can assist management in tracking how much time employees or contractors/consultants spend on a project or how many hours are worked. Restaurant operations can use the point-of-sale system to track employee time and attendance. This system typically can provide summary reports that can be used to record payroll in QuickBooks.

Click **Next.**

In the Do you have employees? window, click **Yes.**

Select **We have W-2 employees.**

Select **We have 1099 contractors.**

> Many restaurants outsource payroll. For purposes of this book, the payroll feature is enabled to allow the user to process manual payroll using QuickBooks. See page 28 for additional information.

Click **Next.**

In the Do you want to track multiple currencies in QuickBooks? window, click **No.**

Click **Next.**

In the Using accounts in QuickBooks window, click **Next.**

In the Select a date to start tracking your finances window, select **Beginning of this fiscal year: 01/01/2008.**

Click **Next.**

In the Add your bank account window, click **Yes.**

Enter the operating bank account at this time. An operating account is used to record day-to-day income and expense transactions. Additional bank accounts can be created at any time. This may include a savings account or an investment account.

In the Enter your bank account information window—for the example presented in this book—enter the following data:

Bank account name:	Checking Account
Bank account number:	1111111111

Select **Before, 01/01/2008.**

Click **Next.**

In the Enter your bank statement information window, enter **December 31, 2007.**

Do not enter an ending balance.

Click **Next.**

In the Review bank accounts window, when prompted Do you want to add another bank account?, select **No, I'm done or will add more later.**

Click **Next.**

In the Review income and expense accounts window, place a checkmark next to every account on the list (see Figure 2-2).

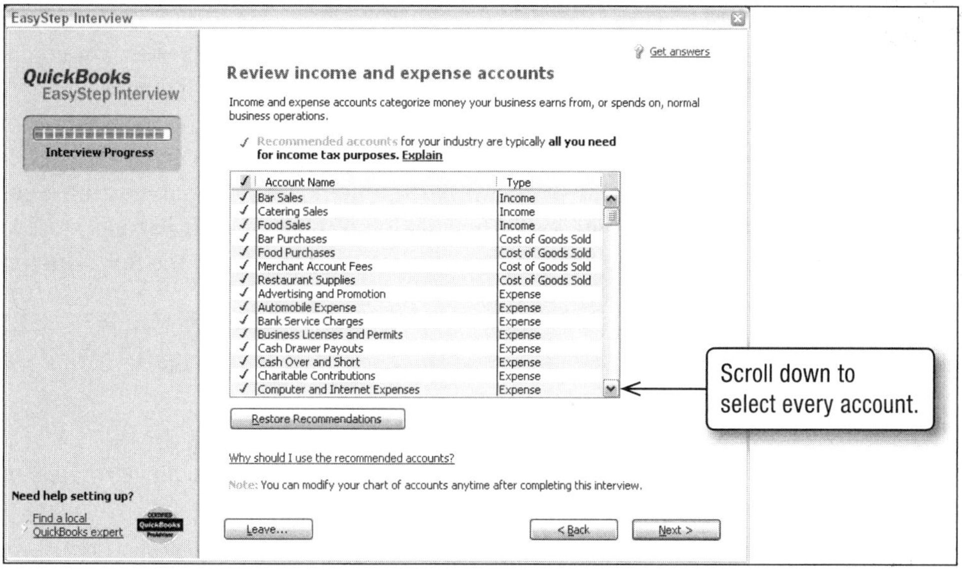

Figure 2-2.

QuickBooks creates a list of accounts based on the industry type selected. New accounts can be added at any time. See Chapter 3 for information on how to add a new account.

It is important to check and accept all income and expense accounts. Using the accounts selected, QuickBooks creates a Chart of Accounts (see page 46 for additional information). If accounts are not selected, the user may be required to add a substantial number of new accounts to the Chart of Accounts. Accounts can be added, edited, or inactivated at any time.

Click **Next.**

In the Congratulations! You've completed the EasyStep Interview window, click **Finish.**

Backing Up and Restoring QuickBooks Files

Once a QuickBooks working file (.QBW) is established, it is imperative to start backing up. It is critical for a restaurant to back up to multiple locations on a regular basis. A failure to back up data on a regular basis subjects your business to the unnecessary risk of lost and unrecoverable data. It is virtually impossible for a manager to recreate from memory the multitude of transactions that occur on a regular basis in the operation of a restaurant. The loss of payroll, payables, receivables, inventory, and other critical business information can subject the enterprise to significant time and expense to recreate the lost data. On a worst-case basis, your restaurant could find itself in violation of state and federal regulations for its inability to produce reliable information and data. Regular backups may be required on a daily or weekly basis depending on the restaurant. One objective of an effective backup schedule is to minimize the amount of data that must be recreated in the event of data loss. The location to which backup data is stored and frequency of the backups are up to management, but the following are a few things to consider:

- Regular backup to a hard drive (or the same storage device) is not recommended. Drives do crash.
- Backup files can be stored on tapes, CDs, or flash drives. Two backup files should be created. These storage devices should be rotated and replaced on a regular basis.
- One backup file should be stored at an off-site location. One option for off-site storage is the use of a remote server, such as the QuickBooks Online Backup Service. Restaurant operators can use the service for a fee. See *www.intuit.com* for details.
- Backups should be scheduled and conducted on a regular basis once a frequency schedule is identified.

Creating a Backup File

Click the **File** drop-down menu.

Select **Save Copy or Backup.**

In the What type of file do you want to save? window, select **Backup copy.**

Click **Next.**

In the Do you want to save your backup copy locally or online? window, select **Local backup.**

Click **Next.**

In the When do you want to save your backup copy? window, select **Save it now.**

Select a **file location and file name.**

Click **Save.**

Click **OK.**

QUICKBOOKS TIP

The current QuickBooks company file name uses a .QBW extension. The backup company file uses a .QBB extension. A user can choose to schedule future backups. After the initial backup file is created, the steps for subsequent backup files will vary.

This backup file is a compressed file. The backup file must be restored for a user to be able to access it. You must be in single-user mode to restore a file.

Restoring QuickBooks Files

A QuickBooks company backup file (.QBB) can be restored by clicking the **File** drop-down menu and selecting **Open or Restore Company.**

Select **Restore a backup copy** and click **Next.**

In the Is the backup copy stored locally or online? window, select **Local backup.**

Click **Next.**

After file location and file name have been identified, click **Open.**

In the Where do you want to restore the file? window, click **Next.**

In the Save Company File as window, select a **file location and file name.**

Click **Save.**

QuickBooks should display a window to confirm that the data has been restored successfully.

Establishing Company Preferences

The Preferences feature allows the user to customize a QuickBooks file to a particular need and style. Some users may collect sales tax, use QuickBooks to process payroll, or track inventory, while others may not. Once established, most preferences can be changed as needed. Preference options may vary depending on the version of QuickBooks in use. A restaurant should identify which preferences are appropriate for its particular business. Based on the responses to questions in the EasyStep Interview, certain preferences have already been turned on while others may need to be activated. Depending on the individual organization, the preferences will vary to meet the organization's specific needs. For Aroma Ristorante, the following additional preferences have been identified.

To access Preferences, click the **Edit** drop-down menu.

Select **Preferences.**

Accounting Preferences

Select **Accounting**, and click the **Company Preferences** tab. Place a check-mark next to Use account numbers (see Figure 2-3).

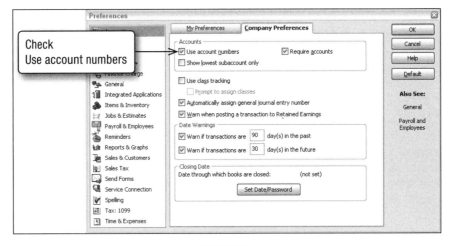

Figure 2-3.

HELPFUL TIP
Using account numbers allows a user more flexibility in report preparation.

Checking Preferences

Select **Checking,** and click the **My Preferences** tab.

Place a checkmark next to each option under **Select Default Accounts to Use.**

Select **Checking Account** from the drop-down list for all options (see Figure 2-4).

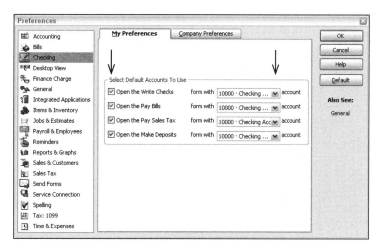

Figure 2-4.

Select **Checking,** and click the **Company Preferences** tab.

Place checkmarks next to both **Open the Create Paychecks** and **Open the Pay Payroll Liabilities.** Select **Checking Account** from the drop down list for both options (see Figure 2-5).

Figure 2-5.

Items & Inventory Preferences

Select **Items & Inventory.**

Click the **Company Preferences** tab (see Figure 2-6).

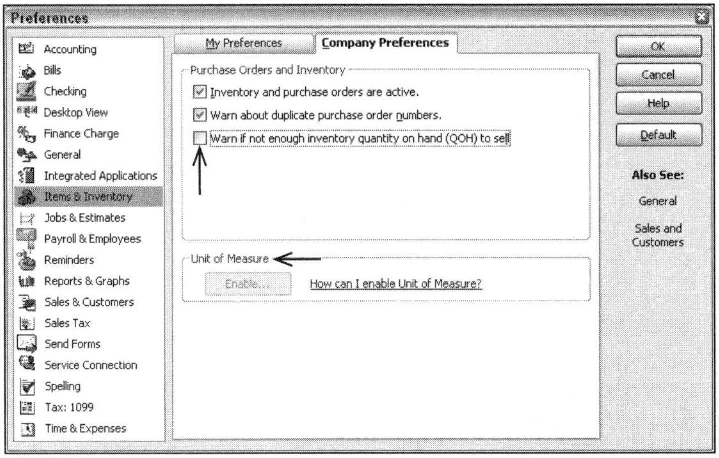

Figure 2-6.

Clear the **Warn if not enough inventory quantity on hand (QOH) to sell** checkbox. This will allow a user to use the inventory feature to create Customer Invoices without having to view warning windows.

HELPFUL TIP

Certain QuickBooks versions support different units of measure per item. This feature is useful for food and beverage inventory.

Reports & Graphs Preferences

Select **Reports & Graphs.**

Click the **Company Preferences** tab (see Figure 2-7).

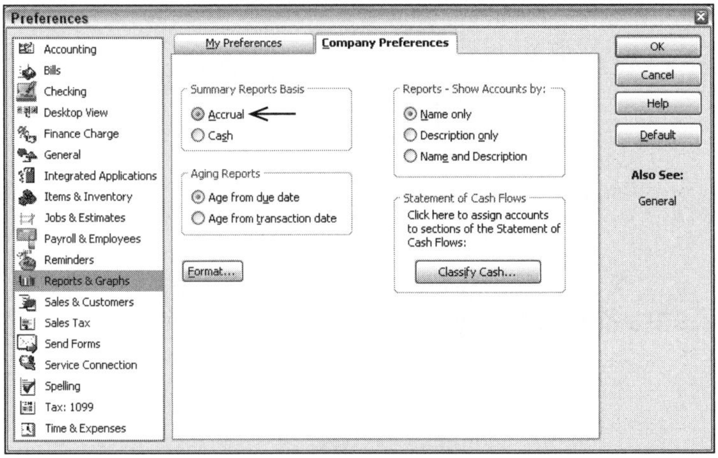

Figure 2-7.

ACCOUNTING TIP

Accrual basis accounting records revenue when it is earned and expenses when they are incurred. *Cash basis* accounting records revenue when the cash is received and expenses when cash is disbursed.

Make sure **Accrual** is selected for the Summary Reports Basis in the window.

Sales & Customers Preferences

Select **Sales & Customers.**

Click the **Company Preferences** tab (see Figure 2-8).

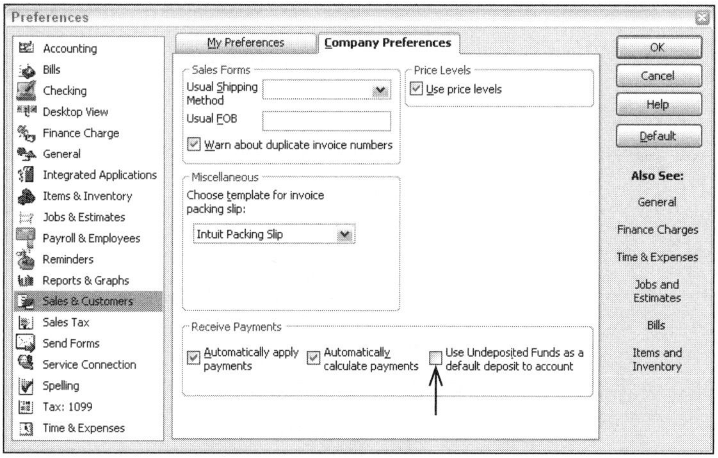

Figure 2-8.

Clear the **Use Undeposited Funds as a default deposit to account** in the Receive Payments section of the window.

When payments are received, the Undeposited Funds account can be used as a default account to record the payments until they are deposited in the bank and/or the checks have been cleared. Once deposited, the payment is transferred from the Undeposited Funds accounts to the appropriate bank account. For the purposes of this book, Aroma Ristorante will record all payments directly into the checking account.

Sales Tax Preferences

Select **Sales Tax.**

Click the **Company Preferences** tab (see Figure 2-9).

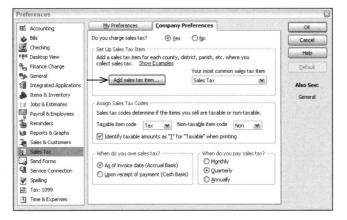

Figure 2-9.

Click **Add sales tax item.**

In the New Item window, select **Sales Tax Item** from the Type drop-down list (see Figure 2-10).

Figure 2-10.

In the New Item window, enter the following information:

Type:	Sales Tax Item
Sales Tax Name:	Sales Tax
Description:	Sales Tax
Tax Rate (%):	8.25%
Tax Agency:	Select **Add New** from the drop-down list and add NYS Sales Tax Department, PO Box 5550, Capital City, NY 11112

Setting Up an Additional Bank Account

Chart of
Accounts

Click the **Chart of Accounts** icon on the Home page.

Click the **Account** button in the lower-left corner of the desktop.

Select **New.**

Select **Bank.**

Click **Continue.**

In the Add New Account window, enter the following information (see Figure 2-11):

Account Type:	Bank
Number:	10500
Account Name:	Savings Account
Bank Acct. No.:	2222222222

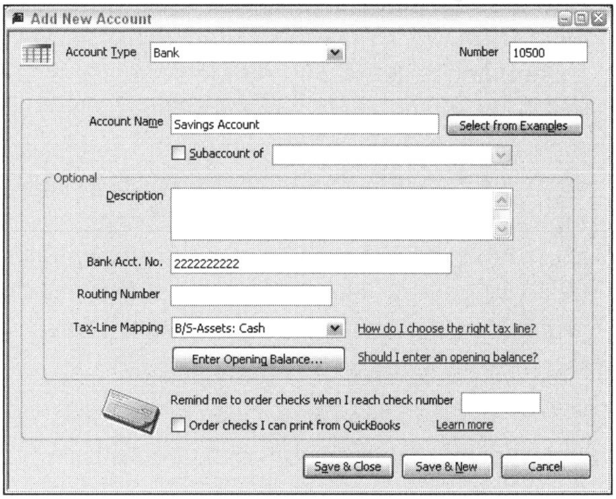

Figure 2-11.

Click **Save & Close.**

Recording Opening Balances

For businesses that have engaged in previous transactions before adopting QuickBooks, it will be necessary to enter this information into QuickBooks by entering opening balances. An *opening balance* is the value of or the amount of money in an account as of the first day QuickBooks is used. A business may have opening balances for customers, vendors, and various general ledger accounts, such as fixed assets, sales, expenses, and so on. Beginning balances are recorded in a variety of ways, depending on the type.

Setting Up QuickBooks to Manually Accept Payroll

In the EasyStep Interview (earlier in the chapter), **Yes** should be selected when prompted if you want to use QuickBooks to help you with payroll. *Most restaurants do not use QuickBooks to manually process payroll.* At a minimum, restaurateurs should subscribe to Intuit's Standard Payroll, which calculates employees' earnings, deductions, and payroll taxes. The service also includes filling out federal and state tax forms. QuickBooks offers different levels of payroll services (see page 140). A fee is assessed for all levels of payroll services. For purposes of this book, manual payroll is used to expose the reader to the payroll process and procedures. The following payroll setup is for Aroma Ristorante and uses the restaurant's profile that was identified in Chapter 1. Payroll setup will vary to meet an organization's needs.

This restaurant operates in Capital City, New York. QuickBooks will create a company file that offers different options based on the state selected during the set-up process.

If a user decides to manually process payroll using QuickBooks, the following payroll setup is required. If not, ignore the payroll setup procedures. Payroll options can be edited after the initial payroll setup is completed by clicking the **Employees** drop-down menu and selecting **Payroll Setup.**

Turning On Manual Payroll

Click the **Help** drop-down menu.

Select **QuickBooks Help.**

Click the **Search** tab.

Enter **manual payroll** in the search field.

Click the **arrow** icon.

Select the topic **Process payroll manually (without a subscription to QuickBooks Payroll).**

Select the **Set your company file to use the manual payroll calculations setting** link.

If you are sure you want to manually calculate your payroll taxes in Quick-Books, click the **Set my company file to use manual calculations** link.

Payroll Setup

In order to process payroll, it is necessary to complete the entire QuickBooks Payroll Setup in order. A user can make changes to the payroll setup at any time. The payroll setup process will accomplish the following:

- Identify the types of employee compensation, such as hourly wage, salary, and so on.
- Identify the types of employee benefits offered by the restaurant, such as health insurance, dental insurance, retirement, and vacation and sick time.
- Identify other deductions, such as wage garnishments, mileage reimbursements, and so on.
- Set up employees and payroll items that should appear on the employee paychecks.
- Set up federal, state, and payroll taxes.
- Enter previous payroll history for employees if the restaurant is starting to use QuickBooks in the middle of the year.

Click the **Employees** drop-down menu.

Select **Payroll Setup.**

In the Welcome to QuickBooks Payroll Setup window (see Figure 2-12), click **Continue.**

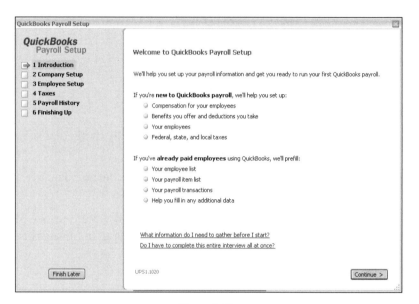

Figure 2-12.

In the Company Setup: Compensation Benefits window, click **Continue.**

In the Tell us how you compensate your employees window (see Figure 2-13), select the following:

- **Salary**
- **Hourly wage and overtime**
- **Bonus, award, or one-time compensation**
- **Tips**

HELPFUL TIP

Employee tips are included in gross wages and subject to payroll taxes. Reported tips are included in an employee's paycheck when the employee turns in tips to the manager or guests charge tips on credit cards. Reported Cash Tips should be used when employees keep tips and report tip amounts to their employer. Reported Paycheck Tips should be used when tips are paid to the employees through their paychecks.

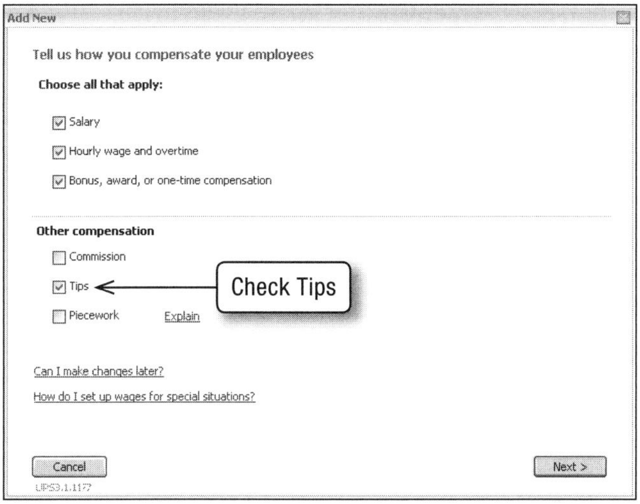

Figure 2-13.

Click **Next.**

In the Tell us how you track tips window, select **Reported cash tips.**

Click **Finish.**

In the Review your Compensation list window (see Figure 2-14), click **Continue.**

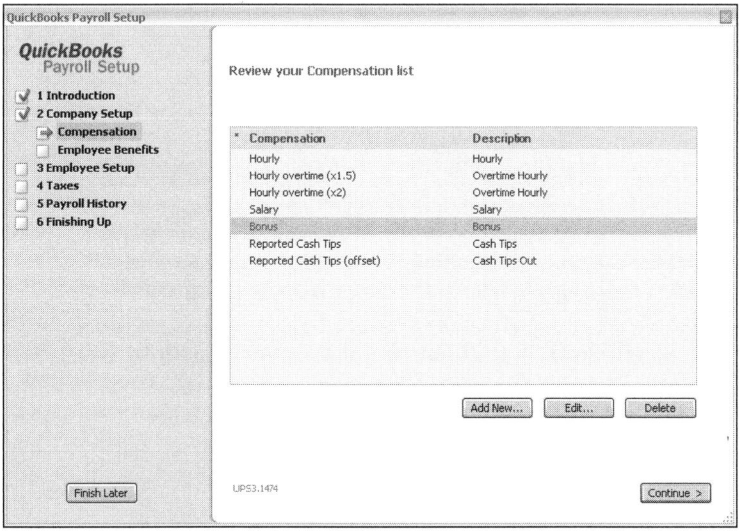

Figure 2-14.

In the Set up employee benefits window, click **Continue.**

In the Set up insurance benefits window, select **Health insurance** and **Dental insurance**, and click **Next.**

In the Tell us about health insurance window, select **Bvoth the employee and company pay portions.**

Select **Payment is deducted after taxes.**

Click **Next.**

In the Set up the payment schedule for health insurance window, enter **Premium Health Company** in the Payee (Vendor) field.

Select **Quarterly** Payment frequency (see Figure 2-15).

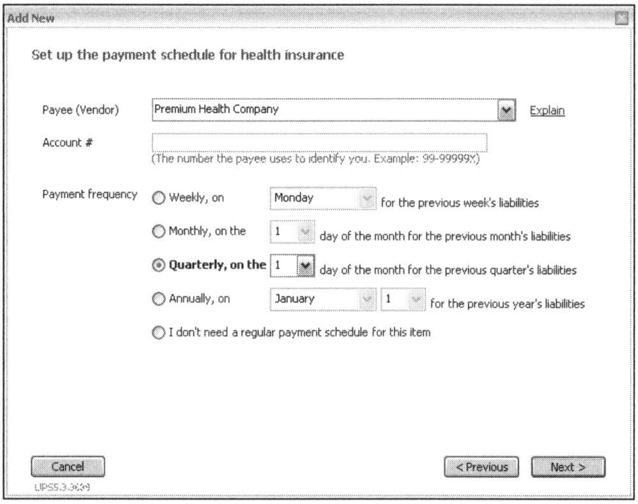

Figure 2-15.

Click **Next.**

In the Tell us about dental insurance window, select **Both the employee and company pay portions.**

Select **Payment is deducted after taxes.**

Click **Next.**

In the Set up the payment schedule for dental insurance window, enter **Northeast Dental Insurance, Inc.** in the Payee (Vendor) field.

Select **Quarterly** Payment frequency (see Figure 2-16).

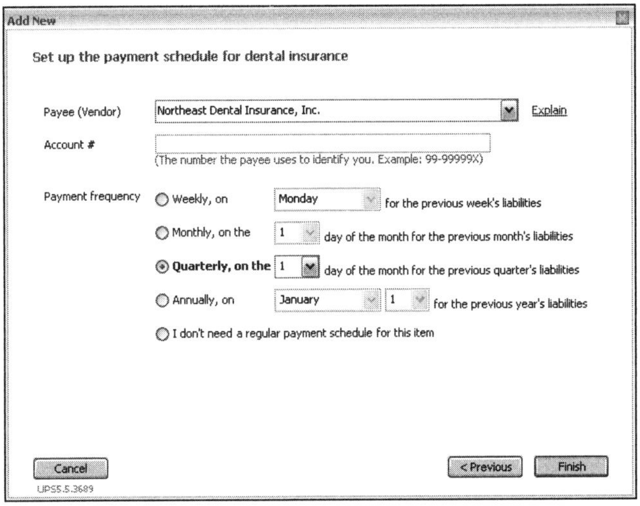

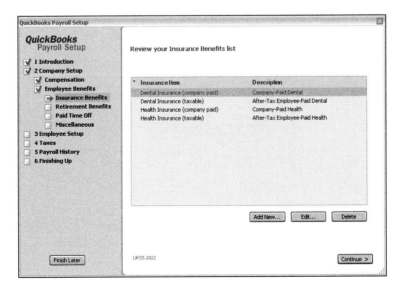

Figure 2-16.

Click **Finish.**

In the Review your Insurance Benefits list window (see Figure 2-17), click **Continue.**

Figure 2-17.

In the Tell us about your company retirement benefits window, select **My company does not provide retirement benefits.**

Click **Finish.**

In the Review your Retirement Benefits list window, click **Continue.**

In the Set up paid time off window (see Figure 2-18), select **Paid sick time off** and **Paid vacation time off.**

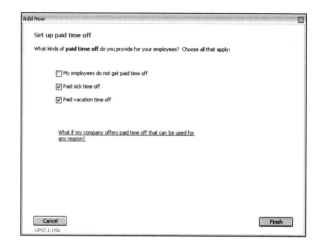

Figure 2-18.

Click **Finish.**

In the Review your Paid Time Off list window (see Figure 2-19), click **Continue.**

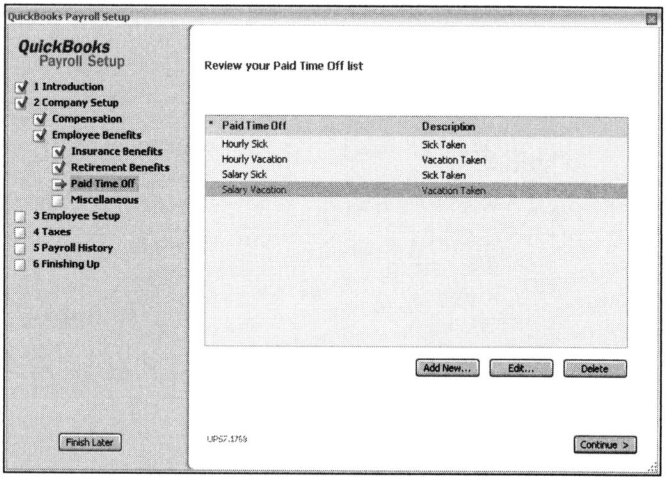

Figure 2-19.

In the Set up additions and deductions window, select **Mileage reimbursement** and **Wage garnishment** (see Figure 2-20).

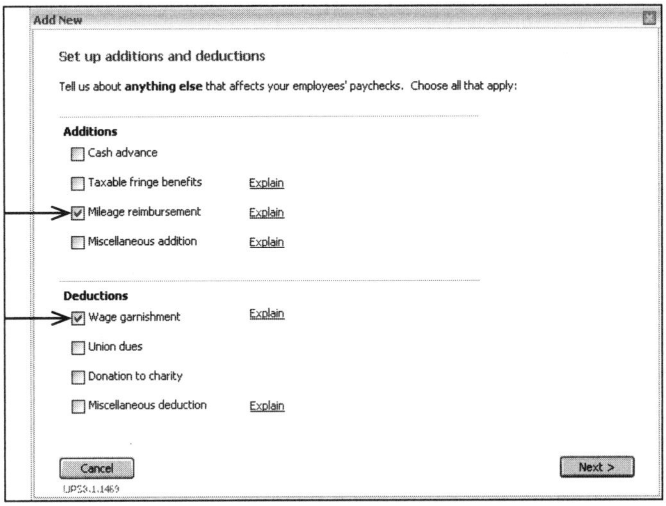

Figure 2-20.

Click **Next.**

In the Set up the payment schedule for wage garnishment window, do not enter any information.

Click **Finish**.

In the Review your Additions and Deductions list window, click **Continue.**

In the Set up your employees window, click **Continue.**

HELPFUL TIP

Each Garnishment is paid to a different vendor based on the type of garnishment. For example, child support payments may be made to a local court.

At this time, set up one employee. You must create one employee record during payroll setup to set deductions and vendors that will be used to process payroll for all employees. Additional employee records are created in Chapter 6.

Enter the following information in the Enter employee's name and address window (see Figure 2-21).

First name:	Mary
Last name:	Hoffman
Employee status:	Active
Address:	544 C Street, Apartment # 201
City:	Capital City
State:	New York
Zip Code:	11112
Phone:	555-888-0202

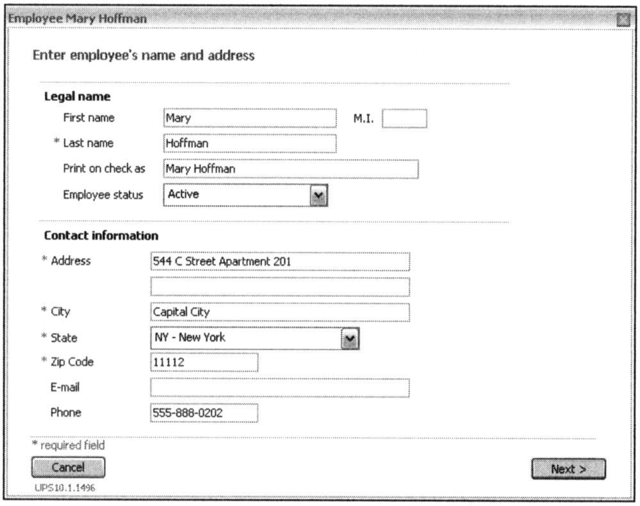

Figure 2-21.

Click **Next.**

In the Enter Mary Hoffman's hiring information window (see Figure 2-22), enter the following information:

Employee Tax Type:	Regular
Social Security #:	000-33-4444
Hire date:	01/1/2008
Birth date:	11/5/1987
Gender:	Female

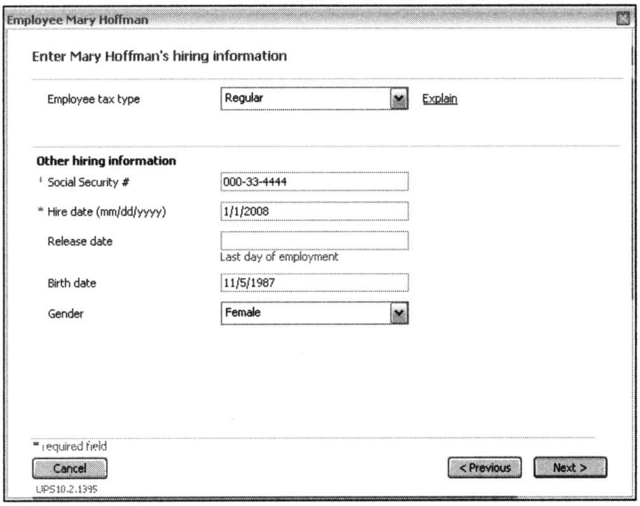

Figure 2-22.

Click **Next.**

In the Tell us about wages and compensation for Mary Hoffman window (see Figure 2-23), enter the following information:

Pay frequency:	Twice a month (Semimonthly)
Hourly wage:	$8.00
Hourly overtime (x1.5):	$12.00

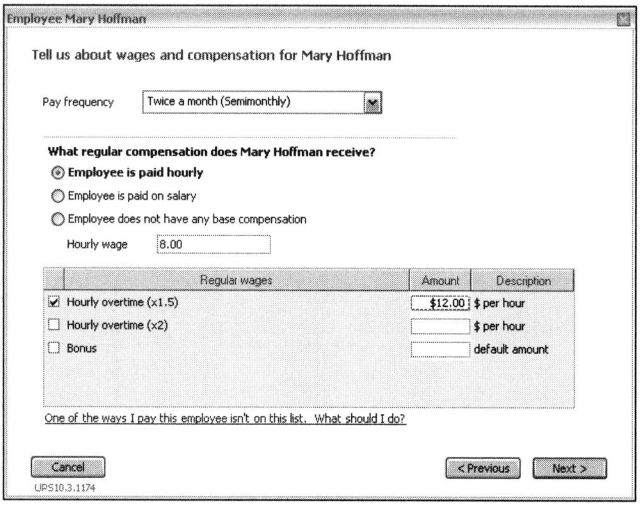

Figure 2-23.

Click **Next.**

In the Tell us about benefits for Mary Hoffman window (see Figure 2-24), enter the following information.

Dental Insurance (company paid):	$25.00
Health Insurance (company paid):	$75.00
Dental Insurance (taxable):	$7.00
Health Insurance (taxable):	$25.00

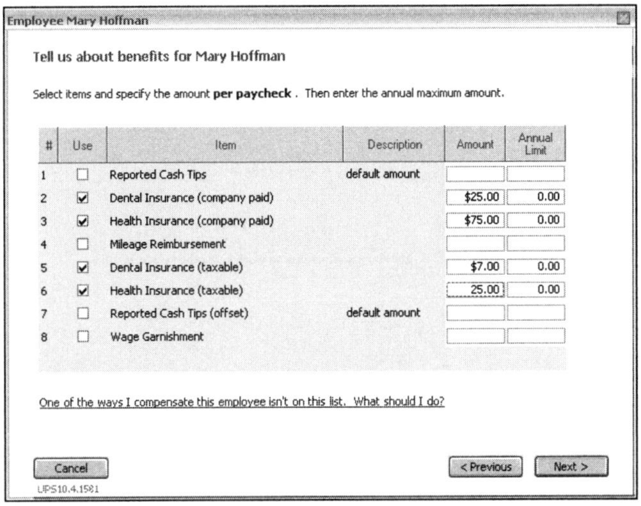

Figure 2-24.

Click **Next**.

Do not enter any information in the How is sick time off calculated for Mary Hoffman? window.

Note that Aroma Ristorante offers sick and vacation paid time off for full-time employees at 90 days of employment. Sick time will not be set up at this time.

Click **Next**.

Do not enter any information in the How is vacation time off calculated for Mary Hoffman? window.

As mentioned previously, Aroma Ristorante offers sick and vacation paid time off for full-time employees at 90 days of employment. Vacation time will not be set up at this time.

Click **Next**.

In the Set up Mary Hoffman's direct deposit information window, do not select direct deposit information. Click **Next**.

In the Tell us where Mary Hoffman is subject to taxes window (see Figure 2-25), enter the following information:

State subject to withholding:	NY-New York
State subject to unemployment tax:	NY-New York

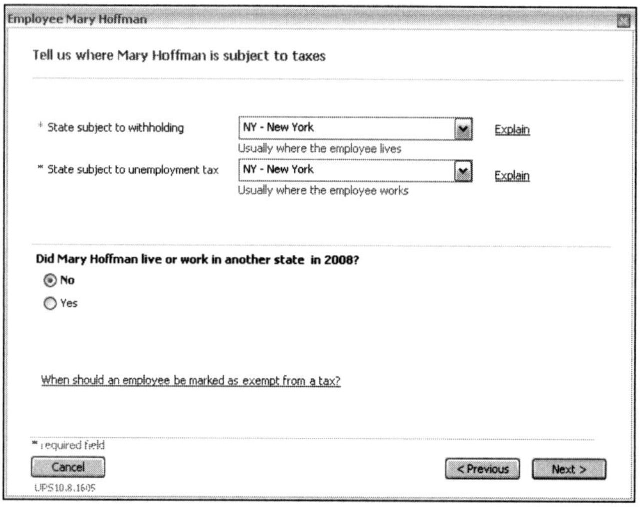

Figure 2-25.

Click **Next**.

In the Enter federal tax information for Mary Hoffman window (see Figure 2-26), enter the following information:

Filing Status:	Single
Allowances:	0
Extra Withholding:	Leave blank

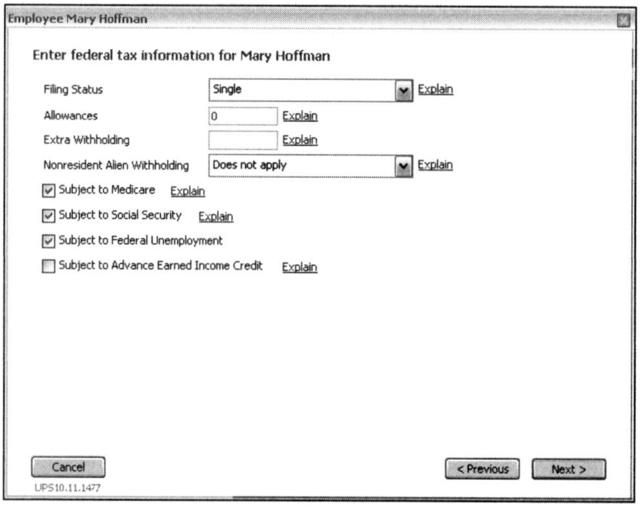

Figure 2-26.

The employee is subject to the following taxes:

- Medicare
- Social Security
- Federal Unemployment

Click **Next.**

In the Enter state tax information for Mary Hoffman window (see Figure 2-27), enter the following information:

Filing Status:	Single
Allowances:	0
Extra Withholding:	Leave blank

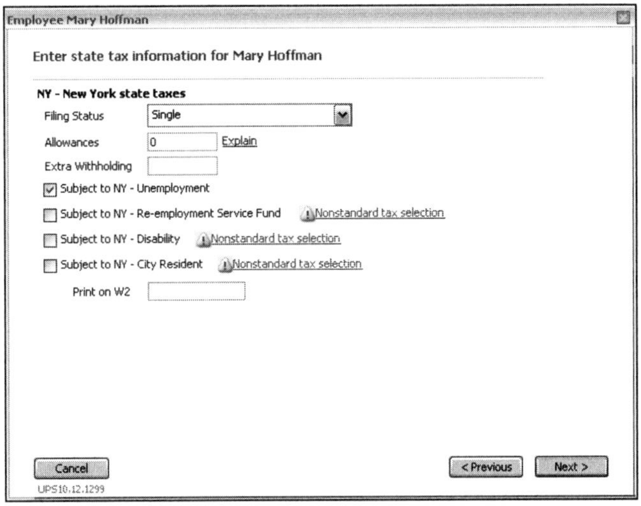

Figure 2-27.

Indicate that the employee is subject to the following taxes:

NY-Unemployment

Click **Next.**

Do not enter any information in the Enter additional state tax information for Mary Hoffman window.

Mary Hoffman is not subject to any additional New York State taxes.

Click **Finish.**

In the Review your Employee list window, click **Continue.**

In the Set up your payroll taxes window, click **Continue.**

In the Here are the federal taxes we set up for you window, click **Continue.**

Do not enter any information in the NY-Disability payments window.

Click **Next.**

In the NYS Employment Taxes payments window, enter **5.4%** for the NY-Unemployment Company Rate.

Click **Finish.**

In the Review your state taxes window, click **Continue.**

In the Set up payment schedule for Federal 940 window, enter the following information:

Payee:	United States Treasury
Payment (deposit) frequency:	Quarterly

Click **Next.**

In the Set up payment schedule for Federal 941/944 window, enter the following information:

Payee:	United States Treasury
Payment (deposit) frequency:	Quarterly

Click **Next.**

In the Set up payment for NY Disability Insurance window, do not enter any information.

Click **Next.**

In the Set up payment schedule for NY UI and Re-employment Service Fund window, enter the following information:

Payee:	NYS Employment Taxes
Payment (deposit) frequency:	Quarterly

Click **Next.**

In the Set up payment schedule for NY Withholding, NYC and Yonkers window, enter the following information:

Payee:	NYS Income Tax
Payment (deposit) frequency:	Quarterly

Click **Finish.**

In the Review your Scheduled Tax Payments list window, click **Continue.**

In the Enter payroll history for the current year window, click **Continue.**

In the Determine if you need to enter payroll history window, click **No.**

If a restaurant begins to use QuickBooks at any other time except for the beginning of the fiscal/calendar year and has issued paychecks, it is necessary to enter year-to-date payroll amounts.

Click **Continue.**

Setup is complete, **Click Finish.**

At this point, payroll is set up and QuickBooks allows the user to manually process payroll. Adding additional employee records and payroll processing are addressed in Chapter 6.

Working with Lists

Access the Chapter 3 data file from the CD-ROM that accompanies this book or download the file from the web site.

Chapter Outline

Using Lists

QuickBooks lists enable the user to organize, store, and report on specific information about the business. Lists can be created for vendors, customers, classes, items, accounts (Chart of Accounts), and so on. Once established, these lists enable the user to process business transactions and create reports. After a list has been created, it can be edited as needed.

Using the Chart of Accounts

The Chart of Accounts is a complete list of a restaurant's accounts. The Chart of Accounts is used to organize, categorize, and report on various business transactions. It is essential that the Chart of Accounts is customized to suit the unique needs of each restaurant, ensuring the preparation of useful financial reports.

During the EasyStep Interview, QuickBooks provides a customized Chart of Accounts for a restaurant, caterer, or bar. The Chart of Accounts is sorted alphabetically by account type. The Chart of Accounts initially created by QuickBooks is a starting point, but it will be necessary to add and/or edit accounts.

The Chart of Accounts can also be organized by account number. Each account is assigned a unique number. This numbering system enables users to easily locate an account and provides greater flexibility in reporting. Accounts can be organized as follows:

Assets (10000s)

Liabilities (20000s)

Equity (30000s)

Income/Sales (40000s)

Cost of Goods Sold (50000s)

Operating Expenses (60000s)

Other Income (70000s)

Other Expenses (80000s)

To utilize the numbering system, the user should turn on Use Account Numbers in Company Preferences—Accounting (see Chapter 2, page 22). QuickBooks assigns a number to each account. Because of the limited number of accounts in the Chart of Accounts created by QuickBooks, an example of an enhanced Chart of Accounts for a table service restaurant is provided on page 60.

Creating and Editing Accounts

As a restaurant progresses through various stages of operations, it may be necessary to create new accounts and edit existing accounts. These changes can be made at any time.

Chart of
Accounts

Click the **Chart of Accounts** icon on the Home page.

Click the **Account** button in the lower-left corner of the desktop (see Figure 3-1).

| File | Edit | View | Lists | Company | Customers | Vendors | Employees | Banking | Reports | Online Services | Window | Help |

Home · Company Snapshot · Customer Center · Vendor Center · Employee Center · Online Banking · Report Center · Payroll · Credit Cards · Services · Live Community · Help · Feedback · Search

Name	Type	Balance Total
◆10000 · Checking Account	Bank	0.00
◆12400 · Food Inventory	Other Current Asset	0.00
◆15000 · Furniture and Equipment	Fixed Asset	0.00
◆17000 · Accumulated Depreciation	Fixed Asset	0.00
◆18700 · Security Deposits Asset	Other Asset	0.00
◆24000 · Payroll Liabilities	Other Current Liabi...	0.00
◆25100 · Employee Tips Payable	Other Current Liabi...	0.00
◆25500 · Sales Tax Payable	Other Current Liabi...	0.00
◆30000 · Opening Balance Equity	Equity	0.00
◆30100 · Capital Stock	Equity	0.00
◆30200 · Dividends Paid	Equity	0.00
◆32000 · Retained Earnings	Equity	
◆41400 · Bar Sales	Income	
◆42100 · Catering Sales	Income	
◆43800 · Food Sales	Income	
◆50900 · Food Purchases	Cost of Goods Sold	
◆51000 · Bar Purchases	Cost of Goods Sold	
◆51800 · Merchant Account Fees	Cost of Goods Sold	
◆53100 · Restaurant Supplies	Cost of Goods Sold	
◆60000 · Advertising and Promotion	Expense	
◆60200 · Automobile Expense	Expense	
◆60400 · Bank Service Charges	Expense	
◆61000 · Business Licenses and Permits	Expense	
◆61200 · Cash Drawer Payouts	Expense	
◆61300 · Cash Over and Short	Expense	

New	Ctrl+N
Edit Account	Ctrl+E
Delete Account	Ctrl+D
Make Account Inactive	
Show Inactive Accounts	
✔ **Hierarchical View**	
Flat View	
Customize Columns...	
Import from Excel ...	
Use	Ctrl+U
Find Transactions in...	
Print List...	Ctrl+P
Re-sort List	

Expense (repeated)

| Account ▾ | Activities ▾ | Reports ▾ | ☐ Include inactive |

Figure 3-1.

Select **New**.

Select **Other Account Types**.

Select **Other Current Asset** from the drop-down list (see Figure 3-2).

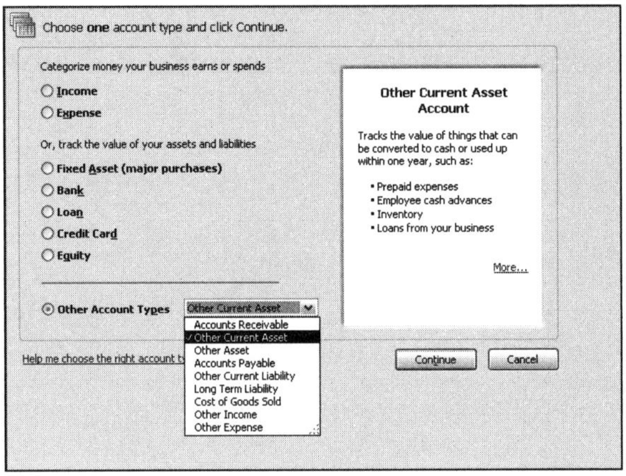

Figure 3-2.

Click **Continue**.

Using the following data, enter the information in the appropriate fields (see Figure 3-3).

DATA: Add an Account Named Retail Inventory.

ACCOUNT TYPE:	Other Current Asset
NUMBER:	12600
ACCOUNT NAME:	Retail Inventory

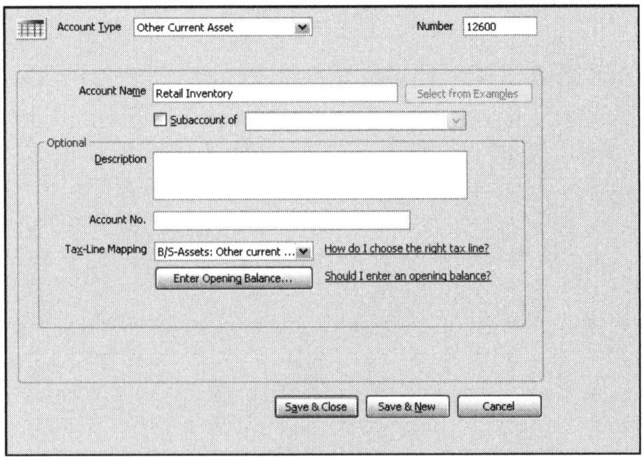

Figure 3-3.

QUICKBOOKS TIP

For existing businesses, opening balances can be entered at this time. See Chapter 2, page 28 for details.

Click **Save & Close**.

Using the following data, add the following accounts to the Chart of Accounts.

DATA: Add an Account Named Other Expense.

ACCOUNT TYPE:	Other Expense
NUMBER:	80100
ACCOUNT NAME:	Other Expense

DATA: Add an Account Named Other Income.

ACCOUNT TYPE:	Other Income
NUMBER:	70000
ACCOUNT NAME:	Other Income

Creating a New Subaccount

Chart of Accounts

Click the **Chart of Accounts** icon on the Home page.

Click the **Account** button in the lower-left corner of the desktop.

Select **New**.

Click **Continue**.

Select **Other Account Types** and select **Other Current Asset** from the drop-down list (see Figure 3-4).

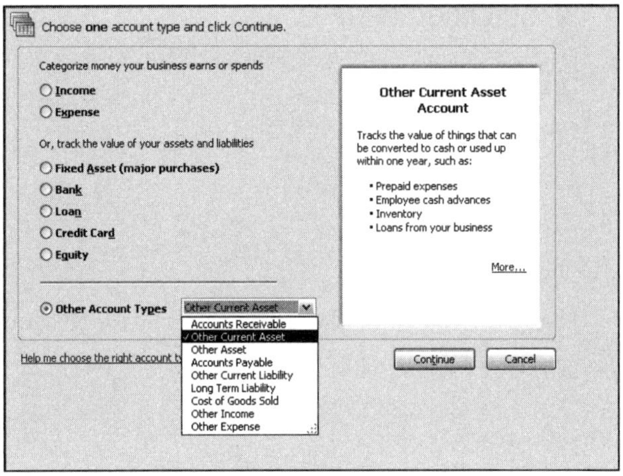

Figure 3-4.

Using the following data, enter the information in the appropriate fields (see Figure 3-5).

DATA: Add Beer as Subaccount of Beverage Inventory.

ACCOUNT TYPE:	Other Current Asset
NUMBER:	12510
ACCOUNT NAME:	Beer
SUBACCOUNT OF:	12500 Beverage Inventory

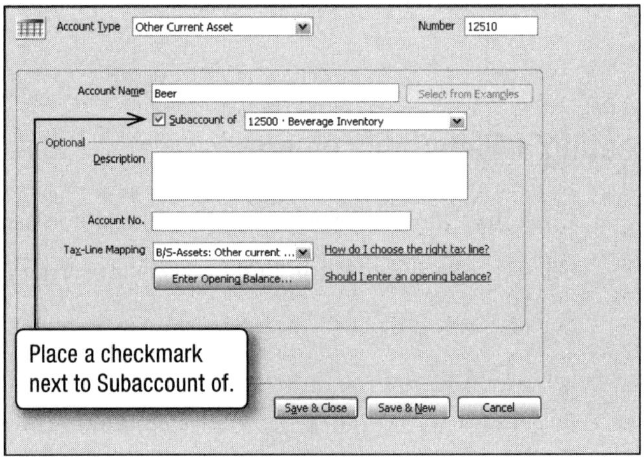

Figure 3-5.

Click **Save & Close**.

Editing an Account

Click the **Chart of Accounts** icon on the Home page.

Left-click the account to be edited.

Click the **Account** button in the lower-left corner of the desktop.

Select **Edit Account**.

Make the appropriate edits.

Click **Save & Close**.

Deleting Accounts

Deleting an account removes it from the Chart of Accounts. QuickBooks does not allow an account to be deleted if it has been used in any transaction or has an item assigned to it. Accounts that cannot be deleted could be inactivated and hidden from the Chart of Accounts. Accounts that have never been used and will not be used in the future should be deleted.

Click the **Chart of Accounts** icon on the Home page.

Left-click the account to be deleted.

Click the **Account** button in the lower-left corner of the desktop.

Select **Delete Account**.

Click **OK**.

The account is removed from the Chart of Accounts.

Accounts cannot be deleted if subaccounts are attached. Thus, you must delete all subaccounts before primary accounts.

Making an Account Inactive

Making an account inactive keeps the information associated with the account. The inactive account can be hidden from the Chart of Accounts and can be reactivated for future use. The user can choose to display inactive accounts in the Chart of Accounts, but the accounts are not available for use in drop-down lists.

Click the **Chart of Accounts** icon on the Home page.

Left-click the account to be made inactive.

Click the **Account** button in the lower-left corner of the desktop.

Select **Make Account Inactive**.

Creating a Vendor from the Vendor Center

Vendors are companies or individuals who provide goods or services to a restaurant, such as food and beverage vendors, accountants, law firms, telephone companies, tax agencies, and so on. Vendor records hold contact information, account numbers, payment terms, payments, and balances. The purpose of the Vendor Center is to have all vendors, vendor information, and transactions in a single location. Creating a vendor list enables the user to create transactions without having to enter vendor information each time.

Click the **Vendor Center** icon.

Click the **New Vendor** icon.

Using the following data, enter the information in the appropriate fields (see Figure 3-6).

DATA: Add a New Vendor to the Vendor List.	
VENDOR NAME:	Quality Food Vendor
COMPANY NAME:	Quality Food Vendor
ADDRESS:	4356 Lexington Avenue Capital City, NY 11112
PHONE:	555-444-4000
TERMS:	Due on receipt

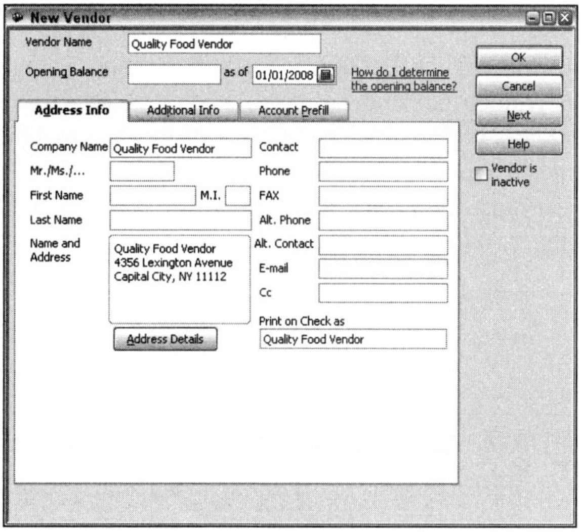

Figure 3-6.

Instructional Guide

*Enter the vendor name in the Company Name field **first**. Three additional*

Click the **Additional Info** tab and select **Due on receipt** from the Terms drop-down list (see Figure 3-7).

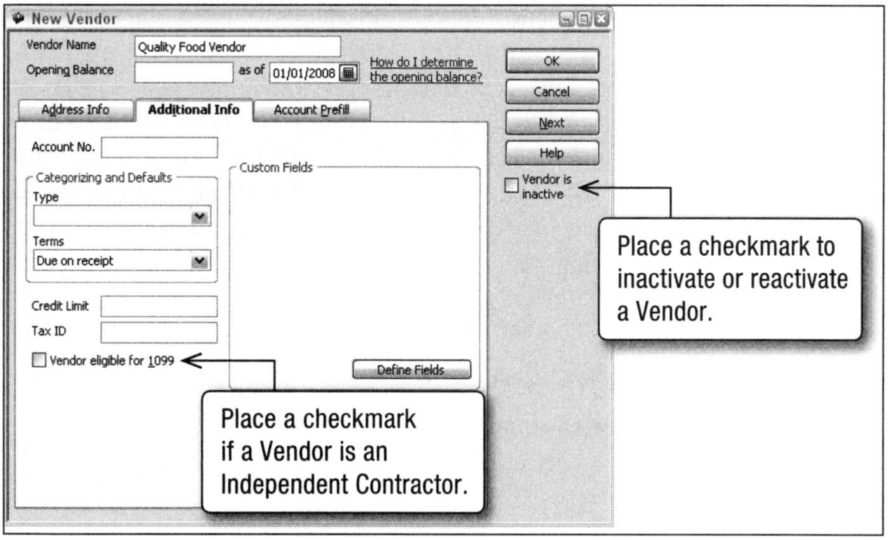

Figure 3-7.

Click **OK**.

A vendor can be an independent contractor. An independent contractor is an individual (not a corporation) whom a restaurant pays for goods delivered or services performed. The restaurant does not withhold any taxes from the payment. Independent contractors who are paid $600 or more during a calendar year must receive a Form 1099-MISC. (See Figure 3-7). See Chapter 10, page 210 for further information.

Using the following data, enter the information in the appropriate fields.

DATA: Add a New Vendor to the Vendor List.	
VENDOR NAME:	North Publishing Company
COMPANY NAME:	North Publishing Company
ADDRESS:	345 River Road
	Capital City, NY 11121
PHONE:	555-333-2222
TERMS:	Net 15

Creating a Customer from the Customer Center

Customers are individuals or businesses who pay the restaurant for goods and services provided. In certain cases, customer lists are not needed unless a restaurant bills a customer for services rendered and needs to create an invoice. Customer lists are useful for restaurants that provide catering and banquet services and can also be maintained for marketing purposes. Customer records contain contact and payment information. The purpose of the Customer Center is to have all customer information and transactions in a single location.

Click the **Customer Center** icon.

Click the **New Customer & Job** icon.

Select **New Customer**.

Using the following data, enter the information in the appropriate fields (see Figure 3-8).

DATA: Add a New Customer to the Customer List.

CUSTOMER NAME:	Bankers Association of Capital City
COMPANY NAME:	Bankers Association of Capital City
FIRST NAME:	Lynn
LAST NAME:	Brown
ADDRESSES:	1385 America Avenue, Capital City, NY 10000
PHONE:	555-515-5151
TERMS:	Due on receipt
PREFERRED SEND METHOD:	Mail
TAX CODE:	Tax
TAX ITEM:	Sales Tax
PREFERRED PAYMENT METHOD:	MasterCard
CREDIT CARD NO:	5454545454545454
EXP. DATE:	11/2015
NAME ON CARD:	Lynn Brown

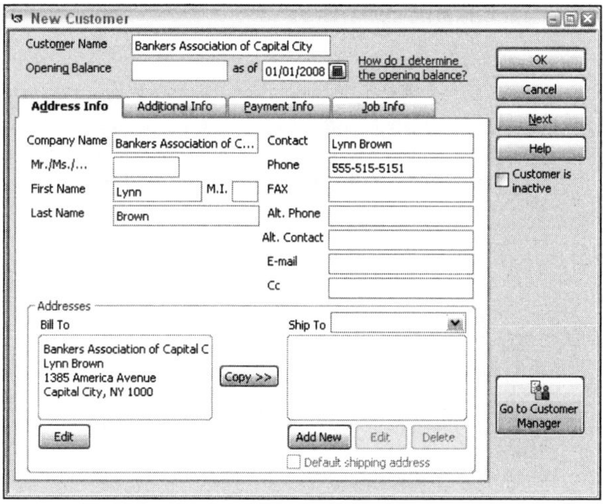

Figure 3-8.

Instructional Guide

*Enter the company name in the Company Name field **first**. Two additional fields are populated, resulting in less data entry.*

Click the **Additional Info** tab and enter the appropriate information (see Figure 3-9).

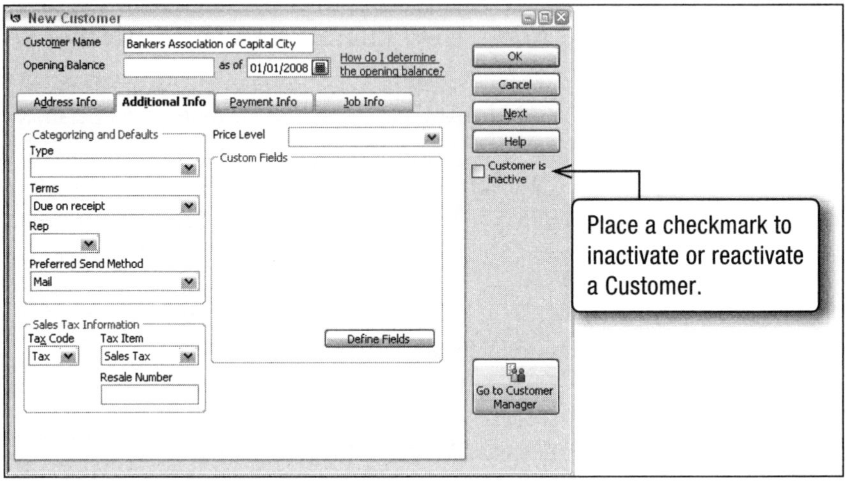

Figure 3-9.

Click the **Payment Info** tab and enter the remaining information
(see Figure 3-10).

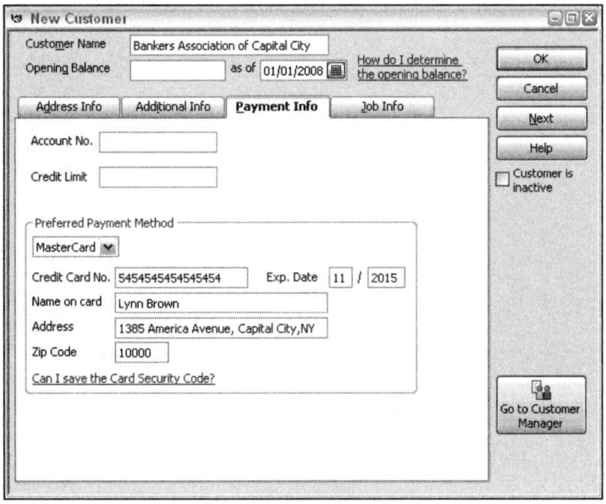

Figure 3-10.

QUICKBOOKS TIP

For tax-exempt customers, assign non-taxable sales in the Tax Code field. An example is
not-for-profit organizations.

Click **OK**.

HELPFUL TIP

Credit card information can be stored in the customer record and credit cards can be processed from the QuickBooks application. Credit card transactions can also be processed through a restaurant's point-of-sale system.

Creating an Item

An *item* can be anything that a restaurant buys or sells, or information that appears on a Customer Invoice or Purchase Order. These items may include: menu items, discounts, sales tax, or prepayments. If items are not entered into QuickBooks first, Customer Invoices and Purchase Orders cannot be created.

QuickBooks categorizes items by different types. The most frequently used types for restaurants are as follows:

- **Service:** Used when a restaurant purchases items that are not set up as inventory items, such as catering items (for example, a house bottle of red wine), or provides a service.
- **Inventory Part:** Used for goods purchased, tracked as inventory, and resold. It can be used for a restaurant's food and beverage items, as well as for retail items, such as cookbooks. (The inventory tracking feature must be enabled during the EasyStep Interview or Company Preferences. See Chapter 2, page 17.)
- **Non-Inventory Part:** Used for purchased goods that are not tracked as inventory, such as office supplies.
- **Other Charge:** Used for miscellaneous charges, such as set-up fees, delivery charges, shipping charges, or finance charges.
- **Discount:** Used for an amount to be subtracted from a subtotal.
- **Payment:** Used for recording partial payments.
- **Sales Tax:** Used for assessing a single tax at a specific rate.

Click the **Items & Services** icon on the Home page.

Click the **Item** button in the lower-left corner of the desktop.

Select **New**.

Using the following data, enter the information in the appropriate fields (see Figure 3-11).

DATA: Add an Item to the Item List.

TYPE:	Inventory Part
ITEM NAME/NUMBER:	Aroma Cookbook
DESCRIPTION:	Aroma Ristorante Cookbook
COST:	$12.50
COGS ACCOUNT:	80600 Retail Expense
PREFERRED VENDOR:	North Publishing Company
TAX CODE:	Tax
ASSET ACCOUNT:	12600 Retail Inventory
INCOME ACCOUNT:	70010 Retail Income
REORDER POINT:	24
AS OF:	01/01/2008

Figure 3-11.

Click **OK**.

Using the following data, enter the information in the appropriate fields.

DATA: Add an Item to the Item List.

TYPE:	Service
ITEM NAME/NUMBER:	Caesar Salad Small
DESCRIPTION:	Caesar Salad Half Pan
RATE:	$25.00
TAX CODE:	Tax
ACCOUNT:	42110 Catering Sales – Food

Editing and Deleting a Vendor, Customer, and Item

To edit or delete a vendor, customer, or item from the list, do the following:

Select the **Vendor, Customer,** or **Item** record (left-click).

Click the **Edit** drop-down menu.

Select **Edit** or **Delete** from the drop-down menu.

Identifying The Role of Classes

The Class Tracking feature enables a restaurant to report income and expenses by departments, locations, or specific divisions, such as on-premise or off-premise catering. This function must be enabled in the Accounting Company Preferences. Once enabled, the user has the option of assigning individual transactions to a specific class and preparing reports by class. This function can be particularly useful for restaurants with multiple locations. The same reporting objectives can also be achieved by developing a more detailed Chart of Accounts.

Preparing Lists

Lists can be accessed by using the list drop-down menu or by accessing a center (i.e., customer, vendor, employee center, and so on) and clicking the **Print** icon to access the drop-down list.

Examples of lists include the following:

- **From Customer Center:** Customer & Job Transaction List, Customer Invoice List, and Received Payments List
- **From Vendor Center:** Vendor List, Vendor Transaction List, Purchase Order List, Bill List, and Bill Payment List
- **From Employee Center:** Employee Information List and Paycheck List

Within a center, many of these lists can be viewed as a report after selecting a transaction type and right-clicking in the window and selecting **View as a Report.** These reports can be modified to suit individual needs. It is suggested to print these lists as reports to allow modifications such as date ranges or selecting only certain fields to be displayed. For further information on Customizing Reports, see Chapter 4, page 99.

Sample Chart of Accounts for a Table Service Restaurant

Account Number	Account Name	QuickBooks Type
10000	Checking Account	Bank
10050	Visa / MasterCard	Bank
10075	Amex	Bank
10100	Advance Deposits	Bank
10150	Over / Short	Bank
10160	Petty Cash	Bank
10500	Savings Account	Bank
10700	Accounts Receivable	Accounts Receivable
10800	Allowance for Doubtful Accounts	Accounts Receivable
10950	Cash in Drawer	Other Current Asset
12000	Undeposited Funds	Other Current Asset
12050	Interest Receivable	Other Current Asset
12100	Inventory Asset	Other Current Asset
12400	Food Inventory	Other Current Asset
12500	Beverage Inventory	Other Current Asset
12510	Beer	Other Current Asset
12520	Wine	Other Current Asset
12530	Liquor	Other Current Asset
12540	Other	Other Current Asset
12600	Retail Inventory	Other Current Asset
12700	Supplies Inventory	Other Current Asset
12800	Employee Advances	Other Current Asset
13100	Prepaid Expenses	Other Current Asset
15000	Furniture and Equipment	Fixed Asset
15025	Bar Equipment	Fixed Asset
15050	Kitchen Equipment	Fixed Asset
15075	Office Equipment	Fixed Asset
15100	China, Silver, Glassware, Linen	Fixed Asset
15150	Smallwares	Fixed Asset
15175	Computer Equipment	Fixed Asset
15200	Buildings and Improvements	Fixed Asset
15300	Land	Fixed Asset
15400	Custom Software	Fixed Asset
15900	Leasehold Improvements	Fixed Asset
16400	Vehicles	Fixed Asset

Account Number	Account Name	QuickBooks Type
17000	Accumulated Depreciation	Fixed Asset
17010	Furniture and Equipment	Fixed Asset
17020	Bar Equipment	Fixed Asset
17030	Kitchen Equipment	Fixed Asset
17040	Office Equipment	Fixed Asset
17050	China, Silver, Glassware, Linen	Fixed Asset
17060	Smallwares	Fixed Asset
17065	Computer Equipment	Fixed Asset
17070	Buildings and Improvement	Fixed Asset
17080	Custom Software	Fixed Asset
17090	Leasehold Improvements	Fixed Asset
17095	Vehicles	Fixed Asset
18500	Cost of Liquor License	Other Asset
18700	Security Deposits Asset	Other Asset
20000	Accounts Payable	Accounts Payable
21000	Interest Payable	Other Current Liability
24000	Payroll Liabilities	Other Current Liability
24010	Social Security	Other Current Liability
24020	Medicare	Other Current Liability
24030	Federal Unemployment	Other Current Liability
24040	State Unemployment	Other Current Liability
24050	Federal Income Tax	Other Current Liability
24060	State Income Tax	Other Current Liability
24070	Health and Dental	Other Current Liability
25100	Employee Tips Payable	Other Current Liability
25200	Gift Certificates Outstanding	Other Current Liability
25300	Gift Certificates Redeemed	Other Current Liability
25500	Sales Tax Payable	Other Current Liability
26000	Notes Payable – Current	Other Current Liability
27000	Unearned Revenue	Other Current Liability
28000	Notes Payable	Long-Term Liability
30000	Opening Balance Equity	Equity
30100	Capital Stock	Equity
30200	Dividends Paid	Equity
32000	Retained Earnings	Equity
41400	Beverage Sales	Income
41410	Beer	Income
41420	Wine	Income
41430	Liquor	Income

Account Number	Account Name	QuickBooks Type
42100	Catering Sales	Income
42110	Food	Income
43800	Food Sales	Income
43900	Sales Comps, Discounts, & Promo	Income
50000	Cost of Goods Sold	Cost of Goods Sold
50900	Food Purchases	Cost of Goods Sold
51000	Bar Purchases	Cost of Goods Sold
51010	Beer	Cost of Goods Sold
51020	Wine	Cost of Goods Sold
51030	Liquor	Cost of Goods Sold
51040	Other	Cost of Goods Sold
51800	Merchant Account Fees	Cost of Goods Sold
60000	Advertising and Promotion	Expense
60200	Automobile Expense	Expense
60400	Bank Service Charges	Expense
60500	Bad Debt Expense	Expense
61000	Business Licenses and Permits	Expense
61200	Cash Drawer Payouts	Expense
61400	Charitable Contributions	Expense
61700	Computer and Internet Expenses	Expense
62000	Continuing Education	Expense
62400	Depreciation Expense	Expense
62410	Furniture and Equipment	Expense
62420	Bar Equipment	Expense
62430	Kitchen Equipment	Expense
62440	Office Equipment	Expense
62450	China, Silver, Glassware, Linen	Expense
62460	Smallwares	Expense
62465	Computer Equipment	Expense
62470	Buildings and Improvements	Expense
62480	Custom Software	Expense
62490	Leasehold Improvements	Expense
62495	Vehicle	Expense
62500	Dues and Subscriptions	Expense
62600	Equipment Rental	Expense

Account Number	Account Name	QuickBooks Type
63300	Insurance Expense	Expense
63310	General Liability Insurance	Expense
63320	Health Insurance	Expense
63330	Life and Disability Insurance	Expense
63360	Worker's Compensation	Expense
63500	Janitorial Expense	Expense
63550	Kitchen Utensils and Tableware	Expense
64000	Linen and Dry Cleaning Expense	Expense
64200	Maintenance Fee	Expense
64300	Meals and Entertainment	Expense
64700	Miscellaneous Expense	Expense
64800	Music and Entertainment	Expense
64900	Office Supplies	Expense
65200	Outside Services	Expense
66000	Payroll Expenses	Expense
66005	Manager	Expense
66010	Chef	Expense
66015	Sous Chef	Expense
66020	Service and Bus Staff	Expense
66030	Host	Expense
66040	Bartender	Expense
66050	Kitchen Staff	Expense
66055	Expeditor	Expense
66058	Dishwasher	Expense
66060	Social Security	Expense
66065	Medicare	Expense
66070	Federal Unemployment	Expense
66075	State Unemployment	Expense
66080	Employee Benefits	Expense
66085	Workers' Compensation	Expense
66090	Catering	Expense
66095	Other	Expense
66500	Postage and Delivery	Expense
66600	Printing and Reproduction	Expense
66700	Professional Fees	Expense
66710	Accounting	Expense
66720	Legal	Expense
67100	Rent Expense	Expense

Account Number	Account Name	QuickBooks Type
67200	Repairs and Maintenance	Expense
67300	Start-up Costs	Expense
67500	Supplies Expense	Expense
68000	Taxes—Property	Expense
68100	Telephone Expense	Expense
68400	Travel Expense	Expense
68500	Uniforms	Expense
68600	Utilities	Expense
70000	Other Income	Other Income
70010	Retail Income	Other Income
70050	Gift Certificates Unredeemed	Other Income
70100	Insurance Proceeds Received	Other Income
70200	Interest Income	Other Income
70500	Proceeds from Sale of Assets	Other Income
80000	Ask My Accountant	Other Expense
80100	Other Expense	Other Expense
80300	Interest Expense	Other Expense
80500	Political Contributions	Other Expense
80600	Retail Expense	Other Expense
90000	Estimates	Non-Posting
90100	Purchase Orders	Non-Posting

Chapter Review Problems

1. Add the following accounts to the Chart of Accounts.

Account Number	Account Name	Type
12700	Supplies Inventory	Other Current Asset
15100	China, Silver, Glassware, Linen	Fixed Asset
26000	Notes Payable – Current	Other Current Liability
27000	Unearned Revenue	Other Current Liability
28000	Notes Payable	Long Term Liability
60500	Bad Debt Expense	Expense

2. Add the following subaccounts to the Chart of Accounts.

Account Number	Account Name	Subaccount	Type
10100	Advance Deposits	Checking Account	Bank
12520	Wine	Beverage Inventory	Other Current Asset
17010	Furniture and Equipment	Accumulated Depreciation	Fixed Asset
42110	Food	Catering Sales	Income
51010	Beer	Beverage Purchases	COGS

3. Add the following vendors to the Vendor List.

DATA:

Safety Plus Insurance
367 Langley Lane
Morristown, MI 44444
999-666-6000
TERMS: Net 30

DATA:

Food Works, Inc.
183 78th Street
Capital City, NY 11110
555-450-1111
TERMS: Net 15

4. Add the following customers to the Customer List.

DATA:

Capital City Medical
1820 Pauline Place
Capital City, NY 11100
Dr. Barbara Allen
555-222-9999

TERMS:	Due on receipt
PREFERRED SEND METHOD:	Mail
TAX CODE:	Tax
TAX ITEM:	Sales Tax

DATA:

CMR Consulting Group
1530 Park Avenue
Capital City, NY 11100
Mr. James Garcia
555-555-4242

TERMS:	Due on receipt
PREFERRED SEND METHOD:	Mail
TAX CODE:	Tax
TAX ITEM:	Sales Tax

5. Add the following items to the Item list.

DATA:

TYPE:	Service
ITEM NAME/NUMBER:	Penne Large
DESCRIPTION:	Penne Full Pan
RATE:	$80.00
TAX CODE:	Tax
ACCOUNT:	42110 Catering Sales – Food

DATA:

TYPE:	Noninventory Part
ITEM NAME/NUMBER:	Paper Towel
DESCRIPTION:	Paper Towel – Center Pull, Case
COST:	$24.85
TAX CODE:	Tax
ACCOUNT:	12700 Supplies Inventory

DATA:

TYPE:	Inventory Part
ITEM NAME/NUMBER:	Tomato Crushed #10 Can
DESCRIPTION:	Tomato Crushed #10 Can
COST:	$3.45
COGS ACCOUNT:	50900 Food Purchases
PREFERRED VENDOR:	Quality Food Vendor
TAX CODE:	Tax
ASSET ACCOUNT:	12400 Food Inventory
INCOME ACCOUNT:	43800 Food Sales
REORDER POINT:	12
AS OF:	01/01/2008

DATA:

TYPE:	Inventory Part
ITEM NAME/NUMBER:	Pasta Sauce Sampler
DESCRIPTION:	Pasta Sauce Sampler – 3 Jars
COST:	$5.00
COGS ACCOUNT:	80600 Retail Expense
PREFERRED VENDOR:	Italian Imports Direct
TAX CODE:	Tax
ASSET ACCOUNT:	12600 Retail Inventory
INCOME ACCOUNT:	70010 Retail Income
REORDER POINT:	24
AS OF:	01/01/2008

You can find additional Review Problems at *www.wiley.com/college/murphy*.

Restaurant Purchases, Payables, and Inventory

Access the Chapter 4 data file from the CD-ROM that accompanies this book or download the file from the web site.

Chapter Outline

The Purchasing Process

Working with Purchase Orders

Receiving Goods

Entering Bills

Editing Bills

Voiding and Deleting Bills

Memorizing Bills

Paying Bills

Using Vendor Discounts

Using Vendor Credits

Using the Check Register

Creating and Printing Checks

Editing, Voiding, and Deleting Checks

Inventory Stock Status (Inventory on Hand) and Par Levels

Physical Inventory Worksheets

Making Inventory Adjustments

Other Inventory Management Systems

Reports

Chapter Review Problems

The Purchasing Process

Purchasing is the process of obtaining goods and services for use in the restaurant. Items can be purchased using cash or credit. In addition, the provider may also extend credit to the restaurant. There are different methods that can be used to facilitate the purchase of goods and services. Checks can be written, bills can be directly entered into QuickBooks, or purchase orders can be created and turned into a bill when inventory is received. Bills can be entered and paid immediately, or payment can be made at a later date.

A restaurant's cash flow and liquidity dictates when bills are paid. Some vendors reward businesses with a discount for early payment. A restaurant should establish a Chart of Accounts, Vendor List and Item List prior to processing purchases and payments. An Item List should be used for purchased items that will be tracked as inventory items in QuickBooks. Additional accounts, items, and vendors can be added while processing transactions. New vendors can be added through the Vendor Center (see Chapter 3, page 52).

ACCOUNTING TIP

The fundamental accounting equation states that the total assets of a business are equal to the total liabilities plus the owner's equity of the business. The system of double entry accounting maintains the balance in the equation by having every transaction impact at least two accounts. Each transaction is recorded in the left side of an account (also referred to as the debit side) and the right side of an account (also referred to as the credit side). The total amounts of the debits must be equal to the total amounts of the credits.

An item list was previously created for Aroma Ristorante (see Chapter 3). The restaurant's purchased items are included on the list. The restaurant tracks inventory for food, beverage, and retail items only. The purchase of an inventory item results in an increase in Inventory and Accounts Payable accounts (DEBIT: Inventory; CREDIT: Accounts Payable). When the invoice is paid, Cash and Accounts Payable accounts will decrease (DEBIT: Accounts Payable; CREDIT: Cash). Adjustments to inventory will be made on completion of the physical inventory count, and the related cost of goods sold will be recorded at that time.

Working with Purchase Orders

One of the most critical functions of any restaurant operation is the ability to place orders and receive goods and services from vendors. The documentation utilized for this business process is called a purchase order. A *purchase order* is a document that provides written or electronic confirmation of a restaurant's request for the delivery of a good or service. Each purchase order is assigned a specific number that allows proper tracking of the order from its initial placement to its final receipt. The numbered purchase order also enables the restaurant to verify the accuracy and completeness of the order.

An effective purchase order system can be used to manage costs in a restaurant by controlling the amount of inventory on hand at any given time. Maintaining appropriate inventory levels can improve the cash flow of the operation. Restaurant operations can use a variety of different tools and systems to generate purchase orders and manage inventory, including QuickBooks.

Industry Fact

Many large food and beverage vendors provide inventory management tools to their customers, including web-enabled technology that can create and process purchase orders for the restaurant. Large vendors provide services that place the orders in a timely fashion to ensure that the restaurant has the required inventory items in the proper amounts to meet the consumer demand.

When a purchase order is created in QuickBooks, a non-posting account called Purchase Orders is automatically created in the Chart of Accounts. A *non-posting account* means that the purchase orders do not become a part of the financial statements of the restaurant. The purpose of this non-posting Purchase Order account is to track the restaurant's open purchase orders. QuickBooks can create a purchase order using items from the Item List as long as the items have been entered. Once an item is received and verified, a purchase order can be converted into a bill, which increases inventory and accounts payable.

HELPFUL TIP

Restaurant operators may require vendors to identify the purchase order number on their invoices when submitting them for payment. This practice enables the restaurant to verify the payable with the items purchased and received.

To Create a Purchase Order

Click the **Vendor Center** icon or click the **Purchase Orders** icon on the Home page.

Click the **New Transactions** icon.

Select **Purchase Orders** from the drop-down list.

Aroma Ristorante wants to create a purchase order for their cookbooks that are for sale at the restaurant.

Using the following data, enter the information in the appropriate fields (see Figure 4-1).

DATA: Create a Purchase Order for Aroma Cookbooks.

VENDOR:	North Publishing Company
TEMPLATE:	Custom Purchase Order
DATE:	1/1/2008
PO NUMBER:	108
ITEM:	Aroma Cookbook (Select from the drop-down list)
QTY:	24

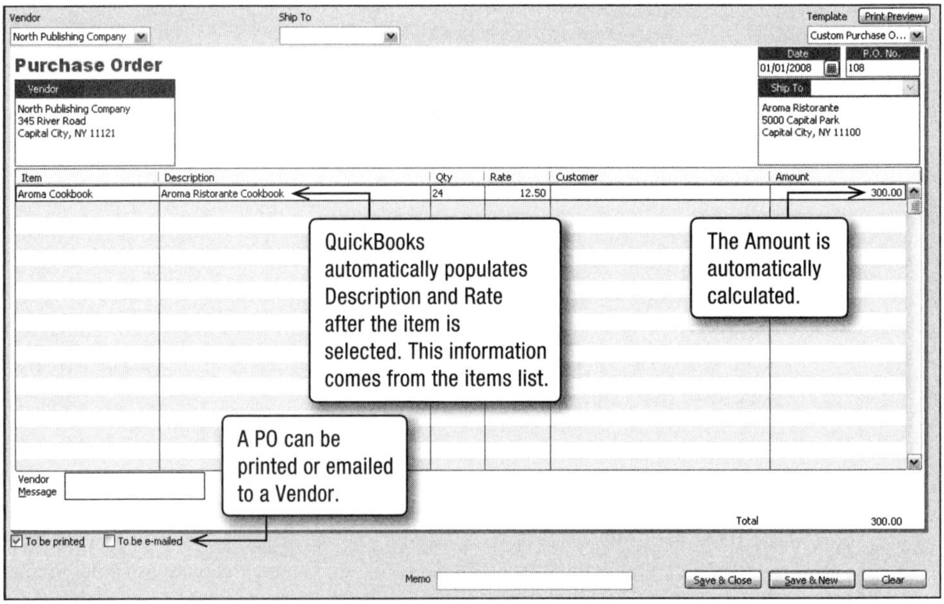

Figure 4-1.

Click **Save & Close**.

Receiving Goods

How a restaurant uses the Item List and inventory features will determine how goods are recorded in QuickBooks. Aroma Ristorante's goods will be recorded in inventory when they are received.

After submitting Purchase Order No.108, 24 cookbooks were received from North Publishing Company, and the bill was included in the shipment.

Receive the Cookbooks into Inventory and Turn the Purchase Order into a Bill

Click the **Vendor Center** icon or click the **Receive Inventory** icon on the Home page.

Click the **New Transactions** icon.

Select **Receive Items and Enter Bill**.

Select **North Publishing Company** from the Vendor drop-down list.

The **Open POs Exist** window will display on the desktop (see Figure 4-2).

Figure 4-2.

Click **Yes**.

Select **PO#108** from the Open Purchase Orders window.

Click **OK**.

In the Enter Bill window, QuickBooks will automatically populate data from the existing Purchase Order (see Figure 4-3).

⊙ Bill ○ Credit				☑ Bill Received			
Bill							
Vendor North Publishing Company ▾		Date	01/15/2008 📖				
Address North Publishing Company 345 River Road Capital City, NY 11121		Ref. No.	64102				
		Amount Due	300.00				
		Bill Due	01/30/2008 📖		← Enter Invoice Number		
Terms Net 15 ▾ Discount Date							
Memo							

Expenses	$0.00	**Items**	$300.00					
Item	Description			Qty	Cost	Amount	Customer:Job	Billable?
Aroma Cookbook	Aroma Ristorante Cookbook			24	12.50	300.00		

Figure 4-3.

Enter the Reference Number (Invoice Number) **64102.**

Enter a date of **1/15/2008.**

Click **Save & Close.**

Twenty-four Aroma Cookbooks have been added to Retail Inventory. As a result, Accounts Payable has increased by $300.00.

QUICKBOOKS TIP

The quantity received can be changed on the Purchase Order if fewer or more items than requested were received from the vendor.

Prices do not always remain the same; and unless the manager has updated the cost of the item in the Item List, prices on the purchase order may differ from the current invoice prices. If this occurs, changes can be made to the purchase order or the bill to reflect the correct price.

If a purchase order was created and the restaurant is not going to receive some or all of the items on the purchase order, the order should be closed. Purchase orders should not be left outstanding because QuickBooks will only display active purchase orders in the non-posting account.

To Close a Purchase Order

Click the **Vendor Center** icon.

Click the **Transactions** tab.

Select **Purchase Orders.**

Double-click the appropriate purchase order.

Select the **Closed** checkbox at the bottom left of the Purchase Order window (see Figure 4-4).

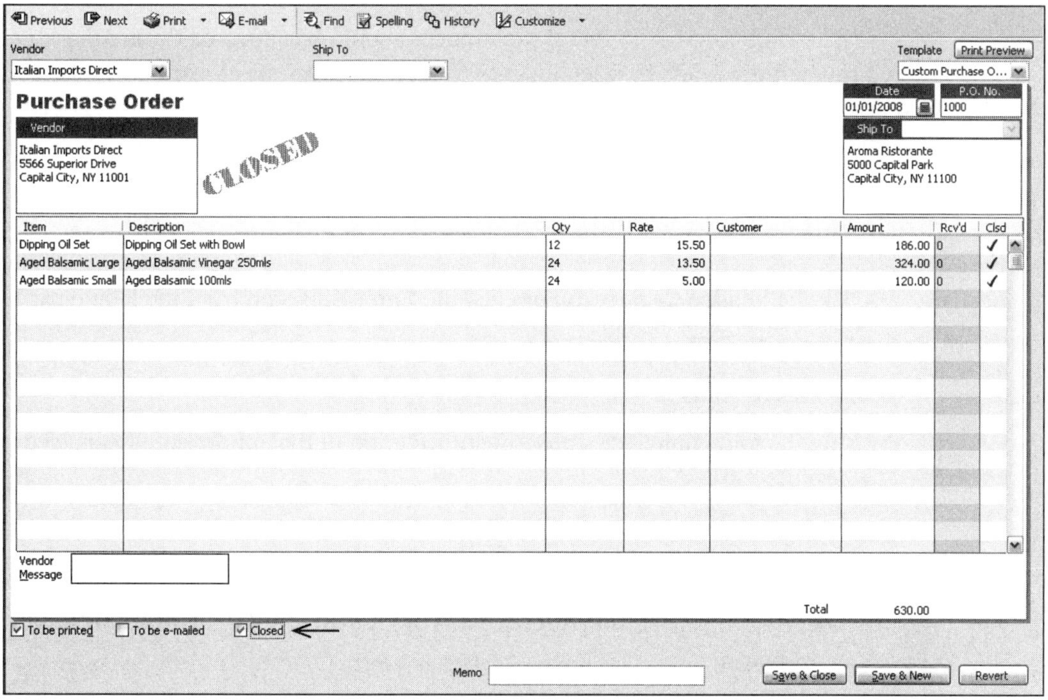

Figure 4-4.

For some businesses with a large quantity and variety of inventory items, the purchase order process is a valuable tool in facilitating efficient inventory management. Conversely, other businesses find that purchase orders slow down the procurement process.

In certain operations, as an internal control procedure, the individual responsible for receiving inventory items is different from the individual responsible for placing the order. This segregation of responsibilities reduces the potential for theft. Accounting personnel compare the receiving report to the purchase order and invoice to ensure payment is made only for items that were received. These procedures help to control inventory costs.

Entering Bills

As previously mentioned, bills can also be entered directly into QuickBooks without the use of purchase orders. Bills can be entered via the Vendor Center or the Accounts Payable Register.

Prior to entering bills, several preferences should be activated during the EasyStep Interview by selecting **Yes** to the following questions: Do you keep track of bills you owe? Do you print checks? Do you track inventory? A bank account must have been previously established (see Chapter 2, page 18).

Enter a Bill—Using Vendor Center

Click the **Vendor Center** icon or click the **Enter Bills** icon from the Home page.

Click the **New Transactions** icon.

Select **Enter Bills.**

Using the following data, enter the information in the appropriate fields (see Figure 4-5).

DATA: Enter the Bill Received from Capital City Utilities, Inc.	
VENDOR:	Capital City Utilities, Inc.
DATE:	1/31/2008
REF NO.:	736541
AMOUNT DUE:	$4,100
ACCOUNT:	68600 Utilities
MEMO:	Electric, Gas, and Water Expense

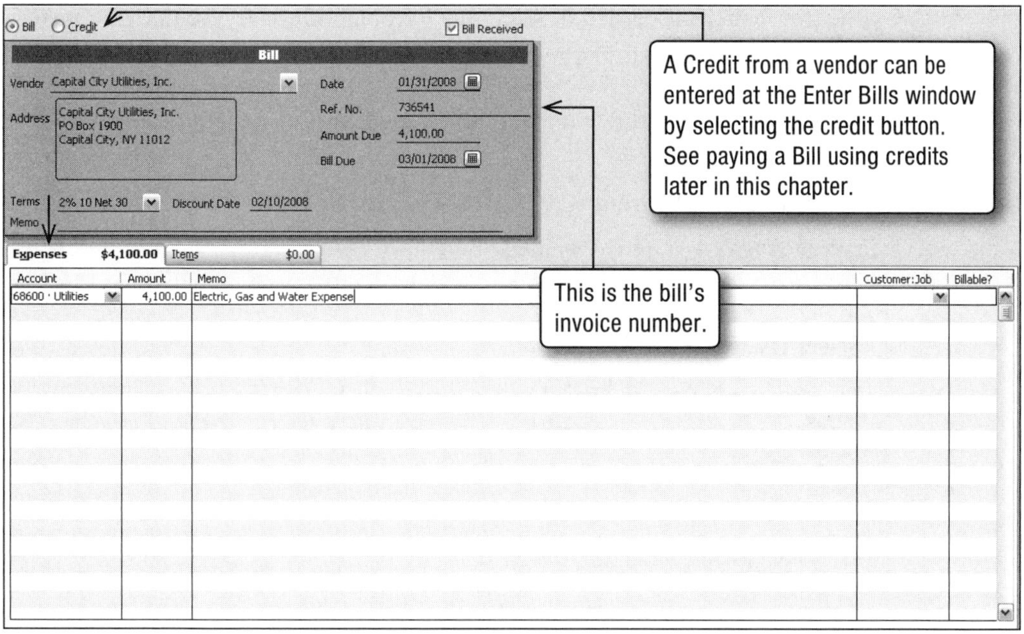

Figure 4-5.

When entering a bill for an expense, click the **Expenses** tab and identify the appropriate expense account. When entering a bill for items to be recorded in inventory, click the **Items** tab and identify the appropriate items.

Click **Save & Close**.

QUICKBOOKS TIP
If a vendor or an account was not previously entered into QuickBooks, this information can be added in this window by selecting the appropriate drop-down list and selecting **Add New** (see Chapter 3).

QUICKBOOKS TIP
If the address and terms of the vendor were identified in the vendor record, these fields will automatically populate. QuickBooks calculates the bill due date based on the terms specified.

Enter a Bill—Using the Accounts Payable Register

Accounts Payable is a list of all the restaurant's unpaid bills. The Accounts Payable account is considered a current liability because these bills should be paid within thirty days. The Accounts Payable Register is a detailed list of all the transactions recorded in Accounts Payable. Bills can be entered, edited, and deleted directly in the register.

Chart of
Accounts

Click the **List** drop-down menu or click the **Chart of Accounts** icon on the Home page.

Select **Chart of Accounts.**

Select **20000 Accounts Payable.**

Click the **Activities** button at the bottom of the window.

Select **Use Register.**

The current date is displayed in the next open line of the register. Click the **Calendar** icon to change the date. The new bill can be entered on the next two lines of the register (see Figure 4-6).

Date	Number	Vendor		Due Date	Billed	✓	Paid	Balance
	Type	Account	Memo					
01/01/2008	98265	Restaurant Equipment, Inc.		Paid	189,350.00			189,350.00
	BILL	-split-						
01/01/2008	852001	Capital City News and Guide		Paid	350.00			189,700.00
	BILL	60000 · Advertising and Promotion						
01/01/2008	03269950	Capital City Telephone Book - Yellow Page		Paid	3,000.00			192,700.00
	BILL	13100 · Prepaid Expenses						
01/02/2008	0023695	Restaurant World, Inc.		Paid	58,450.00			251,150.00
	BILL	-split-						
01/02/2008	0023841	Bobs Sound Barn		Paid	5,000.00			256,150.00
	BILL	-split-						
01/02/2008	333222	Four Star Carpet Cleaning ◀—	Enter bill information here	Paid	500.00			256,650.00
	BILL	67200 · Repairs and Maintenance						

Figure 4-6.

Editing Bills

Bills can be edited using the Vendor Center or the Accounts Payable Register. Corrections can be made to a bill at any time.

Edit a Bill—Using Vendor Center

Click the **Vendor Center** icon.

Click the **Transactions** tab.

Select **Bills.**

All bills are displayed on the right side of the desktop. Find the bill to be edited from the list and double-click on it to display the bill.

Make the appropriate changes.

Click **Save & Close.**

Edit a Bill—Using the Accounts Payable Register

 Click the **List** drop-down menu or click the **Chart of Accounts** icon on the Home page.

Select **Chart of Accounts.**

Select **20000 Accounts Payable.**

Click the **Activities** button at the bottom of the window.

Select **Use Register.**

Locate and edit the appropriate bill.

Click **Record.**

QuickBooks will notify you with a message: You have changed the transaction. Do you want to record your change?

Click **Yes.**

Voiding and Deleting Bills

Bills can be voided or deleted using the Vendor Center or the Accounts Payable Register. Deleting a bill permanently removes the bill from the QuickBooks file. Voiding a bill keeps the bill in the QuickBooks file so it can be viewed, but the bill will have a zero balance.

Void Bill—Using Vendor Center

Click the **Vendor Center** icon.

Click the **Transactions** tab.

Select **Bills.**

A list of bills will be displayed on the right side of the window. Double-click on the bill to be voided.

Click the **Edit** drop-down menu.

Select **Void Bill.**

Click **Save & Close.**

QuickBooks will notify you with a message: You have changed the transaction. Do you want to record your change?

Click **Yes.**

Delete Bill—Using the Accounts Payable Register

Click the **List** drop-down menu or click the **Chart of Accounts** icon on the Home page.

Select **Chart of Accounts.**

Double-click on **20000 Accounts Payable.**

Double-click on the bill to be deleted. (Double-click on the word "BILL" in the type column.)

Click the **Edit** drop-down menu.

Select **Delete Bill.**

QuickBooks will notify you with a message: Are you sure you want to delete this transaction?

Click **Yes.**

Memorizing Bills

QuickBooks has a feature that allows the user to set up memorized transactions that frequently occur. This memorization feature recalls previously entered data, which reduces data entry time. For example, a restaurant may have a variable expense such as a monthly bill for linen service, where the amount is different each month. In this case, only the bill amount, date, and reference number (invoice number) need to be entered each time.

ACCOUNTING TIP

Fixed expenses remain constant for a certain period of time. Variable expenses vary with sales volume.

A restaurant may have a fixed expense such as insurance where the amount is the same each quarter and only the date and reference number change. Memorized transactions can be used to reduce the data entry. QuickBooks will display a prompt to remind a manager when a bill is due. In addition, memorized transactions can be set up to record automatically.

Aroma Ristorante receives a linen bill each week. The linen service amount varies. As a result, the amount of the bill should be left blank. To create and memorize a bill from Best Linen Service, Inc., perform the following:

Click the **Vendor Center** icon.

Click the **New Transactions** icon.

Select **Enter Bills** from the drop-down list.

Select **Best Linen Service, Inc.** from the Vendor drop-down list.

Select Account **64000 Linen and Dry Cleaning Expense** from the Account drop-down list (see Figure 4-7).

Click the **Edit** drop-down menu.

Select **Memorize Bill.**

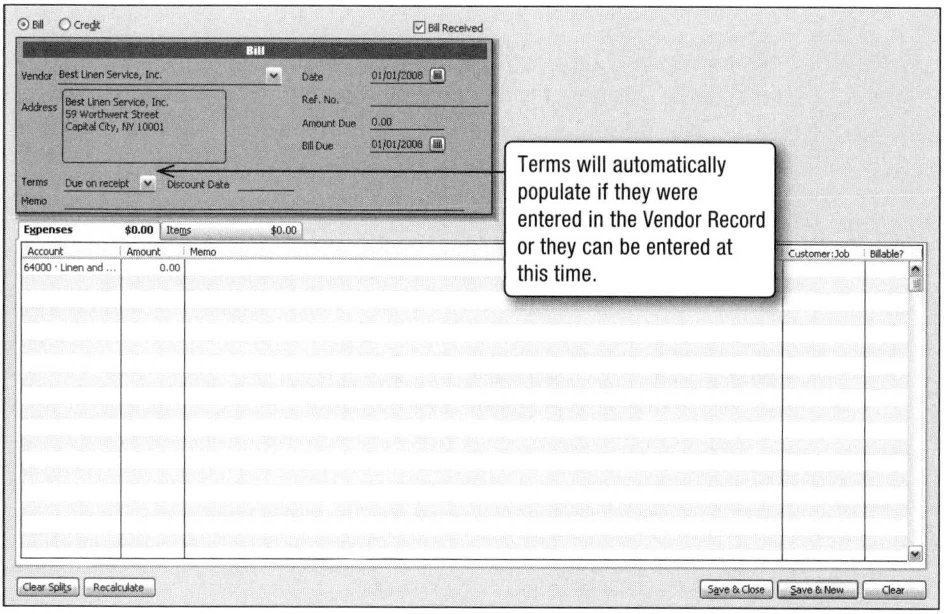

Figure 4-7.

In the Memorized Transaction window, the Name field is automatically populated with the vendor name (see Figure 4-8). This name can be changed. Each memorized transaction is identified in the Memorized Transaction List by a specific name. The name of the transaction should be easily recognizable, distinguishing it from other names in the Memorized Transaction List.

The three options are **Remind Me, Don't Remind Me,** or **Automatically Enter.**

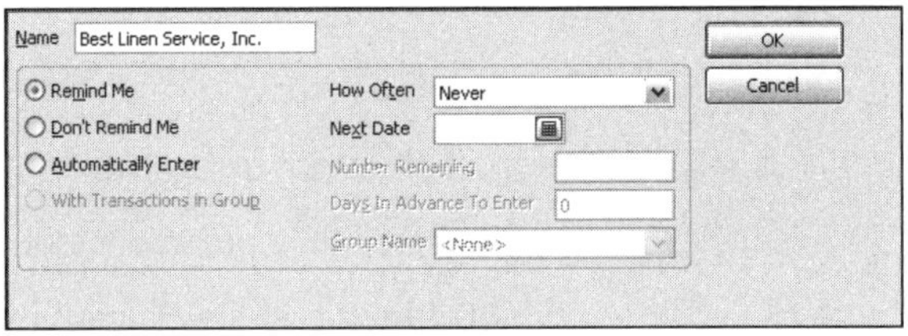

Figure 4-8.

Remind Me

QuickBooks will prompt the restaurant operator to pay the bill at the specified date. This date needs to be identified in the How Often or Next Date field. This option is appropriate for a reoccurring expense, such as utilities.

Don't Remind Me

QuickBooks will not prompt the restaurant operator to pay the bill, yet the transaction will be saved in the Memorized Transaction List. This option is appropriate for an expense from an established vendor that does not occur on a regular basis, such as repairs and maintenance. This enables the manager to recall the transaction only when needed.

Automatically Enter

QuickBooks automatically records the memorized transaction for the restaurant operator. It is necessary to identify how often QuickBooks should enter the transaction and when the next transaction is due. In the number remaining field, a manager can specify the number of times to enter the transaction. This option is appropriate for transactions that are the same amount and are due on a regular schedule, such as rent.

QUICKBOOKS TIP
The date field automatically populates the current date. This date can be changed when the transaction is recalled.

QUICKBOOKS TIP
Groups can be created for related transactions. Memorized transactions can be added to a group, such as a monthly bill group.

By clicking **OK** at the Memorized Transaction window, the transaction will be saved in the Memorized Transaction List.

Paying Bills

Some bills will be entered into QuickBooks from the Pay Bill window, and other expenditures can be paid directly (bypassing the enter bills process) using the Write Checks option. The Write Checks option is suitable for vendors that do not send bills or vendors who expect payment on delivery. A combination of both methods is an appropriate practice for the restaurant operator. Using either method, bills should be entered frequently so a restaurant operator can see the impact of the expense on the financial statements.

Aroma Ristorante would like to pay a bill from Quality Food Vendor.

QUICKBOOKS TIP

When bills are entered in the Pay Bills window, the amount is recorded as an increase in accounts payable. When bills are paid using the Write Checks option, the amount is recorded as a decrease in cash.

Click the **Vendor Center** icon.

Click the **New Transactions** icon.

Select **Pay Bills** or click the **Pay Bills** icon on the Home page (see Figure 4-9).

Select **Show bills Due on or before 1/31/2008.**

Select the **Quality Food Vendor** bill for $877.89.

Select **Check** from the Payment Method drop-down list.

Select **10000 Checking Account** from the Payment Account drop-down list.

Select **1/18/2008** as the Payment Date.

Click **Pay Selected Bills.**

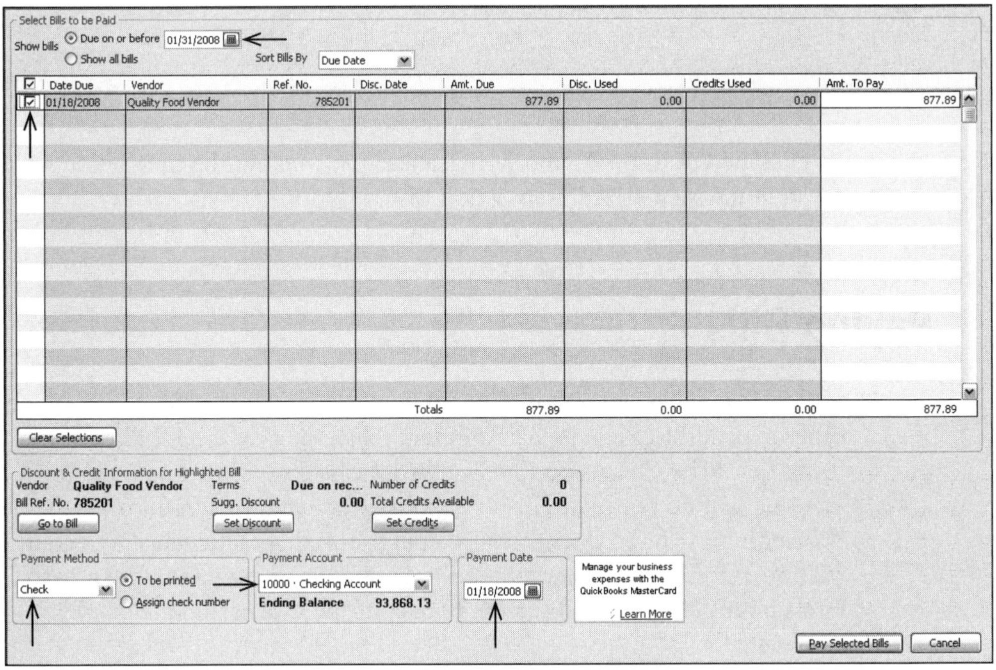

☑	Date Due	Vendor	Ref. No.	Disc. Date	Amt. Due	Disc. Used	Credits Used	Amt. To Pay
☑	01/18/2008	Quality Food Vendor	785201		877.89	0.00	0.00	877.89

Figure 4-9.

In the Payment Summary window, confirm information and click **Done** to record the payment.

If a restaurant uses manual checks instead of checks generated by QuickBooks, the payment can be recorded using these steps and assigning the appropriate check number. If a restaurant is using QuickBooks to print checks, a check could be printed at this time.

A bill payment can be voided or deleted after it has been paid.

To Void or Delete Bill and Payment

In certain cases, bills and/or payments may need to be voided or deleted. For example, duplicate or erroneous bills may need to be deleted or voided.

Click the **Vendor Center** icon.

Click the **Transactions** tab.

Select **Bills** to display bills on the right side of the desktop.

Select the bill by double-clicking on the appropriate bill.

Click the **Edit** drop-down menu.

Select **Void Bill** or **Delete Bill.**

Follow the appropriate QuickBooks instructions, based on the option selected.

> **QUICKBOOKS TIP**
>
> Online Banking: A user can download electronic statements from certain financial institutions into QuickBooks to compare transactions and balances.

Using Vendor Discounts

As previously stated, some vendors reward their customers by extending discounts for early payment of invoices. Taking advantage of early payment terms can reduce costs. Discounts can be applied to bills at the Select Bills to be Paid window.

Pay Bills

Click the **Vendor Center** icon or click the **Pay Bills** icon on the Home page.

Click the **New Transactions** icon.

Select **Pay Bills**.

Select **Show All Bills** to view all unpaid bills entered into QuickBooks.

Select the **Four Star Carpet Cleaning, Inc.** bill for $500.00.

Click **Set Discount** (see Figure 4-10).

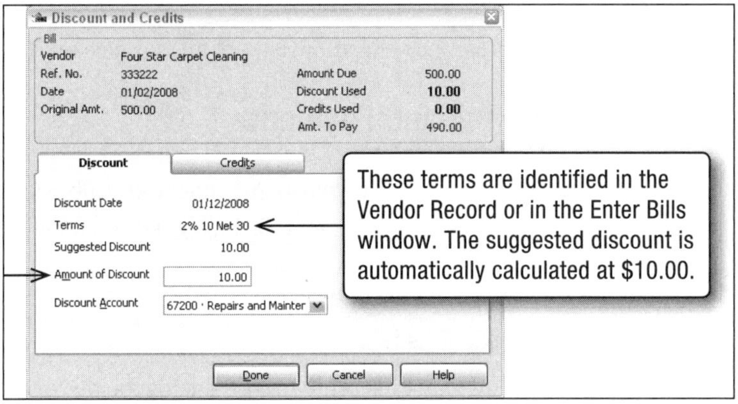

Figure 4-10.

If discounts are not indicated in the vendor record or the Enter Bill window, the amount must be entered in the Amount of Discount field.

Select the **67200 Repairs and Maintenance** account from the drop-down list.

Click **Done**.

Select **10000 Checking Account** from the Payment Account drop-down list.

Select **Check** from the Payment Method drop-down list.

Select a Payment Date of **1/4/2008**.

Click **Pay Selected Bills.**

In the Payment Summary window, confirm the information and click **Done** to record the payment. For additional information on printing checks versus manual checks and on assigning check numbers, see page 90 or QuickBooks Help.

Using Vendor Credits

Vendor credits must be entered first and subsequently applied to a bill. A credit can be applied to an existing bill or a new bill. Partial credits and additional credits can be applied to a bill. Existing credits can be deleted. The credit is applied to the bill when the bill is ready to be paid.

Enter a Credit

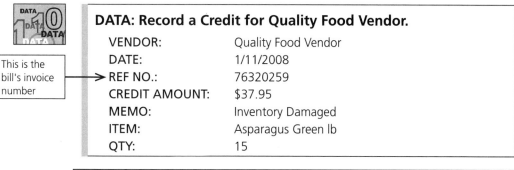
Enter Bills

Click the **Vendor Center** icon or click the **Enter Bills** icon on the Home page.

Click the **New Transactions** icon.

Select **Enter Bills** from the drop-down list.

Click **Credit** to change from a bill to a credit.

Enter the credit information.

Using the data that follows, at the Enter Bills window, enter the information in the appropriate fields (see Figure 4-11).

DATA: Record a Credit for Quality Food Vendor.

VENDOR:	Quality Food Vendor
DATE:	1/11/2008
REF NO.:	76320259
CREDIT AMOUNT:	$37.95
MEMO:	Inventory Damaged
ITEM:	Asparagus Green lb
QTY:	15

This is the bill's invoice number

Figure 4-11.

Click **Save & Close.**

Apply the Credit to an Existing Bill

To reduce the invoice amount, apply the credit to the appropriate invoice.

Click the **Vendor Center** icon or click the **Pay Bills** icon on the Home page.

Click the **New Transactions** icon.

Select **Pay Bills.**

Select **Show All Bills** to view all unpaid bills entered into QuickBooks (see Figure 4-12).

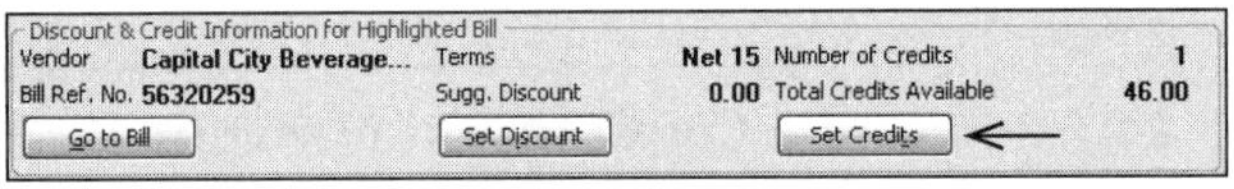

Figure 4-12.

Select the appropriate bill.

Click **Set Credits.**

Select the credit (see Figure 4-13).

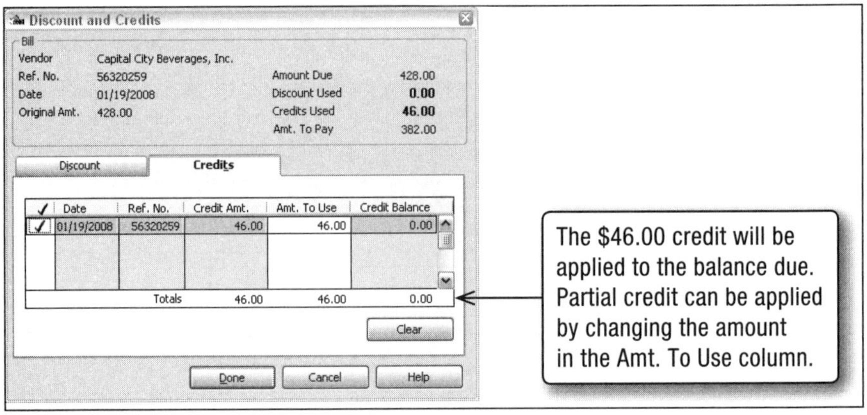

Figure 4-13.

Once a checkmark is placed next to the credit, the credit is applied to the balance due. The amount to be paid to Capital City Beverage is now $382.00.

Click **Done.**

Click **Pay Selected Bills.**

Click **Done.**

Credits can be deleted or voided by clicking the **Vendor Center** icon, clicking the Transactions tab, and selecting **Bills.** Select the appropriate credit by double-clicking on the credit. Once the credit is displayed on the desktop, click the **Edit** drop-down menu and select **Void Credit** or **Delete Credit**.

Using the Check Register

QuickBooks Check Register is very similar to a personal checkbook register. All recorded payments, checks, deposits, and balances are listed, but with QuickBooks a restaurant operator can sort and search for transactions as well as easily make edits to transactions that have already been created. Checks and deposits can be viewed in detail by simply double-clicking on the transaction line in the Check Register.

Accessing the Check Register

Click the **Banking** drop-down menu or click the **Check Register** icon on the Home page.

Select **Use Register.**

Select the **10000 Checking Account** from the window and click **OK.**

Recording a Deposit Using the Check Register

Deposits can also be recorded in the Check Register. These deposits can be refunds from vendors, loan proceeds, or possibly a referral check.

Aroma Ristorante received a refund check from Capital City Florists for a centerpiece that was paid for but never received. The check is for the amount of $50.

On the next open line of the Check Register, enter the following data in the appropriate fields.

DATA: Record the Refund Check from Capital City Florists.	
DATE:	1/10/2008
DEPOSIT NUMBER:	201
PAYEE:	Capital City Florists
DEPOSIT:	$50.00
ACCOUNT:	64700 Miscellaneous Expenses
MEMO:	Refund Check

Click **Record.**

Creating and Printing Checks

Checks can be created and printed from the Write Checks window. The QuickBooks check looks very similar to a regular check and can easily be filled out.

Aroma Ristorante needs to pay rent. The landlord does not send an invoice; therefore a check can be created and printed from the Write Checks window.

Click the **Banking** drop-down menu or click the **Write Check** icon on the Home page.

Select **Write Checks.**

Using the following data, enter the information in the appropriate fields (see Figure 4-14).

DATA: Record the Rent Expense for January.

BANK ACCOUNT:	10000 Checking Account
DATE:	1/1/2008
PAY TO THE ORDER OF:	PE Real Estate (select from the drop-down list)
AMOUNT:	$9,500
MEMO:	Rent for January 2008
ACCOUNT:	67100 Rent Expense

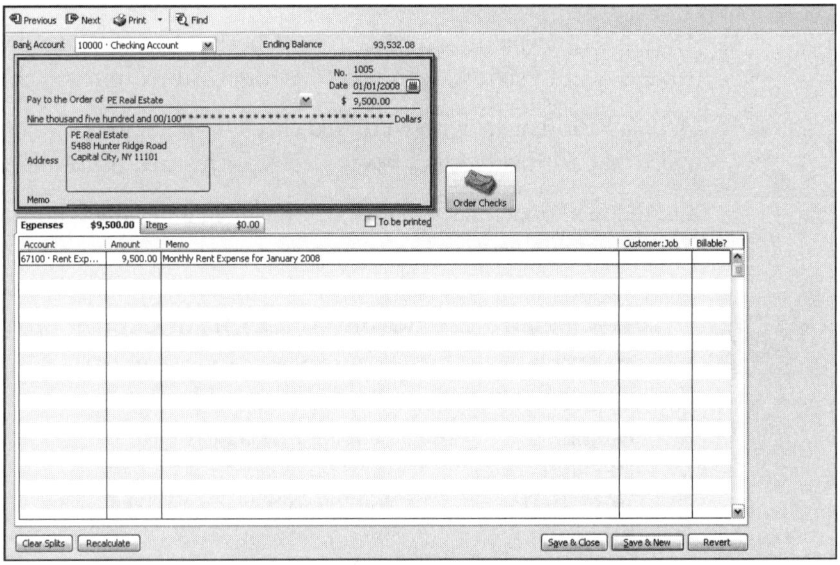

Figure 4-14.

A check can be printed at this time by selecting the **Print** icon at the top of the Write Checks window. To print a check at a later date, see "Print a Check" below.

Click **Save & Close.**

Print a Check

Click the **File** drop-down menu or the **Print Checks** icon on the Home page.

Select **Print Forms.**

Select **Checks.**

In the Select Checks to Print window, select the check(s) you want to print (see Figure 4-15).

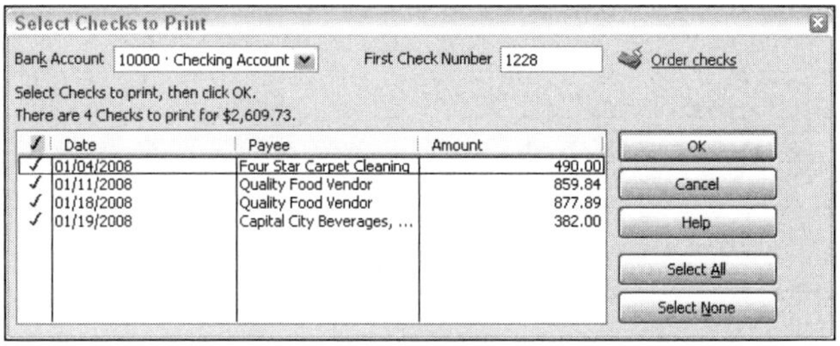

Figure 4-15.

Click **OK.**

Editing, Voiding, and Deleting Checks

Checks can be edited, voided, and deleted from the Check Register window (see Figure 4-16).

Date	Number	Payee		Payment	✓	Deposit	Balance
	Type	Account	Memo				
01/01/2008						1,500.00	1,500.00
	DEP	-split-	Deposit				
01/01/2008						450,000.00	451,500.00
	DEP	30100 · Capital Stock	Deposit				
01/01/2008	1000	Jeffery Jones		5,000.00			446,500.00
	CHK	15025 · Bar Equipment	Bar with Back Display				
01/01/2008	1001	Bob Brown		50,000.00			396,500.00
	CHK	16400 · Vehicles	Used Catering Van				
01/01/2008	1002	Bargain Office Supplies		286.24			396,213.76
	CHK	64900 · Office Supplies					
01/01/2008	1003	NY Liquor License Service, Inc.		2,200.00			394,013.76
	CHK	18500 · Cost of Liquor License					
01/01/2008	1004	Safety Plus Insurance		4,500.00			389,513.76
	CHK	-split-					
01/01/2008	1005	PE Real Estate		9,500.00			380,013.76
	CHK	67100 · Rent Expense					
01/01/2008	1006	Johnson & Associates		1,000.00			379,013.76
	CHK	67300 · Start-Up Costs					
01/01/2008	1007	U.S. Postal Service		100.00			378,913.76
	CHK	66500 · Postage and Delivery					
01/02/2008	1008	Glass and Silver Source Corp.		2,150.00			376,763.76
	CHK	15100 · China, Silver, Glassware, Linen					
01/02/2008	1009	ABC Metalcrafters, Inc.		3,200.00			373,563.76
	CHK	15150 · Smallwares					
01/02/2008	1010	Cutlery USA		2,500.00			371,063.76
	CHK	63550 · Kitchen Utensils and Tableware					
01/03/2008	1012	Restaurant World, Inc.		1,995.00			369,068.76
	CHK	15150 · Smallwares					

Double-click on CHK to edit, void, or delete

Figure 4-16.

Edit a Check

Double-click on the check to be edited from the Check Register window and make appropriate changes.

Click **Save & Close.**

Void a Check

Double-click on the check to be voided from the Check Register window.

Once the check is displayed on the desktop, click the **Edit** drop-down menu.

Select **Void Check.**

QUICKBOOKS TIP

Voided checks can be viewed and/or reversed, while deleted checks are deleted from the QuickBooks company file. A deleted check is permanently removed from the file and it cannot be retrieved. In most cases, it is better to void rather than delete a check.

Delete a Check

Double-click on the check to be deleted from the Check Register window.

Once the check is displayed on the desktop, click the **Edit** drop-down menu.

Select **Delete Check.**

Inventory Stock Status (Inventory on Hand) and Par Levels

An essential element of a profitable restaurant operation is the restaurant operator's ability to manage the inventories required to produce the products expected by the restaurant's customers. Vendors will often use pricing models that encourage owners to purchase larger quantities of an item than are required for a specific inventory cycle. For example, if a restaurant uses ten cases of an inventory item in a month, the vendor may offer a 10 percent discount per case if the restaurant orders twenty cases. While the price savings may be attractive, the restaurant operator will incur inventory carrying costs for the additional items ordered above the normal monthly requirements. Excessive inventory ties up cash that could be used for other expenditures in the operation of the restaurant. On the other hand, if a restaurant does not have a sufficient quantity of a required item on hand, it may not be able to produce items that are listed on its menu. If fresh seafood is not delivered on a regular basis, Aroma Ristorante runs a significant risk of disappointing customers who are partial to seafood.

A manager should establish par levels or reorder points for inventory items in QuickBooks to ensure the proper balance between the quantity required to meet customer demands and the need to minimize excessive inventory quantities. Inventory reports generated by QuickBooks can be used to achieve this balance. These reports can be accessed by clicking the **Reports** drop-down menu and selecting **Inventory** or by accessing the Reports Center. Among the available reports is the Inventory Stock Status by Item (see Figure 4-17).

This report provides a comprehensive list of all items in inventory, identifies the quantity on hand, and indicates the previously established reorder level for each item. For each item, the report lists the preferred vendor, the purchase order if it has been previously created, and the number of items that have been ordered.

Aroma Ristorante
Inventory Stock Status by Item
January 2008

Item Description	Pref Vendor	Reorder Pt	On Hand	Order	On PO	Next Deliv	Sales/Week
Inventory							
Aged Balsamic Large	▶ Aged Balsamic Vin...	Italian Impor...	15	24		0	0 ◀
Aged Balsamic Small	Aged Balsamic 10...	Italian Impor...	15	24		0	0
Angel Hair Pasta	Case Angel Hair D...	Quality Foo...		2		0	0
Aroma Cookbook	Aroma Ristorante ...	North Publis...	24	22	✓	0	0
Asparagus Green lb	Asparagus Green lb	Quality Foo...		-3		0	0
Baby Arugala lb	Baby Arugala lb	Quality Foo...		5		0	0
Balsamic Vinegar Bottle	Balsamic Vinegar ...	Quality Foo...		5		0	0
Beer - Lager Bottle, Case	Beer - Lager Bottle...	Capital City ...		3		0	0
Beer - Porter Bottle, Case	Beer - Porter Bottle...	Capital City ...		2		0	0
Beer -Ale Bottle, Case	Beer -Ale Bottle, C...	Capital City ...		4		0	0
Boneless Prosciutto	Boneless Prosciut...	Quality Foo...		5		0	0
Butter - Unsalted lb	Butter - Unsalted lb	Quality Foo...		12		0	0
Cabernet, Case	Cabernet, Case	Capital City ...		3		0	0
Capers - small 32 oz jar	Capers - small 32 ...	Quality Foo...		6		0	0
Chardonnay, Case	Chardonnay, Case	Capital City ...		2		0	0
Chianti, Case	Chianti, Case	Capital City ...		4		0	0
Chicken Breast Bnlss/Sknlss lb	Chicken Breast Bn...	Quality Foo...		25		0	0
Club Soda	Club Soda	Capital City ...		6		0	0
Coffee Decaf, Case	Coffee Decaf, Case	Java First, I...		2		0	0
Coffee High Test Roast, Case	Coffee High Test R...	Java First, I...		1		0	0
Cranberry Juice, Gallon	Cranberry Juice, G...	Quality Foo...	3	3	✓	0	0
Diet Soda - Box	Diet Soda - Box	Capital City ...		7		0	0
Dipping Oil Set	Dipping Oil Set wit...	Italian Impor...	12	11	✓	0	0
Eggs Large	Eggs Large	Quality Foo...		4		0	0
Espresso Pack, Decaf	Espresso Pack, De...	Java First, I...		2		0	0
Espresso Pack, Regular	Espresso Pack, Re...	Java First, I...		1		0	0
Flour, W 50 lb	Flour, Case	Quality Foo...		2		0	0
Garlic Fresh lb	Garlic Fresh lb	Quality Foo...		20		0	0
Gin Premium - BTL	Gin Premium - BTL	Capital City ...		14		0	0
Gin Well, BTL	Gin Well, BTL	Capital City ...		8		0	0

Figure 4-17.

Physical Inventory Worksheets

QuickBooks has the capability to track inventory levels. Periodically, inventory levels recorded in QuickBooks should be reconciled to the actual inventory amount on hand by performing a physical inventory count. Restaurants should have procedures for tracking and recording their physical inventories. Physical inventory counts should be performed on a regular basis. Restaurant operators recognize that inventories can shrink as the result of breakage, theft, waste, and other production and handling errors. These operational problems with inventory require effective management processes and controls to minimize their financial impact on the restaurant. The frequency of physical counts of inventory may vary from restaurant to restaurant; some conduct an inventory count at the end of each day, others on a weekly basis, and others on a monthly basis. In certain cases, the frequency of inventory counts will depend on the value of the inventory item. Higher value items may be counted on a daily basis, whereas low value items may be counted on a weekly or monthly basis. QuickBooks has the capability to assist with the physical inventory process by producing Physical Inventory Worksheets (see Figure 4-18) that are used to manually record the physical count of each inventory item prior to making inventory adjustments. These worksheets list inventory items in alphabetical order, which can make them somewhat unwieldy for large inventories; however, the report can be exported to Microsoft Excel, which can give the user additional ways to sort or filter the spreadsheet, making the physical inventory count less time consuming.

Report Center

Click the **Reports** drop-down menu or click the **Reports Center** icon on the Home page.

Select **Inventory**.

Select **Physical Inventory Worksheet**.

Aroma Ristorante
Physical Inventory Worksheet
All Transactions

	Item Description	Pref Vendor	On Hand	Physical Count
Inventory				
Aged Balsamic Large	Aged Balsamic Vinegar 250mls	Italian Imports Direct	23	
Aged Balsamic Small	Aged Balsamic 100mls	Italian Imports Direct	23	
Angel Hair Pasta	Case Angel Hair Dry Pasta	Quality Food Vendor	6	
Aroma Cookbook	Aroma Ristorante Cookbook	North Publishing Company	19	
Asparagus Green lb	Asparagus Green lb	Quality Food Vendor	-5	
Baby Arugala lb	Baby Arugala lb	Quality Food Vendor	10	
Balsamic Vinegar Bottle	Balsamic Vinegar Bottle	Quality Food Vendor	8	
Beer - Lager Bottle, Case	Beer - Lager Bottle, Case	Capital City Liquor,Wine and Beer	7	
Beer - Porter Bottle, Case	Beer - Porter Bottle, Case	Capital City Liquor,Wine and Beer	3	
Beer -Ale Bottle, Case	Beer -Ale Bottle, Case	Capital City Liquor,Wine and Beer	8	
Boneless Prosciutto	Boneless Prosciutto 10lbs	Quality Food Vendor	6	
Butter - Unsalted lb	Butter - Unsalted lb	Quality Food Vendor	12	
Cabernet, Case	Cabernet, Case	Capital City Liquor,Wine and Beer	6	
Capers - small 32 oz jar	Capers - small 32 oz jar	Quality Food Vendor	90	
Chardonnay, Case	Chardonnay, Case	Capital City Liquor,Wine and Beer	7	
Chianti, Case	Chianti, Case	Capital City Liquor,Wine and Beer	8	
Chicken Breast Bnlss/Sknlss lb	Chicken Breast Bnlss/Sknlss lb	Quality Food Vendor	20	
Club Soda	Club Soda	Capital City Beverages, Inc.	12	
Coffee Decaf, Case	Coffee Decaf, Case	Java First, Inc.	1	
Coffee High Test Roast, Case	Coffee High Test Roast, Case	Java First, Inc.	1	
Cranberry Juice, Gallon	Cranberry Juice, Gallon	Quality Food Vendor	25	
Diet Soda - Box	Diet Soda - Box	Capital City Beverages, Inc.	8	
Dipping Oil Set	Dipping Oil Set with Bowl	Italian Imports Direct	8	
Eggs Large	Eggs Large	Quality Food Vendor	5	
Espresso Pack, Decaf	Espresso Pack, Decaf	Java First, Inc.	1	
Espresso Pack, Regular	Espresso Pack, Regular	Java First, Inc.	1	
Flour, W 50 lb	Flour, Case	Quality Food Vendor	3	
Garlic Fresh lb	Garlic Fresh lb	Quality Food Vendor	10	
Gin Premium - BTL	Gin Premium - BTL	Capital City Liquor,Wine and Beer	18	
Gin Well -BTL	Gin Well -BTL	Capital City Liquor,Wine and Beer	14	
Herb Oregano oz	Herb Oregano oz	Quality Food Vendor	36	

Figure 4-18.

Once the worksheet has been printed, management can use the worksheet to conduct the physical inventory count. The correct count is recorded directly on the worksheet in the Physical Count column.

Making Inventory Adjustments

Once the physical inventory count is completed, it is critical to adjust the inventory levels in QuickBooks to reflect the actual value of the physical inventory on hand.

Adjusting Quantity on Hand

Click the **Vendors** drop-down menu or click the **Adjust Quantity on Hand** icon on the Home page.

Select **Inventory Activities.**

Select **Adjust Quantity/Value on Hand.**

Select the appropriate **Adjustment Date** and **Adjustment Account** (see Figure 4-19).

Item	Description	Current Qty	New Qty	Qty Difference
Aged Balsamic Large	Aged Balsamic Vinegar 250mls	24		
Aged Balsamic Small	Aged Balsamic 100mls	24		
Angel Hair Pasta	Case Angel Hair Dry Pasta	2		
Aroma Cookbook	Aroma Ristorante Cookbook	22		
Asparagus Green lb	Asparagus Green lb	12		
Baby Arugula lb	Baby Arugula lb	5		
Balsamic Vinegar Bottle	Balsamic Vinegar Bottle	5		
Beer - Lager Bottle, Case	Beer - Lager Bottle, Case	3		
Beer - Porter Bottle, Case	Beer - Porter Bottle, Case	2		
Beer -Ale Bottle, Case	Beer -Ale Bottle, Case	4		
Boneless Prosciutto	Boneless Prosciutto	5		
Butter - Unsalted lb	Butter - Unsalted lb	12		
Cabernet, Case	Cabernet, Case	3		
Capers - small 32 oz jar	Capers - small 32 oz jar	6		
Chardonnay, Case	Chardonnay, Case	2		
Chianti, Case	Chianti, Case	4		
Chicken Breast Bnlss/Sknlss lb	Chicken Breast Bnlss/Sknlss lb	25		
Club Soda	Club Soda	6		
Coffee Decaf, Case	Coffee Decaf, Case	2		
Coffee High Test Roast, Case	Coffee High Test Roast, Case	1		
Cranberry Juice, Gallon	Cranberry Juice, Gallon	3		
Diet Soda - Box	Diet Soda - Box	7		
Dipping Oil Set	Dipping Oil Set with Bowl	11		
Eggs Large	Eggs Large	4		
Espresso Pack, Decaf	Espresso Pack, Decaf	2		
Espresso Pack, Regular	Espresso Pack, Regular	1		

Figure 4-19.

Record the **Correct Count** in the New Qty column.

Click **Save & Close.**

Any significant shortages or overages between Current Quantity and New Quantity should be investigated by management. Once the inventory reconciliation is completed, QuickBooks will automatically adjust the inventory valuation on the Balance Sheet and record the adjustment in the related Cost of Goods Sold account on the Profit and Loss Statement.

Generally most reductions in inventory are attributed to sales and cause an increase in Cost of Goods Sold, but not all inventory items are actually sold to customers. Employee meals reduce inventory, and other inventory losses may be due to shrinkage, waste, and theft. These losses will overstate the Cost of Goods Sold, unless the manager devises a method to identify and record them in a separate account for Shrinkage, Waste, and Theft.

Another approach considers these losses, as well as the cost of such restaurant supplies as "To Go" containers, as part of the cost of doing business; and therefore they are included in Cost of Goods Sold. Whichever approach is utilized, it is important for restaurant operators to be mindful of these costs and develop and implement better internal controls in order to minimize their impact on the restaurant's profits.

ACCOUNTING TIP

A separate account for Shrinkage, Waste, and Theft can be established as a subaccount of Cost of Goods Sold.

ACCOUNTING TIP

Calculating an exact value for inventory is complicated because current inventory items are purchased at different times and at different prices. Inventory valuation methods such as Average Cost Method, Weighted Average, First In First Out (FIFO), and Last In First Out (LIFO) are used to compute the value of the inventory and cost of sales. Inventory valuation directly affects the restaurant's profitability. QuickBooks uses the Average Cost method.

Other Inventory Management Systems

One of the great features of QuickBooks is its ability to meet the general business needs of a wide variety of businesses. That broad appeal does, however, create a need among restaurant operators to find specialized inventory systems that meet the unique needs of the food and beverage industry. For example, most inventory systems record and track raw material inventories and their conversion to finished goods. These systems can track inventory on a FIFO, LIFO, etc., basis depending on the preferences of the business. A restaurant operator has several unique inventory management challenges. For example, a vendor can supply Aroma Ristorante with ten pound blocks of cheese, which the kitchen staff will convert into one pound increments of shredded, sliced, and cubed cheese. Aroma Ristorante wants to track the newly converted cheese inventory by its new configuration. Unfortunately QuickBooks inventory management capabilities would require multiple inputs and adjustments to achieve the desired inventory tracking. QuickBooks Pro 2009 does not currently include the units of measure feature. Other versions of QuickBooks offer this feature. Check *www.intuit.com* for further information.

A number of vendors have developed systems that specifically support the unique requirements of the restaurant industry. In addition to special inventory tracking capability, these systems can also provide recipe and menu costing, purchasing and ordering, nutritional analysis, sales analysis and reporting, and other specialized features.

Several inventory systems are available today specifically designed to meet the needs of the restaurant industry. The software can be costly. Inputting inventory items is an additional expense. Depending on the provider, these inventory management systems can work with the restaurant's POS system or can function as separate software. A list of current inventory management software providers can be found at:

- Hospitality Technology Magazine Buyer's Guide (*www.htmagazine.com*)
- National Restaurant Association Show Exhibitor Guide (*www .restaurant.org*)
- Hospitality Upgrade – Find a Vendor (*www.hospitalityupgrade.com*)

Inventory software could interface with accounting software thus eliminating the need to manually transfer information from one system to another. This scenario is not always possible; therefore changes in inventory levels must be entered manually into QuickBooks via journal entries.

Some restaurant operators choose to use a spreadsheet application to assist them in inventory management, while others manually manage inventory levels without the use of any software.

Reports

QuickBooks has a variety of reports related to purchases, payables, and inventory, each providing management with specific information that can be used to make business decisions relevant to a particular area. A list of available reports can be obtained through the Report Center or by clicking the **Reports** drop-down menu and then selecting the appropriate category. The following reports are examples that may be valuable to a restaurant operator.

QUICKBOOKS TIP

QuickBooks reports can be customized and modified to suit the needs of the user. Modifications can include changing report dates, altering column widths, and deleting fields or columns altogether. Once a report is formatted, it can be memorized so you won't have to reformat the report each time it is generated. Reports can also be customized by selecting Reports and Graphs from Company Preferences. Double-clicking on certain fields within the report can provide related detailed information.

Accounts Payable Summary Report

Click the **Reports** drop-down menu or click the **Report Center** icon.

Select **Vendors & Payables.**

Select **A/P Aging Summary** (see Figure 4-20).

Aroma Ristorante
A/P Aging Summary
As of January 31, 2008

	Current	1 - 30	31 - 60	61 - 90	> 90	TOTAL
ABC Security, Inc.	50.00	0.00	0.00	0.00	0.00	50.00
ATC Phone and Cable Company	345.00	0.00	0.00	0.00	0.00	345.00
Best Point of Sale Company	200.00	0.00	0.00	0.00	0.00	200.00
Bob's Snow Removal	875.00	0.00	0.00	0.00	0.00	875.00
Capital City Beverages, Inc.	488.00	0.00	0.00	0.00	0.00	488.00
Capital City Gazette	20.00	0.00	0.00	0.00	0.00	20.00
Capital City Utilities, Inc.	4,100.00	0.00	0.00	0.00	0.00	4,100.00
Cool Waves Satalite, Inc.	30.00	0.00	0.00	0.00	0.00	30.00
Lightning Speed Internet Service	56.00	0.00	0.00	0.00	0.00	56.00
Restaurant Equipment, Inc.	120.00	0.00	0.00	0.00	0.00	120.00
STK Waste Removal, Inc.	350.00	0.00	0.00	0.00	0.00	350.00
TOTAL	6,634.00	0.00	0.00	0.00	0.00	6,634.00

Figure 4-20.

This report provides an aging of all unpaid bills and the total amount owed to a specific vendor in each age group, such as 0–30 days, 31–60 days and so on. By selecting the **Accounts Payable Aging Detail** report, the manager can view the individual bills that make up the total of each age group. The Vendor and Payable reports section also includes an Accounts Payable graph that provides a visual on how much the restaurant owes in each age group and a pie chart displaying the percentage of the total owed to a vendor.

It is important that management be aware of the amount of bills due past 30 days in order to remain on positive terms with suppliers and to avoid late fees. If bills are excessively late with a particular vendor, the supplier may refrain from extending credit to the restaurant and request a COD (Cash on Delivery) payment term for future purchases.

The report could identify bills that might have been overlooked or forgotten. If there is an issue with cash, management may use the report to determine which bills and vendors should be paid first as soon as additional cash becomes available.

Vendor Balance Summary

Click the **Reports** drop-down menu or click the **Report Center** icon.

Select **Vendors & Payables.**

Select **Vendor Balance Summary** (see Figure 4-21).

Aroma Ristorante
Vendor Balance Summary
As of January 31, 2008

	◦ Jan 31, 08 ◦
ABC Security, Inc.	▶ 50.00 ◀
ATC Phone and Cable Company	345.00
Best Point of Sale Company	200.00
Bob's Snow Removal	875.00
Capital City Beverages, Inc.	488.00
Capital City Gazette	20.00
Capital City Utilities, Inc.	4,100.00
Cool Waves Satellite, Inc.	30.00
Lightning Speed Internet Service	56.00
Restaurant Equipment, Inc.	120.00
STK Waste Removal, Inc.	350.00
TOTAL	**6,634.00**

Figure 4-21.

This report provides the total amount of unpaid bills owed to an individual vendor. To view the individual bills that make up the total amount due, double-click on an amount within the report or view the Vendor Balance Detail Report.

Management should be aware of any large amounts owed to a particular vendor and determine the reason for such a large outstanding balance. When a restaurant's outstanding balance due to suppliers starts to steadily increase over a period of time, suppliers may become concerned as to whether they will receive the total amount due. Some suppliers may decide to decrease the amount of goods supplied to the restaurant until the restaurant reduces its outstanding balance, and this could significantly impair the restaurant's ability to produce certain profitable menu items. Some vendors may be more flexible than others. A large outstanding balance due to an office supplies vendor may not be as detrimental as one due to the utility company.

Unpaid Bills Report

Click the **Reports** drop-down menu or click the **Report Center** icon.

Select **Vendors & Payables.**

Select **Unpaid Bills Detail** (see Figure 4-22).

| Modify Report... | Memorize... | Print... | E-mail ▾ | Export... | Hide Header | Refresh | Cash Advance Services |

Dates Custom ☑ 01/31/2008 🔲 Sort By Default ☑

2:15 PM
03/04/08

Aroma Ristorante
Unpaid Bills Detail
As of January 31, 2008

◦	Type	◦	Date	◦	Num	◦	Due Date	◦	Aging	◦	Open Balance	◦
Capital City Beverages, Inc.												
▶	Bill		01/30/2008				02/14/2008				488.00 ◀	
	Total Capital City Beverages, Inc.										488.00	
	TOTAL										**488.00**	

Figure 4-22.

This report provides a list of all the restaurant's unpaid bills. It also contains an aging column indicating the number of days a bill is overdue. Managers might use this report to decide which bill should be paid. Two different bills can be in the 0–30 days category, yet one bill is only 2 days late in comparison to another that is 22 days late. With this information, the restaurant operator can decide which bill to pay first.

Purchases by Vendor Summary

Report Center

Click the **Reports** drop-down menu or click the **Report Center** icon.

Select **Purchases.**

Select **Purchases by Vendor Summary** (see Figure 4-23).

Modify Report...	Memorize...	Print...	E-mail ▼	Export...		Hide Header	Collapse	Refresh	

Dates | Custom ⌄ | From 01/01/2008 ▦ To 01/31/2008 ▦ | Columns | Total only ⌄ | Sort By | Default ⌄

2:21 PM	Aroma Ristorante
03/04/08	**Purchases by Vendor Summary**
Accrual Basis	January 2008

	◇ **Jan 08** ◇
Capital City Beverages, Inc.	1,218.00
Capital City Liquor,Wine and Beer	8,933.07
Freshest Produce, Inc.	37.95
Italian Imports Direct	1,554.00
Java First, Inc.	1,964.50
North Publishing Company	300.00
Quality Food Vendor	▶ 17,098.13 ◀
TOTAL	**31,105.65**

Figure 4-23.

This report provides the total amount of purchases from a vendor within a specified time period. The detail of the individual bills that make up the total amount purchased from a vendor can be obtained by double-clicking on the amount within the report or viewing the purchases by Vendor Detail report.

This report can highlight high-volume vendors. This information may be used to negotiate more favorable payment terms and discounts.

Purchases by Item Summary

Click the **Reports** drop-down menu or click the **Reports Center** icon.

Select **Purchases**.

Select **Purchases by Item Summary** (see Figure 4-24).

Aroma Ristorante
Purchases by Item Summary
January 2008

	Jan 08	
	Qty	Amount
Inventory		
Aged Balsamic Large	24	324.00
Aged Balsamic Small	24	120.00
Angel Hair Pasta	25	363.75
Aroma Cookbook	24	300.00
Asparagus Green lb	92	232.76
Baby Arugula lb	49	221.48
Balsamic Vinegar Bottle	45	337.05
Beer - Lager Bottle, Case	17	399.84
Beer - Porter Bottle, Case	11	322.08
Beer -Ale Bottle, Case	17	416.16
Boneless Prosciutto	46	3,245.30
Butter - Unsalted lb	72	133.20
Cabernet, Case	7	841.75
Capers - small 32 oz jar	40	206.00
Chardonnay, Case	4	394.56
Chianti, Case	9	918.00
Chicken Breast Bnlss/Sknlss lb	191	727.71
Club Soda	21	252.00
Coffee Decaf, Case	10	395.00
Coffee High Test Roast, Case	14	588.00
Cranberry Juice, Gallon	12	30.00
Diet Soda - Box	11	506.00
Dipping Oil Set	12	186.00
Eggs Large	50	143.00
Espresso Pack, Decaf	5	225.00
Espresso Pack, Regular	7	315.00
Flour, W 50 lb	12	192.60
Garlic Fresh lb	67	60.97
Gin Premium - BTL	54	1,039.50

Figure 4-24.

This report identifies quantity and amount of inventory items purchased within a specified time period. The restaurant operator may use this information to determine future purchasing decisions, such as an item substitution.

Inventory Valuation Summary

Click the **Reports** drop-down menu or click the **Report Center** icon.

Select **Inventory.**

Select **Inventory Valuation Summary** (see Figure 4-25).

Aroma Ristorante
Inventory Valuation Summary
As of January 31, 2008

	Item Description	On Hand	Avg Cost	Asset Value	% of Tot Asset	Sales Price	Retail Value	% of Tot Retail
Inventory								
Aged Balsamic Large	▶ Aged Balsamic Vin...	24	13.50	324.00	4.2%	0.00	0.00	0.0% ◀
Aged Balsamic Small	Aged Balsamic 10...	24	5.00	120.00	1.5%	0.00	0.00	0.0%
Angel Hair Pasta	Case Angel Hair D...	2	14.55	29.10	0.4%	0.00	0.00	0.0%
Aroma Cookbook	Aroma Ristorante ...	22	12.50	275.00	3.5%	0.00	0.00	0.0%
Asparagus Green lb	Asparagus Green lb	12	2.53	30.36	0.4%	0.00	0.00	0.0%
Baby Arugala lb	Baby Arugala lb	5	4.52	22.60	0.3%	0.00	0.00	0.0%
Balsamic Vinegar Bottle	Balsamic Vinegar ...	5	7.49	37.45	0.5%	0.00	0.00	0.0%
Beer - Lager Bottle, Case	Beer - Lager Bottle...	3	23.52	70.56	0.9%	0.00	0.00	0.0%
Beer - Porter Bottle, Case	Beer - Porter Bottle...	2	29.28	58.56	0.8%	0.00	0.00	0.0%
Beer -Ale Bottle, Case	Beer -Ale Bottle, C...	4	24.48	97.92	1.3%	0.00	0.00	0.0%
Boneless Prosciutto	Boneless Prosciut...	5	70.55	352.75	4.5%	0.00	0.00	0.0%
Butter - Unsalted lb	Butter - Unsalted lb	12	1.85	22.20	0.3%	0.00	0.00	0.0%
Cabernet, Case	Cabernet, Case	3	120.25	360.75	4.6%	0.00	0.00	0.0%
Capers - small 32 oz jar	Capers - small 32 ...	6	5.15	30.90	0.4%	0.00	0.00	0.0%
Chardonnay, Case	Chardonnay, Case	2	98.64	197.28	2.5%	0.00	0.00	0.0%
Chianti, Case	Chianti, Case	4	102.00	408.00	5.2%	0.00	0.00	0.0%
Chicken Breast Bnlss/Sknlss lb	Chicken Breast Bn...	25	3.81	95.25	1.2%	0.00	0.00	0.0%
Club Soda	Club Soda	6	12.00	72.00	0.9%	0.00	0.00	0.0%
Coffee Decaf, Case	Coffee Decaf, Case	2	39.50	79.00	1.0%	0.00	0.00	0.0%
Coffee High Test Roast, Case	Coffee High Test R...	1	42.00	42.00	0.5%	0.00	0.00	0.0%
Cranberry Juice, Gallon	Cranberry Juice, G...	3	2.50	7.50	0.1%	0.00	0.00	0.0%
Diet Soda - Box	Diet Soda - Box	7	46.00	322.00	4.1%	0.00	0.00	0.0%
Dipping Oil Set	Dipping Oil Set wit...	11	15.50	170.50	2.2%	0.00	0.00	0.0%
Eggs Large	Eggs Large	4	2.86	11.44	0.1%	0.00	0.00	0.0%
Espresso Pack, Decaf	Espresso Pack, De...	2	45.00	90.00	1.2%	0.00	0.00	0.0%
Espresso Pack, Regular	Espresso Pack, Re...	1	45.00	45.00	0.6%	0.00	0.00	0.0%
Flour, W 50 lb	Flour, Case	2	16.05	32.10	0.4%	0.00	0.00	0.0%
Garlic Fresh lb	Garlic Fresh lb	20	0.91	18.20	0.2%	0.00	0.00	0.0%
Gin Premium - BTL	Gin Premium - BTL	14	19.25	269.50	3.5%	0.00	0.00	0.0%
Gin Well -BTL	Gin Well -BTL	8	11.95	95.60	1.2%	0.00	0.00	0.0%

Figure 4-25.

This report provides information including a list of inventory items, item description, number of items on hand, sales price, asset value, and percentage of total assets. The report may be used to identify large quantities of a particular item on hand, which may suggest slow sales or overordering of inventory. The restaurant operator may decide to offer some type of incentive, such as dinner specials or discounts, in order to move the inventory.

Chapter Review Problems

1. Aroma Ristorante needs to place a liquor, wine, and beer order. Create a Purchase Order, and receive items in inventory. Enter and pay the bill.

DATA	
VENDOR:	Capital City Liquor, Wine, and Beer
DATE:	1/17/2008
PO NUMBER:	111
QUANTITY AND ITEMS:	2 Chardonnay, Case
	1 Pinot Gris, Case
	3 Cabernet, Case
	2 Merlot, Case
	4 Chianti, Case
	2 Lager Bottle, Case
	2 Keg, Domestic
	2 Keg, Lite Domestic
	6 Vodka Premium, BTL
	6 Gin Well, BTL
	12 Gin Premium, BTL

Pay this bill from the 10000 Checking Account.

2. Write a check through the Write Checks window for the following invoice.

DATA	
VENDOR:	ABC Metalcrafters, Inc.
DATE:	1/2/2008
ACCOUNT:	15150 Smallwares
AMOUNT:	$1,296.83
MEMO:	Purchased 4 sauce pans with lids, 3 stock pots with lids, and 6 sauté pans with lids.

Pay this bill from the 10000 Checking Account.

What does QuickBooks do behind the scenes after this transaction has been entered?

3. Aroma Ristorante receives a bill for six months of insurance premiums. Pay the bill through the Check Register.

DATA	
VENDOR:	Safety Plus Insurance, Inc.
DATE:	1/1/2008
AMOUNT DUE:	$4,500.00
MEMO:	$3,750 for Property and Liability Insurance and $750 for Vehicle Insurance

Pay this bill from the 10000 Checking Account.

What account should you use to record this transaction?

4. Aroma Ristorante wrote a check to Restaurant Equipment, Inc., for $12,250. The check was printed within five days of receipt of the bill and has not been mailed. Assume that the vendor payment term is 2% 10 Net 30 and the current interest rate for the checking account is 5% (simple interest).

   a. Should Aroma Ristorante have taken advantage of the early payment terms?

   b. If Aroma Ristorante does not take advantage of the vendor discount, what steps are required to edit the check?

5. The manager took a physical count at the end of the month and recorded it on the Physical Inventory Worksheet. Compare the Quantity On Hand to the Physical Count for each inventory item and identify any significant discrepancies in quantity and value of the inventory item using the prices identified in the item list. What could be the cause of these discrepancies? Identify potential internal control procedures that could be implemented to prevent them (see Figure 4-26).

Aroma Ristorante
Physical Inventory Worksheet

Inventory	Item Description	Pref Vendor	On Hand	Physical Count
Aged Balsamic Large	Aged Balsamic Vinegar 250mls	Italian Imports Direct	23	23
Aged Balsamic Small	Aged Balsamic 100mls	Italian Imports Direct	23	22
Angel Hair Pasta	Case Angel Hair Dry Pasta	Quality Food Vendor	6	6
Aroma Cookbook	Aroma Ristorante Cookbook	North Publishing Company	19	10
Asparagus Green lb	Asparagus Green lb	Quality Food Vendor	10	2
Baby Arugala lb	Baby Arugala lb	Quality Food Vendor	10	10
Balsamic Vinegar Bottle	Balsamic Vinegar Bottle	Quality Food Vendor	8	6
Beer - Lager Bottle, Case	Beer - Lager Bottle, Case	Capital City Liquor,Wine and Beer	7	6
Beer - Porter Bottle, Case	Beer - Porter Bottle, Case	Capital City Liquor,Wine and Beer	3	3
Beer -Ale Bottle, Case	Beer -Ale Bottle, Case	Capital City Liquor,Wine and Beer	8	6
Boneless Prosciutto	Boneless Prosciutto 10lbs	Quality Food Vendor	6	4
Butter - Unsalted lb	Butter - Unsalted lb	Quality Food Vendor	12	11
Cabernet, Case	Cabernet, Case	Capital City Liquor,Wine and Beer	6	6
Capers - small 32 oz jar	Capers - small 32 oz jar	Quality Food Vendor	90	20
Chardonnay, Case	Chardonnay, Case	Capital City Liquor,Wine and Beer	7	6
Chianti, Case	Chianti, Case	Capital City Liquor,Wine and Beer	8	8
Chicken Breast Bnlss/Sknlss lb	Chicken Breast Bnlss/Sknlss lb	Quality Food Vendor	20	32
Club Soda	Club Soda	Capital City Beverages, Inc.	12	12
Coffee Decaf, Case	Coffee Decaf, Case	Java First, Inc.	1	1
Coffee High Test Roast, Case	Coffee High Test Roast, Case	Java First, Inc.	1	1
Cranberry Juice, Gallon	Cranberry Juice, Gallon	Quality Food Vendor	25	8
Diet Soda - Box	Diet Soda - Box	Capital City Beverages, Inc.	8	8
Dipping Oil Set	Dipping Oil Set with Bowl	Italian Imports Direct	8	6
Eggs Large	Eggs Large	Quality Food Vendor	5	4
Espresso Pack, Decaf	Espresso Pack, Decaf	Java First, Inc.	1	1
Espresso Pack, Regular	Espresso Pack, Regular	Java First, Inc.	1	1
Flour, W 50 lb	Flour, Case	Quality Food Vendor	3	3
Garlic Fresh lb	Garlic Fresh lb	Quality Food Vendor	10	9
Gin Premium - BTL	Gin Premium - BTL	Capital City Liquor,Wine and Beer	18	12
Gin Well -BTL	Gin Well -BTL	Capital City Liquor,Wine and Beer	14	9
Herb Oregano oz	Herb Oregano oz	Quality Food Vendor	36	36

Figure 4-26.

You can find additional Review Problems at *www.wiley.com/college/murphy.*

Sales and Receivables

Access the Chapter 5 data file from the CD-ROM that accompanies this book or download the file from the web site.

Chapter Outline

Recording Sales and Receivables

Point-of-Sale Systems Interfaces

Recording Restaurant Sales from a Point-of-Sale System

Creating Customer Invoices

Editing Customer Invoices

Voiding and Deleting Customer Invoices

Printing Customer Invoices

Recording Customer Payments

Recording Credit Memos

Creating Customer Estimates

Recording Advance Deposits

Reports

Chapter Review Problems

Recording Sales and Receivables

A critical function of a restaurant operation is the ability to generate sales. Sales data must be recorded and categorized in order to establish the financial statements for the business. In the restaurant industry, journal entries to the General Ledger and Customer Invoices are the two most common ways to manually record sales in QuickBooks. Depending on the degree of sophistication of the restaurant operation, sales can be captured by a POS (point-of-sale) system or a cash register and subsequently recorded in the General Ledger using journal entries. The type of operation and the systems in place will generally determine which method for recording sales data is most appropriate. QuickBooks provides a user with options for recording sales. They can be recorded directly to the General Ledger or through use of QuickBooks forms, such as Sales Receipts, Billing Statements, and Customer Invoices. When a manager uses any of these QuickBooks forms to record sales, the data from the form is recorded in the appropriate account. This capability within QuickBooks relieves a manager of the burden of recording journal entries in the General Ledger. Details on how to use billing statements to record sales are not covered in this text. Emphasis will be placed on Customer Invoices and Sales Receipts because these methods are often used by food and beverage operations.

Point-of-Sale Systems Interfaces

Today's restaurant managers need current financial data to assist in decision making and help better manage their operations. According to the 9th Annual Restaurant Technology Study (2007), 78 percent of all restaurant operators surveyed indicated that Accounting/Financials was one of the most important features of their point-of-sale system.

HELPFUL TIP

An *interface* is an application that allows independent systems to communicate with one another.

9th Annual Restaurant Technology Study, Tracking Progress & Spotting Trends, 2007

	% INDICATING IMPORTANT	
POS Function	2006	2007
Labor management	78%	81%
Accounting/financials	82%	78%
Business intelligence	72%	74%
Take-out/delivery	56%	58%
CRM/loyalty	53%	58%
Enterprise management	57%	55%

"Restaurant Technology Study 2007," *Hospitality Technology 2007*. Copyright 2007 Hospitality Technology Magazine. All rights reserved.

Realizing the importance of this financial data, many point-of-sale soft-ware companies have developed interfaces or have worked with partners to develop interfaces to third-party accounting applications. These point-of-sale companies have identified specific data that flows from their system into QuickBooks. Integration can include sales data to QuickBooks General Ledger, Accounts Receivable, Accounts Payable, Payroll, Deposits to Bank Reconciliation, and so on. In addition, interfaces also reduce data entry input time and data entry errors that may occur with manual data entry into QuickBooks. Instead of manually transferring data from point-of-sale reports into the QuickBooks General Ledger, it is done electronically.

Many point-of-sale companies currently have interfaces to QuickBooks. Interfaces are continually being written, so you should contact individual point-of-sale companies for information about their software.

Leading Providers in POS Software from Hospitality Technology Magazine's POS Showcase 2007 (www.htmagazine.com)

Action Systems, Inc. (ASI)

Digital Dining/MenuSoft

Firefly Technologies

Micros Systems, Inc.

pcAmerica

Posera/Maitre'D

Radiant Systems, Inc.

Squirrel Systems

Wand Corporation

Hospitality Technology Magazine's POS Showcase, 2007. Copyright © 2007, *Hospitality Technology Magazine*. All rights reserved.

It is essential for restaurant operators to have a good working knowledge of QuickBooks even if their point-of-sale system has an interface to QuickBooks. Not all transactions are recorded electronically.

Aroma Ristorante uses a point-of-sale system that tracks food, beverage, and retail sales. Each of these revenue centers has been set up within the point-of-sale system. After generating weekly sales reports from the point-of-sale system, sales are recorded weekly via a journal entry in QuickBooks.

William A. Oleksinski, Jr.

Founder and President of ReSTAR

The company was started in 1985 and is growing rapidly. ReSTAR, Inc., is a systems integration and consulting company. ReSTAR sells, installs, trains, and supports both Intuit's QuickBooks and Sage's ACCPAC financial software. ReSTAR is also a Development Partner for many accounting manufacturers, such as Intuit, SAGE Software, Microsoft, ADP, and Computer Associates. ReSTAR was awarded the "Developer of the Year" from Computer Associates in 1994 for an interface package called TransManager. ReSTAR has developed a Strategic Alliance Partnership with Aloha Technologies and Radiant Systems; the first Windows-based POS system. ReSTAR has written the endorsed financial integration utility software Aloha TransManager to numerous accounting systems with over 4000+ sites and is being sold through Aloha's 150 resellers worldwide.

"Integrating POS data to QuickBooks provides faster, more reliable access to financial information. It saves time and money by eliminating tedious and error-prone data entry. Sales, Inventory, Vendor Bills, Customer Charges, and Employee Time Keeping are examples of integration functions available.

Having access to the financial information of your food service operation allows a manager to make better, faster decisions about how to run their business. Timely access to the valuable data captured at your store-level POS system can make the difference between a well-managed business and an inefficient one. Better-informed, long-term decisions result in increased customer satisfaction and improved operating results and financial rewards.

An Inventory Control system is critical to a successful food service operation. There can be a considerable upfront investment of time and human resources required to establish a comprehensive Inventory Control System. Aloha TransManager *Plus* (ATM *Plus)* provides a simple approach that focuses on purchasing and tracking of key inventory items that make up a very large portion of the operation's cost of goods. The ATM *Plus* program generates a daily GL Journal Entry of the Product Mix theoretical costs to update cost of goods and inventory accounts in QuickBooks.

Managing a food service operation on a day-to-day basis is a challenging and rewarding experience. Managers that are taught to think as business-minded operators make better long-term decisions about their operations. The use of ATM *Plus t*o generate a one-page Daily P & L including Sales, Cost of Sales, Labor, and Direct Operating expenses allows managers to better and quickly assess performance and go home at night knowing not just that they were busy, but their efforts contributed to the financial success of their operation."

Recording Restaurant Sales from a Point-of-Sale System

When a restaurant's point-of-sale system does not interface with QuickBooks, all sales transactions must be manually recorded into QuickBooks using journal entries. Once the frequency of booking the sales journal entry is determined, the journal entry can be set up using the appropriate accounts. The journal entry can be memorized, making the entry easily retrieved for future use. (See page 80 on how to memorize a transaction.) This will save data entry time because typically only the journal entry date, journal entry number, and amounts will change.

Using Journal Entries to Record Restaurant Sales from a Point-of-sale System

Click the **Company** drop-down menu.

Select **Make General Journal Entries**.

In the Assigning Numbers to Journal Entries window, select **OK**.

QuickBooks automatically assigns numbers to journal entries. This feature can be turned off in Company Preferences – Accounting. See page 22 for information on Preferences.

Using the following data, enter the information in the appropriate fields (see Figure 5-1).

DATA: Record the Sales Data from the Point-of-Sale Report.	
DATE:	1/14/2008
ENTRY NO.:	7
DEBIT ACCOUNT	AMOUNT
10000 Checking Account:	$2,684.04
10050 Checking Account: Visa/MasterCard	$8,869.88
10075 Checking Account: Amex	$608.60
51800 Merchant Account Fees:	$196.62
43900 Sales Comps, Discounts & Promo:	$1,263.76
66080 Payroll Expenses: Employee Benefits	$124.84

25300 Gift Certificates Redeemed:	$0
10150 Checking Account: Over / Short	$1.50
CREDIT ACCOUNT	**AMOUNT**
25200 Gift Certificates Outstanding:	$100.00
43800 Food Sales:	$8,738.80
41410 Beverage Sales: Beer	$449.42
41420 Beverage Sales: Wine	$2,059.86
41430 Beverage Sales: Liquor	$1,011.20
41440 Beverage Sales: Other	$224.71
70010 Retail Income:	$125.00
25500 Sales Tax Payable:	$1,040.25
MEMO:	To Record Weekly Sales

Date 01/14/2008   Entry No. 7

Account	Debit	Credit	Memo	Name	Billable?
10000 · Checking Account	2,684.04		Record Weekly Sales		
10000 · Checking Account:10050 · Visa / Mastercard	8,869.88		Record Weekly Sales		
10000 · Checking Account:10075 · Amex	608.60		Record Weekly Sales		
51800 · Merchant Account Fees	196.62		Record Weekly Sales		
43900 · Sales Comps, Discounts & Promo	1,263.76		Record Weekly Sales		
66000 · Payroll Expenses:66080 · Employee Benefits	124.84		Record Weekly Sales		
25300 · Gift Certificates Redeemed			Record Weekly Sales		
10000 · Checking Account:10150 · Over / Short	1.50		Record Weekly Sales		
			Record Weekly Sales		
25200 · Gift Certificates Outstanding		100.00	Record Weekly Sales		
43800 · Food Sales		8,738.80	Record Weekly Sales		
41400 · Beverage Sales:41410 · Beer		449.42	Record Weekly Sales		
41400 · Beverage Sales:41420 · Wine		2,059.86	Record Weekly Sales		
41400 · Beverage Sales:41430 · Liquor		1,011.20	Record Weekly Sales		
41400 · Beverage Sales:41440 · Other		224.71	Record Weekly Sales		
70010 · Retail Income		125.00	Record Weekly Sales		
25500 · Sales Tax Payable		1,040.25	Record Weekly Sales	NYS Sales Tax Department	

A Vendor should be associated with Sales Tax Payable Account (other current liability).

Save & Close   Save & New   Revert

Figure 5-1.

Click **Save & Close**.

When recording a journal entry, certain accounts may require the user to associate either a vendor or a customer with the account in the name column of the journal entry.

Creating Customer Invoices

Aroma Ristorante provides off-site catering services. An Item List has been previously established (see Chapter 3) for all food and beverage catering items available for sale. A list of current customers was also created. Both of these lists will enable QuickBooks to generate Customer Invoices.

A Customer Invoice is a form that can be used to record a sale when services have been provided and the customer is expected to pay at a later date. It includes such information as the date of sale, customer contact information, items and quantity sold, sales price, tax, and total amount due. This form can be printed or e-mailed from QuickBooks and sent to the customer as an invoice requesting payment. Multiple invoice formats are available in QuickBooks. The service invoice format is an appropriate format for Aroma's catering business. Customer invoices can be customized to suit individual needs. Customizations can include such formats as font size or style, logos, messages, and so on.

When a Customer Invoice is generated, such data as address and payment terms are pulled from the customer record; and such data as price and item description are pulled from the item record. Once a Customer Invoice is completed, QuickBooks automatically records the information in the appropriate accounts.

When Aroma Ristorante caters an event, the sales are recorded using the Customer Invoice form. For example, if a Tiramisu is sold, creating a customer invoice for this transaction will result in an increase in Accounts Receivable and Catering Sales: Food (DEBIT: Accounts Receivable, CREDIT: Catering Sales: Food).

Costs related to catering or banquet items can be recorded in different ways. The cost related to catering or banquet items can be calculated individually and set up in the Item List. Once a Customer Invoice is created, the cost is recorded in QuickBooks at that time. If a catering or banquet event is priced per person, costs may not be associated with menu items but are recorded at a later time. Some restaurant operators choose not to associate a cost with each catering menu item. The cost of goods sold is calculated and recorded at the end of the accounting period. For Aroma Ristorante, the cost of goods sold and inventory adjustments related to sales transactions will be recorded on completion of the physical inventory count (see Chapter 4). This will allow the restaurant to more accurately record the cost, while considering factors such as spoilage, shrinkage, and breakage.

Customer Invoice

Click the **Customer Center** icon.

Click the **New Transactions** icon.

Select **Invoices** from the drop-down list.

Using the following data, enter the information in the appropriate fields (see Figure 5-2).

DATA: Create a Customer Invoice for Bankers Association of Capital City.

CUSTOMER JOB:	Bankers Association of Capital City	
ACCOUNT:	10700 Accounts Receivable	
TEMPLATE:	Intuit Service Invoice	
DATE:	1/ 17/ 2008	
INVOICE NO.:	100	
TERMS:	Due on receipt	
ITEM AND QUANTITY:	Coffee Regular	1
	Caesar Salad Small	2
	Ravioli Small	2
CUSTOMER TAX CODE:	Tax	

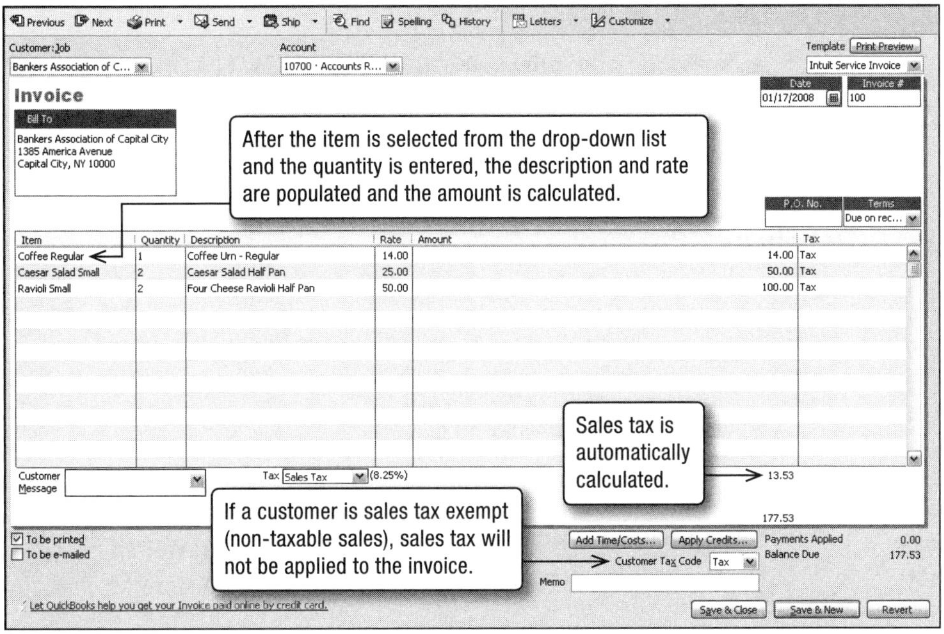

Figure 5-2.

Click **Save & Close**.

Editing Customer Invoices

Customer Invoices can be edited using the Customer Center or the Accounts Receivables Register. Corrections can be made to a Customer Invoice as needed.

Editing a Customer Invoice—Using the Customer Center

Click the **Customer Center** icon.

Click the **Transactions** tab.

Select **Invoices**.

All Customer Invoices are displayed on the right side of the window. Locate the invoice to be edited from the list and double-click on it to display the invoice.

Make the appropriate changes.

Click **Save & Close**.

QuickBooks will notify you with a message: You have changed the transaction. Do you want to record your change?

Click **Yes**.

Editing a Customer Invoice—Using the Accounts Receivable Register

Accounts Receivable is a list of all the restaurant's unpaid Customer Invoices. The Accounts Receivable Register is a detailed list of all the transactions recorded in Accounts Receivable. Customer Invoices can be entered, edited, and deleted directly using the register.

Click the **List** drop-down menu or the **Chart of Accounts** icon on the Home page.

Select **Chart of Accounts**.

Double-click on the **10700 Accounts Receivable** Account.

Locate and edit the appropriate invoice.

Click **Save & Close**.

QuickBooks will notify you with a message: You have changed the transaction. Do you want to record your change?

Click **Yes**.

Voiding and Deleting Customer Invoices

Customer Invoices can be voided or deleted using the Customer Center or the Accounts Receivable Register. Deleting a Customer Invoice permanently removes the invoice from the QuickBooks file. Voiding a Customer Invoice keeps the invoice in the QuickBooks file so it can be viewed, but the Customer Invoice balance will be zero.

Voiding a Customer Invoice—Using the Customer Center

Click the **Customer Center** icon.

Click the **Transactions** tab.

Select **Invoices**.

Double-click on the Customer Invoice to be voided from the list on the right side of the window to display the Customer Invoice.

Click the **Edit** drop-down menu.

Select **Void Invoice**.

Click **Save & Close**.

QuickBooks will notify you with a message: You have changed the transaction. Do you want to record your change?

Click **Yes**.

Deleting a Customer Invoice—Using the Accounts Receivable Register

Click the **List** drop-down menu or the **Chart of Accounts** icon on the Home page.

Select **Chart of Accounts**.

Double-click on **10700 Accounts Receivable** account.

Double-click on the Customer Invoice to be deleted.

Click the **Edit** drop-down menu.

Select **Delete Invoice**.

QuickBooks will notify you of a message: Are you sure you want to delete this transaction?

Click **OK**.

QuickBooks keeps track of all business transactions that are recorded, as well as any and all modifications made to the transaction. It tracks the change, the date of the change, and the individual who recorded the change. This information can be useful to management if a situation arises where information was altered without prior approval. A report can be generated that lists the transaction and the changes made to the transaction. This report can be generated by clicking the **Reports** drop-down menu, selecting **Accountant & Taxes**, and selecting **Audit Trail.**

Printing Customer Invoices

Customer Invoices can be printed using Print Forms or the Customer Center.

Click the **File** drop-down menu.

Select **Print Forms.**

Select **Invoices**.

Place a checkmark next to the invoices to be printed.

Click **OK**.

OR

Click the **Customer Center** icon.

Click the **Transactions** tab.

Select **Invoices**.

Double-click on the Customer Invoice to be printed.

In the Create Invoices window, click the **Print** icon.

Click **Save & Close**.

Recording Customer Payments

Regardless of when the sale is recorded in QuickBooks, all cash receipts should be deposited on a daily basis to prevent theft and increase the availability of cash to pay for other expenditures.

Click the **Customer Center** icon or click the **Receive Payments** icon on the Home page.

Click the **New Transactions** icon.

Select **Receive Payments**.

Using the following data, enter the information in the appropriate fields (see Figure 5-3).

DATA: Record a Payment Received from Bankers Association of Capital City.	
RECEIVED FROM:	Bankers Association of Capital City
A/R ACCOUNT:	10700 Accounts Receivable
DATE:	1/28/2008
PMT METHOD:	Check
CHECK NO.:	10268
AMOUNT:	$177.53
DEPOSIT TO:	10000 Checking Account

Previous Next   History ▾   Get Online Pmts

Customer Payment   A/R Account 10700 · Accounts Re... ▾

Received From Bankers Association of Capital City ▾   Customer Balance   638.68

Amount   177.53   Date   01/28/2008

Pmt. Method   Check   ▾   Check #   10268

Memo   Deposit to 10000 · Checking Ac... ▾

> When a customer is selected from the drop-down list, all outstanding invoices for that customer are displayed.

See how QuickBooks Merchant Service can help simplify selling online. See how

☐ Process credit card payment when saving

Find a Customer/Invoice...

✓	Date	Number	Orig. Amt.	Amt. Due	Payment
✓	01/17/2008	100	177.53	177.53	177.53
	01/24/2008	102	461.15	461.15	0.00
	Totals		638.68	638.68	177.53

This customer has credits available. To apply credits click Discount & Credits...

Available Credits   653.84

Amounts for Selected Invoices

Un-Apply Payment   Amount Due   177.53

Discount & Credits...   Applied   177.53

Discount and Credits Applied   0.00

Save & Close   Save & New   Clear

Figure 5-3.

Click **Save & Close**.

QUICKBOOKS TIP

It is important to place a checkmark next to the outstanding invoice(s) to which the payment should be applied. If a payment is posted to an incorrect invoice, it will be incorrectly shown on the Accounts Receivable (A/R) Aging Report (see page 129 later in this chapter).

When payments are received from customers, by selecting the appropriate account in the "Deposit To" field, funds can be immediately recorded in the checking account, or they can be recorded into a holding account called Undeposited Funds. If a restaurant holds onto the funds for a period of time prior to depositing the funds in the bank, it is appropriate to record the funds in the Undeposited Funds account and transfer the funds to the checking account when the deposit is actually made and checks have been cleared. The Undeposited Funds account or the checking account can be designated as the default account when establishing Company Preferences (see Chapter 2, page 25). Because Aroma Ristorante will be making prompt and daily bank deposits, the checking account was selected as the default account.

When necessary, the "Deposit To" account can be changed when entering the customer payment.

Partial payments may also be made by customers. To record a partial payment, create a partial payment item in the Item List. Select the appropriate Customer Invoice, record the partial payment item, and record the amount in the amount column on the invoice. The balance due will decrease on the Customer Invoice.

Recording Credit Memos

A customer may be granted credit for a particular transaction. A customer credit causes a decrease in the amount due to the restaurant. For example, an incorrect invoice may have already been sent to the customer; and in lieu of voiding it and creating another invoice, the restaurant may choose to render a credit to the customer's account. Customer credits can be retained as an available credit or applied to an invoice, or a refund can be issued to the customer.

Refunds & Credits

Click the **Customer Center** icon or click the **Refunds & Credits** icon on the Home page.

Click the **New Transactions** icon.

Select **Credit Memos/Refunds**.

Using the following data, enter the information in the appropriate fields (see Figure 5-4).

DATA: Enter a Credit for Bankers Association of Capital City.	
CUSTOMER JOB:	Bankers Association of Capital City
ACCOUNT:	10700 Accounts Receivable
DATE:	1/31/2008
TEMPLATE:	Custom Credit Memo
CREDIT NO.:	200
ITEM:	Coffee Regular
QTY:	1
MEMO:	Customer did not receive Coffee $14.00

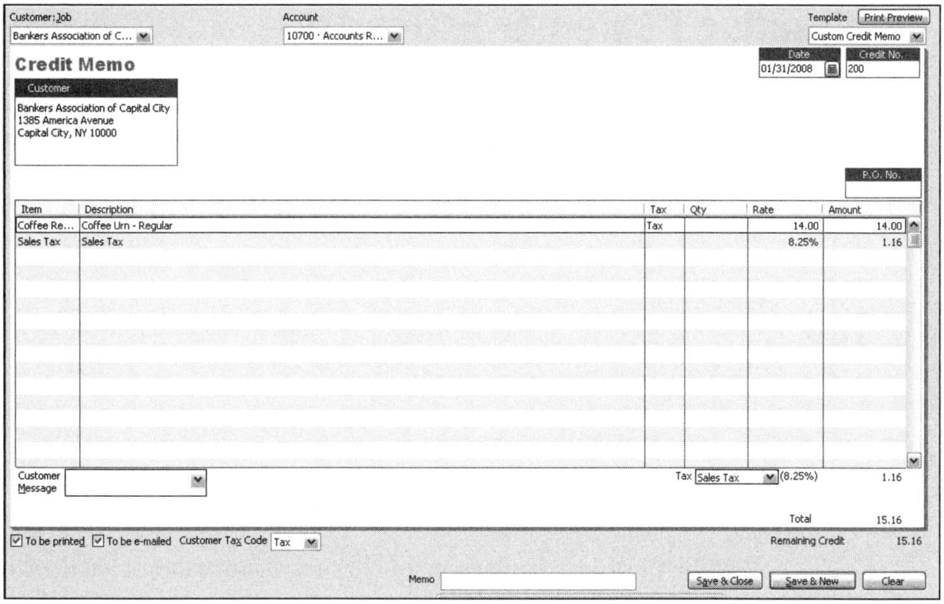

Figure 5-4.

Click **Save & Close**.

After clicking **Save & Close,** the Available Credit window appears, and one of the following three options must be selected: Retain as an available credit, Give a refund, or Apply to an invoice (see Figure 5-5).

- **Retain as an available credit:** A negative amount will be entered in the Accounts Receivable register to be used at a later date.

- **Give a refund:** Opens the Issue a Refund window and a cash, credit card, or check refund will be issued to the customer.

- **Apply to an invoice:** Opens the Apply Credit window and applies the credit to the invoice if the customer has an open invoice. If not, the credit is retained as an available credit.

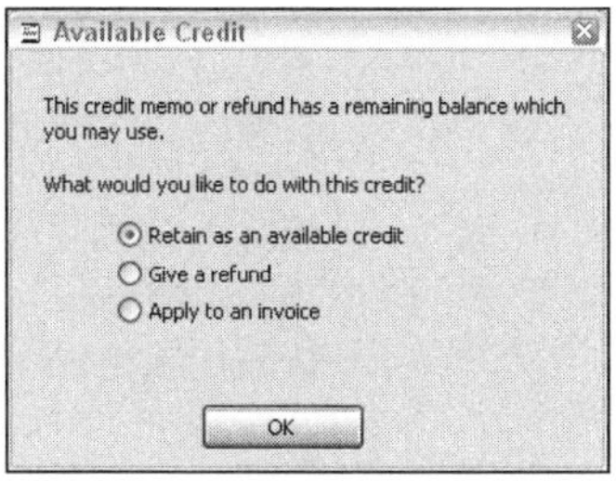

Figure 5-5.

Creating Customer Estimates

Customer Estimates can be prepared for catering and banquet services. Once an estimate has been created, it can be e-mailed and/or printed for the customer. Estimates can be saved in QuickBooks and can be turned into a Customer Invoice after the catering or banquet service has been completed.

QUICKBOOKS TIP

Prior to creating Customer Estimates, activate the estimates function under Jobs & Estimates Company Preferences (see Chapter 2, page 21).

Customer Estimate

Estimates

Click the **Customer Center** icon or click the **Estimates** icon on the Home page.

Click the **New Transactions** icon.

Select **Estimates**.

Using the following data, enter the information in the appropriate fields (see Figure 5-6).

DATA: Create an Estimate for Capital City Medical for a Catering Event.		
CUSTOMER JOB:	Capital City Medical	
DATE:	January 20, 2008	
TEMPLATE:	Custom Estimate	
ESTIMATE NO.:	100	
ITEM AND QTY:	Iced Tea	10
	Coffee Regular	2
	Caesar Salad Large	2
	Tomato/Mozzarella Salad Large	1
	Ravioli Small	1
	Penne Large	1
	Rosemary Chicken Large	1
	Tiramisu	1
MEMO:	For Off-Site Catering Event on 1/31/2008	

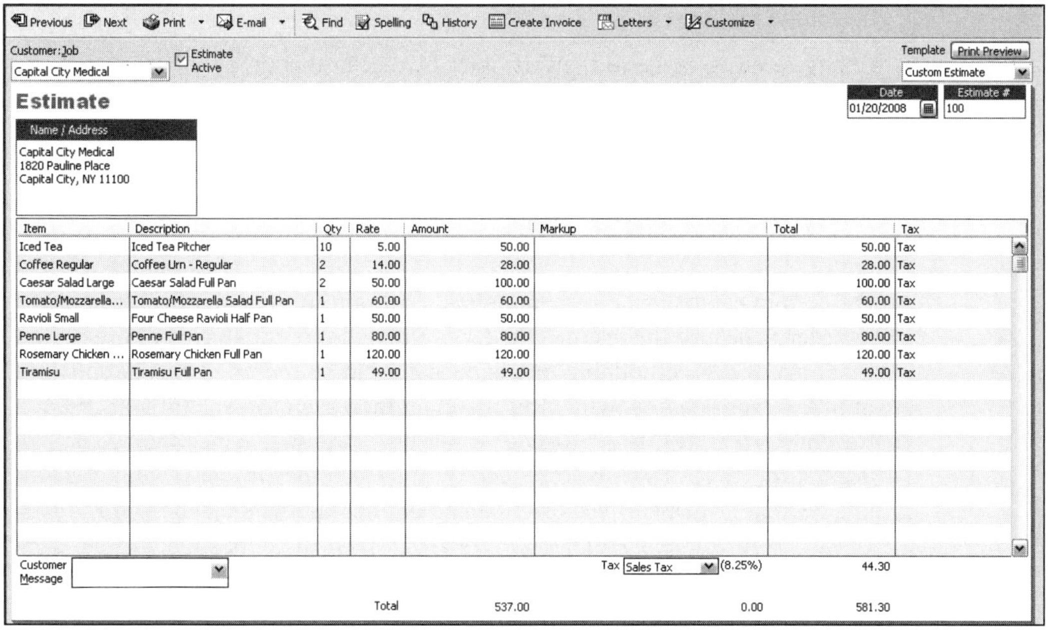

Figure 5-6.

Click **Save & Close**.

Create an Invoice from an Estimate

Click the **Customer Center** icon or click the **Create Invoices** icon on the Home page.

Click the **New Transactions** icon

Select **Invoices** from the drop-down menu.

Using the drop-down list, select **Customer Job.**

Once a Customer Job is selected, active estimates are displayed in the Available Estimates window (see Figure 5-7).

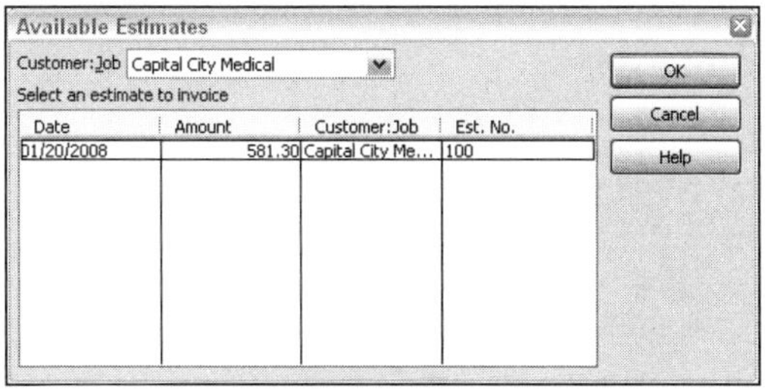

Figure 5-7.

Select the **Estimate** and click **OK**.

Changes can be made to the Customer Invoice at this time.

Click **Save & Close**.

Recording Advance Deposits

For certain events, such as banquets, the restaurant may require a deposit in order to secure the event. The deposit may be refundable or nonrefundable. If it is refundable, the deposit should be recorded as a liability until the event occurs, which results in an increase in Cash and Unearned Revenue (DEBIT: Cash; CREDIT: Unearned Revenue). Once the event occurs, the deposit will be recorded on the Customer Invoice, which results in a decrease in Unearned Revenue and an increase in Revenue (DEBIT: Unearned Revenue; CREDIT: Revenue/Sales). If the deposit is nonrefundable, the deposit can be recorded as revenue at the appropriate time (DEBIT: Cash, CREDIT: Revenue/Sales). In some cases, the deposit is refundable until a specified date, after which it becomes nonrefundable. This prevents the restaurant from incurring costs as a result of the subsequent cancellation of an event.

Refundable Advance Deposit

Click the **Customer Center** icon.

Click the **New Transactions** icon.

Select **Sales Receipts**.

Using the following data, enter the information in the appropriate fields (see Figure 5-8).

DATA: Enter a Refundable Advance Deposit from Best Marketing, Inc.

CUSTOMER JOB:	Best Marketing, Inc.
TEMPLATE:	Custom Sales Receipt
DATE:	1/26/2008
SALE NO.:	102
CHECK NO.:	122268
PAYMENT METHOD:	Check
ITEM:	Advance Deposit—Refundable
AMOUNT:	$500.00
DEPOSIT TO:	10100 Checking Account: Advance Deposits
MEMO:	Off-Site Catering Event on 3/29/2008

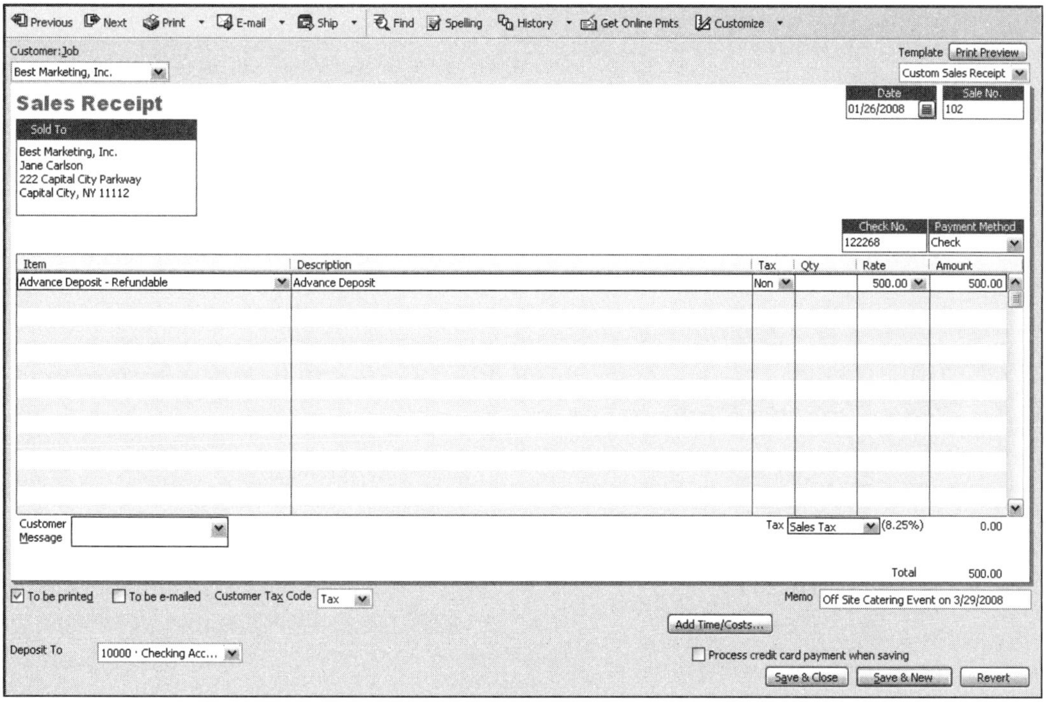

Figure 5-8.

Click **Save & Close**.

QUICKBOOKS TIP

An item for refundable and nonrefundable advance deposits must be set up in the Item List as a service. The refundable advance deposit should be associated with the Unearned Revenue account, and the nonrefundable advance deposit should be associated with the Catering Sales account. If the restaurant wants to track advance deposits in a separate account, an Advance Deposit account can be set up as a subaccount of the Checking account.

To apply an advance deposit to a Customer Invoice, first create the Customer Invoice. On the last line of the invoice, enter the advance deposit item in the items column. Enter –1 in the quantity column and enter the amount of the original deposit in the rate column. At this point, the deposit will show as a reduction on the customer invoice, and the Unearned Revenue and Revenue/Sales accounts will be adjusted accordingly.

Nonrefundable Advance Deposit

Click the **Customer Center** icon.

Click the **New Transactions** tab.

Select **Sales Receipts**.

Using the following data, enter the information in the appropriate fields.

DATA: Enter a Nonrefundable Advance Deposit from Quality Custom Furniture, Inc.

CUSTOMER JOB:	Quality Custom Furniture, Inc.
DATE:	1/31/2008
TEMPLATE:	Custom Sales Receipt
SALE NO.:	103
ITEM:	Advance Deposit—Nonrefundable
AMOUNT:	$200
PAYMENT METHOD:	Check
CHECK NO.:	45638
DEPOSIT TO:	10100 Checking Account: Advance Deposits
MEMO:	Off-Site Catering Event on 2/15/2008

Reports

QuickBooks has a variety of reports relating to sales, customers, and receivables, each of which provides management with specific information that can be used to make business decisions related to a particular area. A detailed list of available reports can be obtained through the **Report Center** or by clicking the **Reports** drop-down menu and then selecting the appropriate category. The following sections include some examples of reports that may be useful to the restaurant manager.

Accounts Receivable Aging Summary

Click the **Reports** drop-down menu.

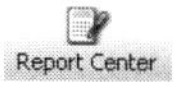

This report can also be accessed through the Report Center.

Select **Customers & Receivables.**

Select the **A/R Aging Summary** (see Figure 5-9).

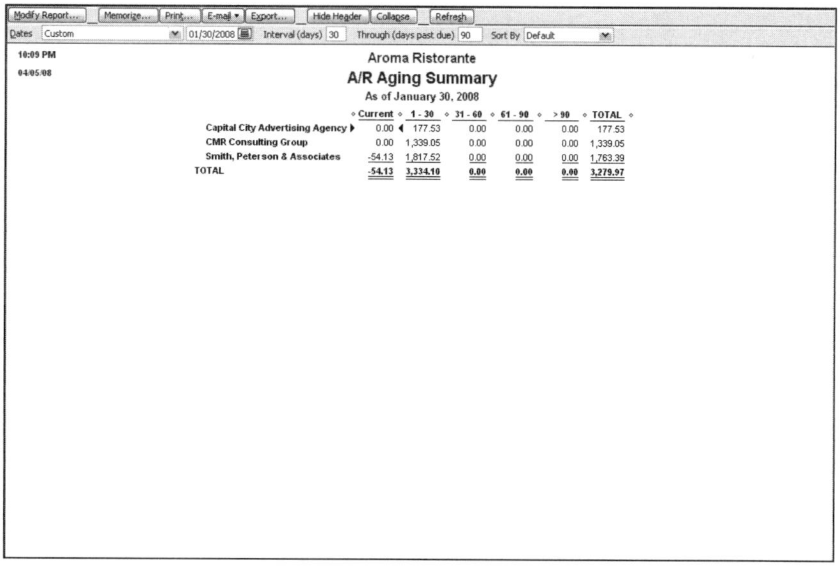

	Current	1 - 30	31 - 60	61 - 90	> 90	TOTAL
Capital City Advertising Agency	0.00	177.53	0.00	0.00	0.00	177.53
CMR Consulting Group	0.00	1,339.05	0.00	0.00	0.00	1,339.05
Smith, Peterson & Associates	-54.13	1,817.52	0.00	0.00	0.00	1,763.39
TOTAL	-54.13	3,334.10	0.00	0.00	0.00	3,279.97

Figure 5-9.

This report provides the total amount owed by a specific customer in each age group, such as 0–30 days, 31–60 days, and so on. By selecting the Accounts Receivable Aging Detail report, the manager can view the individual invoices that make up the total of each age group. The Customers & Receivables reports section also includes an Accounts Receivable graph that provides a visual of how much customers owe the restaurant sorted by customer and a pie chart displaying the percentage of the total due from each customer.

It is important that management be aware of the receivables past due 30 days. Overdue receivables directly impact the restaurant's cash flow and its ability to pay its bills on a timely basis. This report can identify which customer's receivables are significantly overdue and can allow management to decide to potentially forgo further extension of credit to a particular customer.

Customer Balance Summary

Click the **Reports** drop-down menu.

This Report can also be accessed through the Report Center.

Select **Customers & Receivables**.

Select **Customer Balance Summary** (see Figure 5-10).

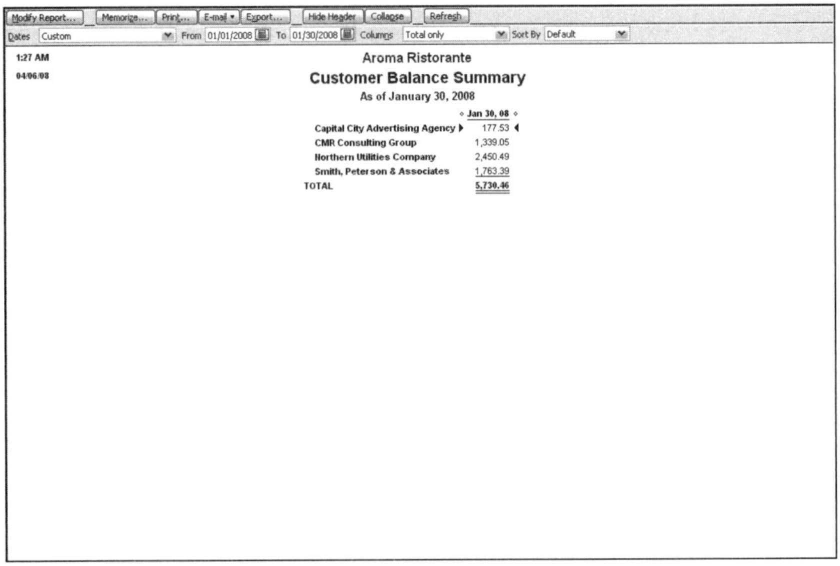

Figure 5-10.

This report shows all unpaid customer balances sorted by customer. To view the invoices that make up the total, select the **Customer Balance Detail Report** or double-click on **Customer Balance** in the Customer Balance Summary Report. Management should be aware of which customers owe the most money and investigate the cause of all significant balances due.

Collections Report

Click the **Reports** drop-down menu.

This Report can also be accessed through the Report Center

Select **Customers & Receivables**.

Select **Collections Report** (see Figure 5-11).

| Modify Report... | Memorize... | Print... | E-mail ▾ | Export... | Hide Header | Refresh |

Dates Custom ▾ 01/31/2008 📅 Past due 1 Sort By Default ▾

10:05 AM
05/05/08

Aroma Ristorante
Collections Report
As of January 31, 2008

	Type	Date	Num	P. O. #	Terms	Due Date	Aging	Open Balance
Capital City Advertising Agency								
Joan Nellson								
555-616-6161								
▸	Invoice	01/22/2008	203		Due on ...	01/22/2008	9	177.53 ◂
Total Capital City Advertising Agency								177.53
CMR Consulting Group								
James Garcia								
555-555-4242								
	Invoice	01/22/2008	101		Due on ...	01/22/2008	9	1,339.05
Total CMR Consulting Group								1,339.05
Northern Utilities Company								
Jerry Martin								
555-666-6565								
	Invoice	01/30/2008	204			01/30/2008	1	2,450.49
Total Northern Utilities Company								2,450.49
Smith, Peterson & Associates								
James Smith								
555-333-0000								
	Credit Memo	01/30/2008	202			01/30/2008	1	-54.13
Total Smith, Peterson & Associates								-54.13
TOTAL								**3,912.94**

Figure 5-11.

This report provides a list of overdue invoices sorted by customer along with the customer contact names and phone numbers. Management can use this information to contact individual customers and request payment without having to print out the customer contact and phone list.

Sales by Customer Summary

Click the **Reports** drop-down menu.

Report Center

This Report can also be accessed through the Report Center.

Select **Sales**.

Select **Sales by Customer Summary** (see Figure 5-12).

| Modify Report... | Memorize... | Print... | E-mail ▼ | Export... | Hide Header | Collapse | Refresh |

Dates Custom ▼ From 01/01/2008 To 01/31/2008 Columns Total only ▼ Sort By Default ▼

1:41 PM
04/10/08
Accrual Basis

Aroma Ristorante
Sales by Customer Summary
January 2008

	◦ Jan 08 ◦
Bankers Association of Capital City ▶	576.00 ◀
Best Marketing, Inc.	500.00
Capital City Advertising Agency	164.00
Capital City Medical	515.00
Capital City Web Design, Inc.	1,000.00
CMR Consulting Group	1,237.00
Northern Utilities Company	2,818.00
Quality Custom Furniture, Inc.	200.00
Smith, Peterson & Associates	1,629.00
TOTAL	**8,639.00**

Figure 5-12.

This report provides the total sales from a specific customer. Management should be aware of which customers provide the most business and make sure the customer is continuously provided satisfactory service. Management may decide to offer a discount or other special service on a future sale as a reward for customer loyalty. Management can also develop plans to increase sales among customers with lower sales histories.

Sales by Item Detail

Click the **Reports** drop-down menu.

Report Center

This Report can also be accessed through the Report Center.

Select **Sales**.

Select **Sales by Item Detail** (see Figure 5-13).

Modify Report...	Memorize...	Print...	E-mail ▾	Export...		Hide Header	Refresh

| Dates | Custom | ▾ | From | 01/01/2008 | To | 01/31/2008 | Sort By | Default | ▾ |

3:34 PM
03/27/08
Accrual Basis

Aroma Ristorante
Sales by Item Detail
January 2008

Type	Date	Num	Memo	Name	Qty	Sales Price	Amount	Balance
Penne Large								
Invoice	01/31/2008	103	Penne Full Pan	Capital City Medical	1	80.00	80.00	80.00
Total Penne Large							80.00	80.00
Ravioli Large								
Invoice	01/22/2008	101	Four Cheese Ravio...	CMR Consulting Group	2	100.00	200.00	200.00
Total Ravioli Large							200.00	200.00
Ravioli Small								
Invoice	01/17/2008	100	Four Cheese Ravio...	Bankers Association of Capit...	2	50.00	100.00	100.00
Invoice	01/31/2008	103	Four Cheese Ravio...	Capital City Medical	1	50.00	50.00	150.00
Total Ravioli Small							150.00	150.00
Red Wine								
Invoice	01/22/2008	101	Bottle House Chianti	CMR Consulting Group	10	15.00	150.00	150.00
Total Red Wine							150.00	150.00
Rosemary Chicken Large								
Invoice	01/31/2008	103	Rosemary Chicken...	Capital City Medical	1	120.00	120.00	120.00
Total Rosemary Chicken Large							120.00	120.00
Rosemary Chicken Small								
Invoice	01/22/2008	101	Rosemary Chicken...	CMR Consulting Group	2	60.00	120.00	120.00
Total Rosemary Chicken Small							120.00	120.00
Tiramisu								
Invoice	01/22/2008	101	Tiramisu Full Pan	CMR Consulting Group	3	49.00	147.00	147.00
Invoice	01/24/2008	102	Tiramisu Full Pan	Bankers Association of Capit...	3	49.00	147.00	294.00
Invoice	01/31/2008	103	Tiramisu Full Pan	Capital City Medical	1	49.00	49.00	343.00
Total Tiramisu							343.00	343.00

Figure 5-13.

This report provides such information as the quantity sold of a particular item, the total amount sold of an item, and the item's percentage of total sales. If an item has a low sales history, perhaps management might decide to offer an incentive to increase sales or discontinue selling that item. Management should be aware of which items are the most popular and therefore should not be removed from the menu. This information can also be used to forecast sales and inventory purchases.

Chapter Review Problems

1. Aroma Ristorante needs to prepare an estimate for an off-site catering event for Smith, Peterson, and Associates. Create an estimate, create an invoice from the estimate, and record a Check Payment in Full from the customer.

DATA:		
CUSTOMER JOB:	Smith, Peterson, and Associates	
DATE:	1/28/2008	
TEMPLATE:	Custom Estimate	
ESTIMATE NO.:	101	
ITEM AND QTY:	Iced Tea	8
	Coffee Regular	2
	Coffee Decaf	2
	Caesar Salad Large	3
	Tomato/Mozzarella Salad Large	2
	Veal Medallions Large	3
	Penne Large	2
	Rosemary Chicken Large	2
	Tiramisu	4
	Cheesecake	3
MEMO:	For Off-Site Catering Event on 1/30/2008	

2. Using a journal entry, record the following sales data.

DATA from a Point-of-Sale Report:	
DATE:	1/21/2008
ENTRY NO.:	8
DEBIT ACCOUNT	**AMOUNT**
10000 Checking Account:	$4,855.38
10050 Checking Account: Visa/MasterCard:	$11,673.52

10075 Checking Account: Amex:	$800.96
51800 Merchant Account Fees:	$258.77
43900 Sales Comps, Discounts & Promo:	$246.45
66080 Payroll Expenses: Employee Benefits:	$164.30
25300 Gift Certificates Redeemed:	$0
10150 Over/Short:	$42.18
CREDIT ACCOUNT	**AMOUNT**
25200 Gift Certificates Outstanding:	$150.00
43800 Food Sales:	$11,501.00
41410 Beverage Sales: Beer:	$591.48
41420 Beverage Sales: Wine:	$2,710.95
41430 Beverage Sales: Liquor:	$1,330.83
41440 Beverage Sales: Other:	$295.74
70010 Retail Income:	$98.00
25500 Sales Tax Payable:	$1,363.56
MEMO:	To Record Weekly Sales

3. Record a Credit Memo for Smith, Peterson, and Associates and retain as an available credit for a future invoice.

DATA:	
CUSTOMER JOB:	Smith, Peterson, and Associates
DATE:	1/30/2008
TEMPLATE:	Custom Credit Memo
CREDIT NO.:	202
ITEM:	Caesar Salad Large
QTY:	1
MEMO:	Overcharged Caesar Salad Large ($50) for Catering Job on 1/28/2008

4. a. Aroma Ristorante will provide catering services for the Northern Utilities Company Annual Awards Dinner on January 30, 2008 and received a $600 refundable deposit from Northern Utilities Company on January 11, 2008. Record the receipt of the refundable advance deposit.

DATA:	
CUSTOMER JOB:	Northern Utilities Company
TEMPLATE:	Custom Sales Receipt
DATE:	1/11/2008
SALE NO.:	105
PAYMENT METHOD:	Check
CHECK NO.:	268955
ITEM:	Advance Deposit—Refundable
AMOUNT.:	$600.00
DEPOSIT TO:	10100 Checking Account: Advance Deposits
MEMO:	Off-Site Catering Job on 1/30/2008

b. On January 30, 2008, Aroma Ristorante catered the Annual Awards Dinner for Northern Utilities Company and submitted an invoice for payment. Create a Customer Invoice for the event and apply $600 advance deposit to the Customer Invoice.

DATA:		
BILL TO:	Northern Utilities Company	
DATE:	1/30/2008	
INVOICE NO.:	204	
ITEM AND QTY:	Cheese Plate	5
	Red Wine	20
	White Wine	15
	Caesar Salad Large	5
	Tomato/Mozzarella Salad Large	5

	Filet Large	4
	Penne Large	6
	Tiramisu	3
	Coffee Regular	2
	Coffee Decaf	2

5. a. On January 25, 2008 Aroma Ristorante received a $1,000 nonrefundable advance deposit from Capital City Web Design, Inc. for an event to be held on January 31, 2008. Record the nonrefundable deposit.

DATA:	
CUSTOMER JOB:	Capital City Web Design, Inc.
TEMPLATE:	Custom Sales Receipt
DATE:	1/25/2008
SALE NO.:	106
PAYMENT METHOD:	Check
CHECK NO.:	30259
ITEM:	Advance Deposit—Nonrefundable
DEPOSIT AMOUNT.:	$1,000.00
DEPOSIT TO:	10100 Checking Account: Advance Deposits
MEMO:	Off-Site Catering Job on 1/29/2008

b. On January 29, 2008, Capital City Web Design, Inc., decided to cancel the event. Is the restaurant required to record a transaction for the cancellation on January 29, 2008?

6. Assume the restaurant recorded a refundable advance deposit from a customer and subsequently the event was canceled and the deposit was returned. How should this transaction be recorded?

You can find additional Review Problems at *www.wiley.com/college/murphy.*

Payroll

Access the Chapter 6 data file from the CD-ROM that accompanies this book or download the file from the web site.

Chapter Outline

Payroll and the Restaurant Industry

QuickBooks Payroll Options

Creating a New Employee Record

Editing an Employee Record

Creating Employee Paychecks

Editing, Voiding, and Deleting Paychecks

Releasing Employees and Inactivating Employee Records

Outsourcing Payroll

Reports

Chapter Review Problems

Payroll and the Restaurant Industry

In the restaurant industry, labor costs are a significant component of a restaurant's costs. According to the Restaurant Industry Operations Report 2006/2007 Edition published by the National Restaurant Association, average labor cost represents 34 percent of sales. Labor costs includes salary and wages; tips; vacation and sick time; retirement benefits; health, dental, and life insurance; incentives and bonuses; job training; employee meals; workman's compensation; and payroll taxes. Payroll taxes include Social Security, Medicare, and federal and state unemployment insurance.

Industry Fact

By 2007, 72 percent of restaurants in the United States were using a computer to manage employee time and attendance.

Source: 6th Annual Restaurant Technology Study, *Hospitality Magazine* (*www.htmagazine.com*)

QUICKBOOKS TIP

You can compare outsourced payroll (such as ADP or Paychex) to QuickBooks payroll by accessing the following web page: *payroll.intuit.com/payrolloutsourcing*.

Payroll can be a labor-intensive, time-consuming, and often confusing process. Given the direct impact of labor cost on the financial success of the restaurant, it is important for a manager to control these costs through hiring practices, labor scheduling, job training, and accurate financial records. Should management decide to process payroll in-house, it is imperative that the restaurant manager be knowledgeable about payroll laws and reporting requirements. Improper payroll processing can result in employee morale problems, underpayments and overpayments, and compliance problems, which may result in significant tax penalties and interest.

Some restaurant operators alleviate this pressure by allowing an outside company to process payroll and file the required payroll reports. In that case, management will receive payroll reports each payroll period and the payroll process simply involves recording a journal entry to transfer the information from the report into QuickBooks.

QuickBooks Payroll Options

Payroll can be recorded manually in QuickBooks. Employers are responsible for obtaining the most recent payroll tax information from the appropriate federal and state agencies. This information is used to manually calculate an employee's payroll withholdings. These withholdings are inputted manually to create paychecks through the Employee Center. Federal and state payroll tax forms must be prepared manually.

So that you can see the payroll process, Aroma Ristorante will manually process payroll. To use QuickBooks to manually process payroll, the payroll set-up process must be completed (see Chapter 2, page 28). As part of the payroll setup, an employee record has been created. Employee records should be created for all remaining employees for Aroma Ristorante. QuickBooks frequently enhances payroll options, so for the latest options and features on QuickBooks Payroll, access the following web page: *payroll.intuit. com/payrollservices*.

QuickBooks Basic Payroll

Employers download the most current federal and state tax tables into the QuickBooks application and enter employee hours. QuickBooks then calculates the earnings, deductions, and payroll taxes for each employee. Payroll checks can be printed. The employer is responsible for tax filings and tax deposits.

QuickBooks Enhanced Payroll

In addition to the features outlined in the Basic Payroll, payroll data flows automatically to tax forms; and this option allows employers to track workers compensation information and also has additional time-tracking options.

QuickBooks Assisted Payroll

In addition to features outlined in the Enhanced Payroll, Intuit will file and submit the payroll tax deposit for federal and state payroll liabilities, as well as print and mail year end forms such as W-2s and 1099s.

QuickBooks Online Payroll

QuickBooks Online Payroll allows managers and accountants to run payroll anywhere there is Internet access.

QUICKBOOKS TIP

Learn more about QuickBooks payroll including: Payroll 101 Guide, Dealing with the Government, Hiring Tips, etc. by accessing *payroll.intuit.com*. Post and review QuickBooks payroll-related questions at the QuickBooks Payroll Center Forum at *www .quickbooksgroup.com/forums*.

Creating a New Employee Record

Using the following data, enter the information in the appropriate fields.

> ### DATA: Create a New Employee Record for Peter Petrov.
>
> Peter Petrov was hired as a full-time manager on January 1, 2008. Mr. Petrov was born on 6/15/1983 and his Social Security number is 000-11-0000. He resides at 25 Fulton Street, Capital City, New York, 11112. His telephone number is 555-666-1234. He is compensated $45,000 annually and is paid semimonthly. His federal and state filing status is as follows: Married, 2 Allowances, No Extra Withholdings, and No local taxes. Mr. Petrov works in New York State and is subject to New York State Withholding. State Unemployment Insurance (SUI) is paid by the company. Health and dental insurance benefits are paid by both employee and employer. The employee deductions are $25 for health insurance and $7 for dental insurance per pay period. The employer contributes $75 for health insurance and $25 for dental insurance per pay period.

Click the **Employee Center** icon.

Click the **New Employee** icon.

In the Personal tab, enter the appropriate information (see Figure 6-1).

Figure 6-1.

Click the **Address and Contact** tab, and enter the appropriate information (see Figure 6-2).

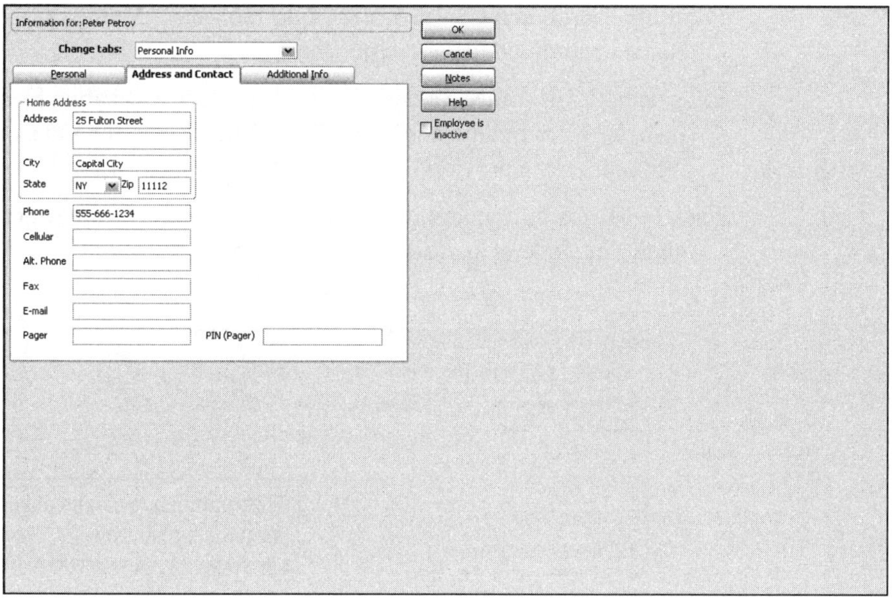

Figure 6-2.

Click the **Change tabs** drop-down list and select the **Payroll and Compensation Info** tab (see Figure 6-3).

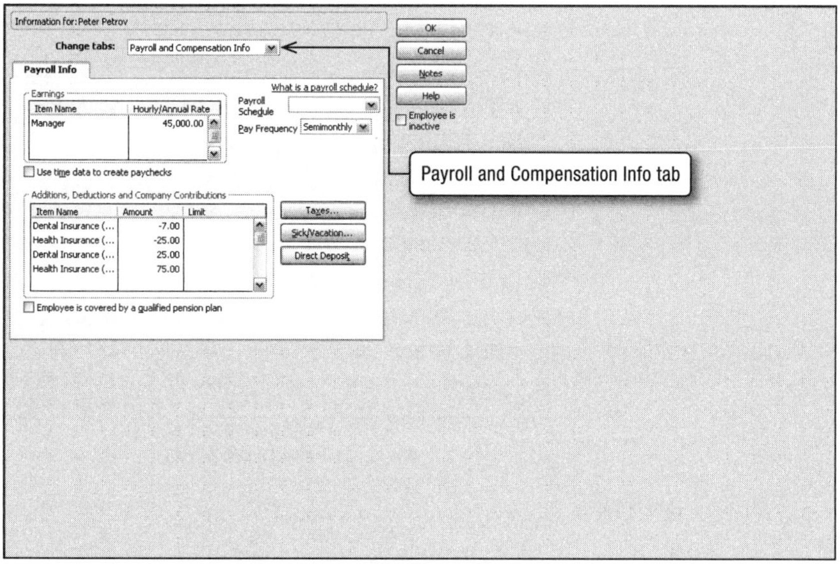

Figure 6-3.

From the Payroll and Compensation Info tab, select **Manager** from the Item Name drop-down list and enter the **Annual Rate.**

Enter **Health Insurance Taxable, Dental Insurance Taxable, Health Insurance (company paid)**, and **Dental Insurance (company paid)**. Deductions are provided in the data box on page 142.

Click the **Taxes** button and enter the information in the appropriate fields under the Federal and State tabs (see Figures 6-4 and 6-5).

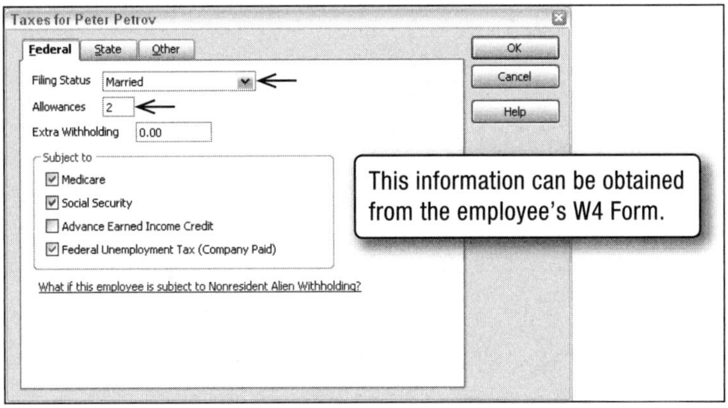

Figure 6-4.

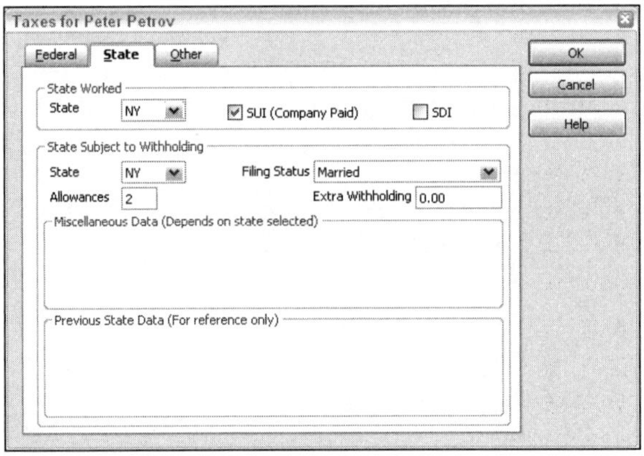

Figure 6-5.

Click **OK**.

When prompted, QuickBooks added the following taxes to this employee (see Figure 6-6).

Figure 6-6.

Click **OK**.

QuickBooks may automatically add these taxes. If the taxes are not applicable, click **Other Tab** and delete them.

Click the **Change tabs** drop-down list, select the **Employment Info** tab, and enter **Hire Date** (see Figure 6-7).

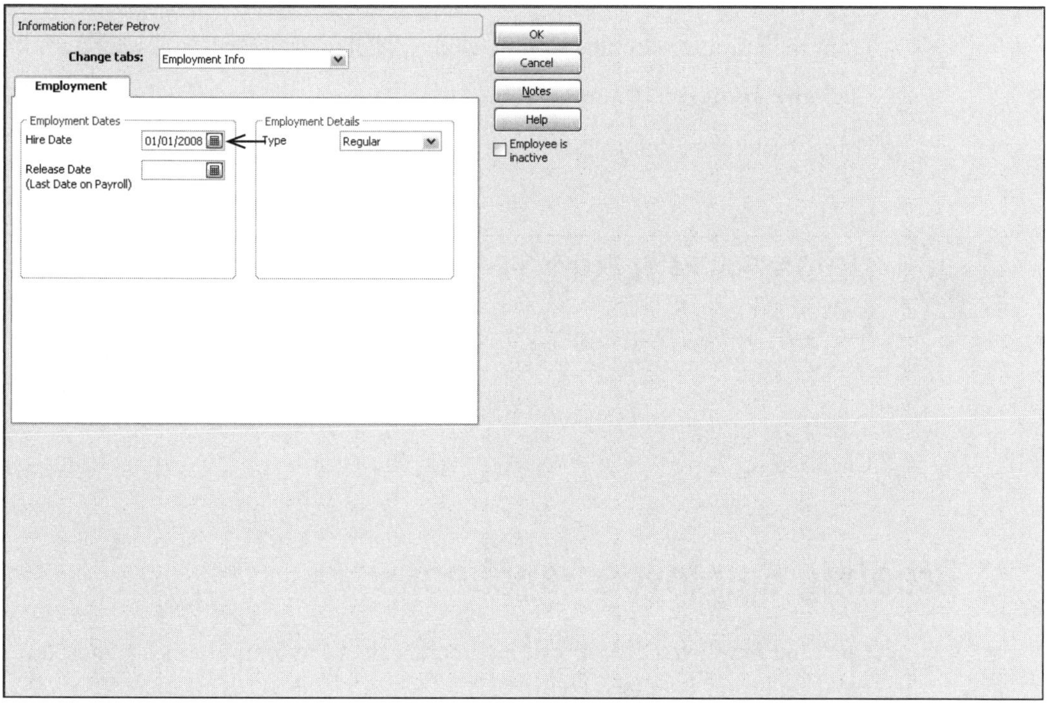

Figure 6-7.

Click **OK** to return to the Employee Center.

Using the following data, enter the information in the appropriate fields.

DATA: Create a New Employee Record for Amy Jameson.

Amy Jameson was hired as full-time Kitchen Staff on January 1, 2008. Mrs. Jameson was born on 12/1/1979 and her Social Security number is 000-22-0000. She resides at 49 Plainview Avenue, Capital City, New York 11112. Her telephone number is 555-777-5678. She is compensated $13.50 per hour and is paid semimonthly. Her overtime rate is $20.25 per hour. Her federal and state filing status is as follows: Married, 1 Allowance, No Extra Withholdings, and No local taxes. Ms. Jameson works in New York State and is subject to New York State Withholding. State Unemployment Insurance (SUI) is paid by the company. She receives health and dental insurance. The employee deductions are $25 for health insurance and $7 for dental insurance per pay period. The employer contributes $75 for health insurance and $25 for dental insurance per pay period.

Editing an Employee Record

From the Employee Center, double-click on **Peter Petrov**'s Employee Record.

Click the **Address and Contact** tab.

Using the information that follows, edit the employee record.

DATA: Edit Peter Petrov's Employee Record.

As of January 15, 2008, Peter Petrov now resides at 402 Market Street, Capital City, NY 11112. His new phone number is 555-999-0000.

Click **OK**.

Creating Employee Paychecks

Click the **Employee** drop-down menu and select **Pay Employees**, or click the **Pay Employees** icon (see Figure 6-8).

Enter the following:

Pay Period Ends:	01/15/2008
Check Date:	01/15/2008

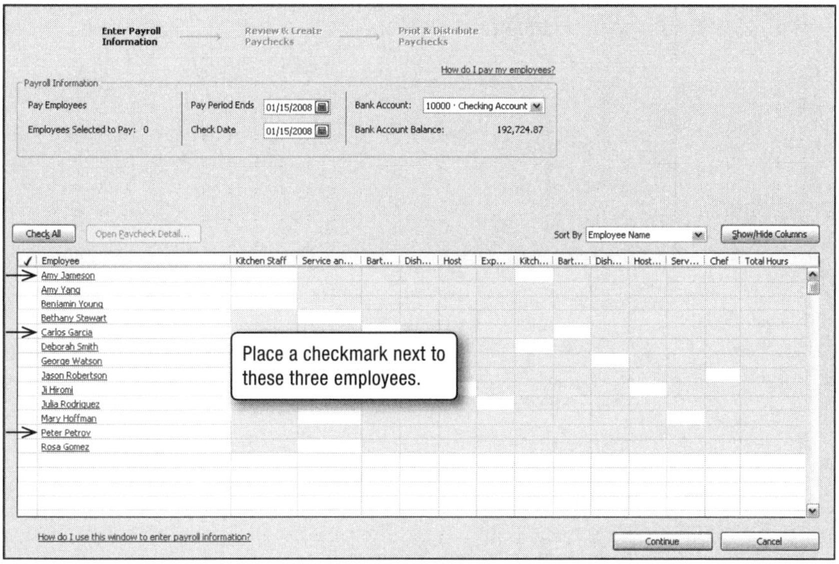

Figure 6-8.

Select **10000 Checking Account** from the Bank Account drop-down list.

Place a checkmark next to **Amy Jameson, Carlos Garcia,** and **Peter Petrov** to create a paycheck for these three employees.

Double-click on **Amy Jameson** to display her paycheck and use the payroll information listed to create her paycheck (see Figure 6-9).

Payroll for January 1, 2008, to January 15, 2008

	Amy Jameson	Peter Petrov	Carlos Garcia
Earnings			
Regular Hours	75.5	80	80
Overtime Hours			2.5
Other Payroll Items			
Dental Insurance (company paid)	$25	$25	$25
Health Insurance (company paid)	$75	$75	$75
Dental Insurance (taxable)	$7	$7	$7
Health Insurance (taxable)	$25	$25	$25
Reported Paycheck Tips			$212.00
Extra Withholding			$20.00

Company Summary			
Social Security	$63.19	$116.25	$75.45
Medicare	$14.78	$27.19	$17.65
Federal Unemployment	$8.15	$15.00	$9.74
NY Unemployment	$55.04	$101.25	$65.72
Employee Summary			
Federal Withholding	$54.00	$156.00	$78.00
Social Security	$63.19	$116.25	$75.45
Medicare	$14.78	$27.19	$17.65
NY Income Tax	$30.10	$84.88	$42.20

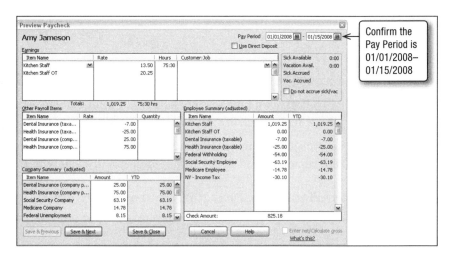

Figure 6-9.

Create paychecks for Carlos Garcia and Peter Petrov using the steps just outlined.

When recording Carlos Garcia's paycheck, enter his tips earned by using the Cash Tips and Reported Cash Tips (offset) in the Other Payroll Items window. Record the additional withholding of $20.00 in the Other Payroll Items section (see Figure 6-10).

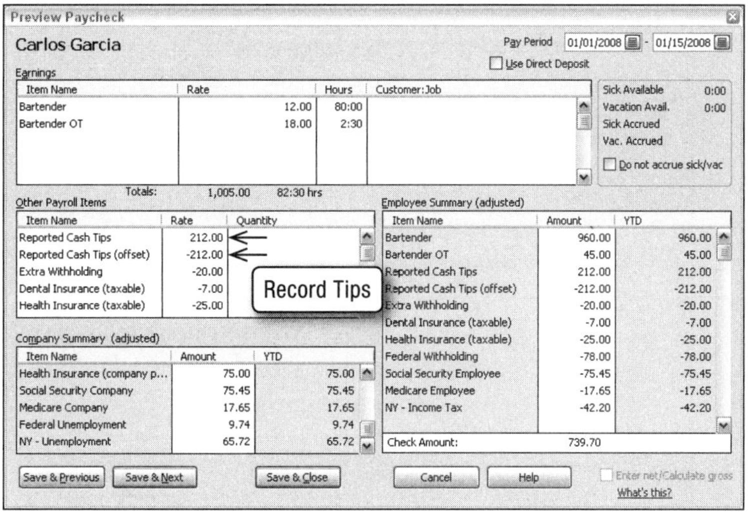

Figure 6-10.

HELPFUL TIP

In most restaurants, employees receive tips from customers. Federal and state regulations established tip reporting requirements. These regulations often allow employers to apply a tip credit against the minimum wage of employees who receive tips, such as servers and bartenders.

HELPFUL TIP

Reported Cash Tips should be used when employees keep tips and report tip amounts to their employer. Reported Paycheck Tips should be used when tips are paid to the employees on their paychecks. Reported Tips: Employee tips are included in gross wages and subject to payroll taxes. Reported tips are included in an employee's paycheck when the employee turns in tips to the manager or guests charge tips on credit cards.

After the three paychecks have been recorded (see Figure 6-11), click the **Continue** button in the Enter Payroll Information window.

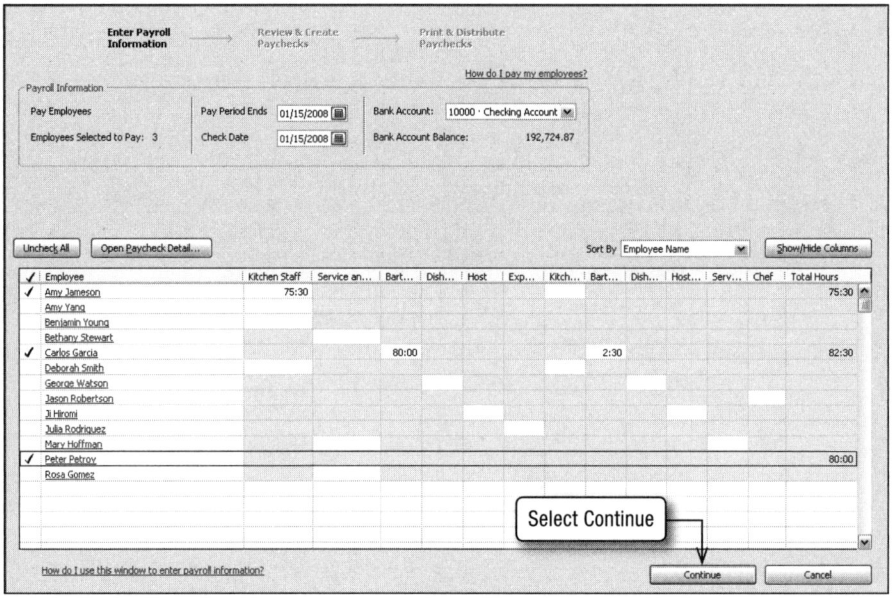

Figure 6-11.

Create Paychecks   In the Review & Create Paychecks window, click the **Create Paychecks** button. Paychecks can be printed at this time (see Figures 6-12 and 6-13).

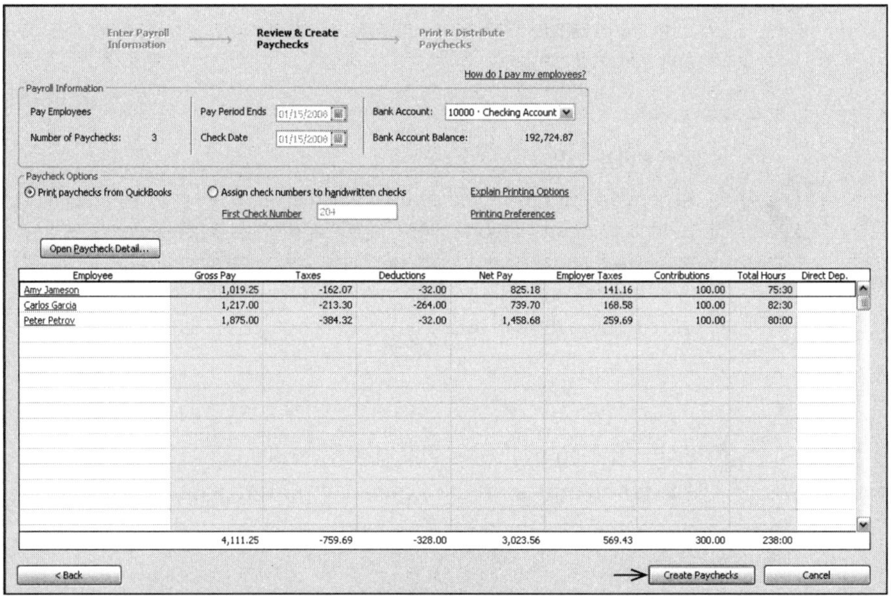

Figure 6-12.

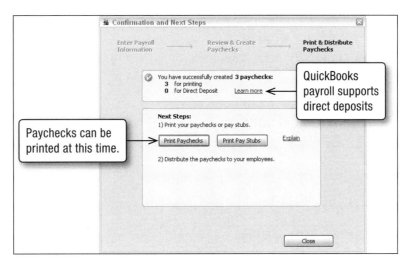

Figure 6-13.

Click **Close**.

Editing, Voiding, and Deleting Paychecks

Editing a Paycheck

Click the **Employee** drop-down menu.

Select **Edit/Void Paychecks**.

Select the appropriate **Date Range**, including start and end date.

Select the **Employee Paycheck**.

Click the **Edit** button.

Click the **Paycheck Detail** button.

Enter the appropriate changes.

Click **OK**.

Click **Save & Close**.

Voiding a Paycheck

Click the **Employee** drop-down menu.

Select **Edit/Void Paychecks.**

Select the appropriate **Date Range,** including start and end date.

Select an employee paycheck to be voided.

Click the **Void** button.

Click **Done**.

QUICKBOOKS TIP

Paychecks can be deleted prior to processing. Voiding an incorrect paycheck and reissuing the paycheck may mean that an employer has to refile payroll tax forms.

Deleting a Paycheck

Click the **Employee** drop-down menu.

Select **Edit/Void Paychecks**.

Select the appropriate **Date Range**, including start and end date.

Double-click on the employee paycheck to be deleted.

Click the **Edit** drop-down menu.

Select **Delete Paycheck**.

QuickBooks will notify you with a message: "Are you sure you want to delete this paycheck?"

Click **OK**.

Releasing Employees and Inactivating Employee Records

Releasing an Employee

Click the **Employee Center** icon. Active employees are displayed on the left side of the window.

Double-click on an Employee Name to access the employee record.

In the Change tabs drop-down list, select the **Employment Info** tab and enter a **Release Date** (see Figure 6-14).

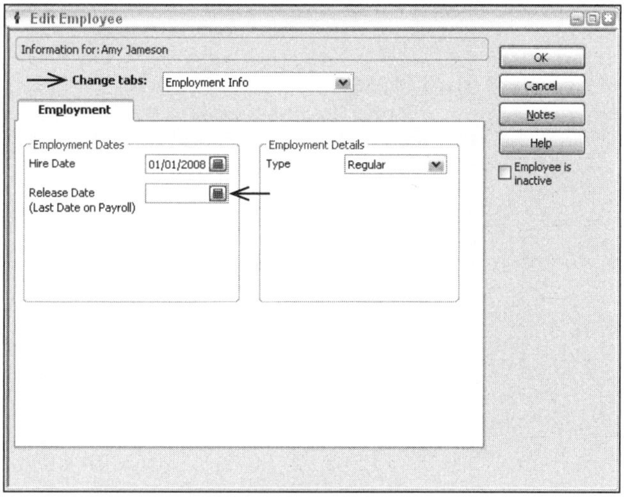

Figure 6-14.

Click **OK**.

QUICKBOOKS TIP

Employees should be released when they are no longer employed at a restaurant. Released employees do not show up as employees to be paid. Inactivating employees removes them from the employee list but does not delete the employees from the company file.

Inactivating an Employee Record

Click the **Employee Center** icon. Active employees are displayed on the left side of the window.

Double-click on an Employee Name to access the employee record.

On the **Personal Info** tab, place a checkmark next to **Employee is inactive** (see Figure 6-15).

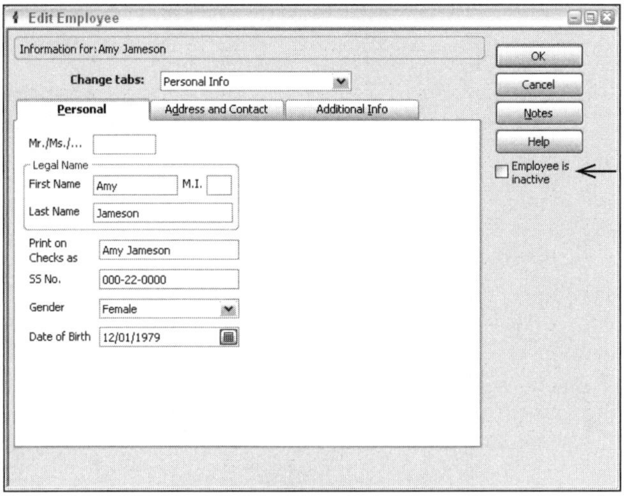

Figure 6-15.

Click **OK**.

Outsourcing Payroll

For restaurants that outsource payroll to companies such as ADP or Paychex, QuickBooks can be used to record payroll transactions via journal entries if there is not an interface to QuickBooks. After submission of employee payroll data to the outside payroll company, a restaurant would receive a detailed report including payroll expenses and related taxes. From this report, this data can be recorded in QuickBooks using a journal entry. (Aroma Ristorante *does not need to record this journal entry* because it is using the QuickBooks Manual Payroll feature.)

Follow these instructions to record a journal entry if outsourcing payroll:

Click the **Company** drop-down menu.

Select **Make Journal Entries**.

Enter the date and journal entry number.

Example of a Journal Entry to Record Semimonthly Payroll

January 15, 2008		
ACCOUNT	DEBIT	CREDIT
Payroll Expenses: Manager	$1,875.00	
Payroll Expenses: Chef	$1,750.00	
Payroll Expenses: Service and Bus Staff	$1,034.00	
Payroll Expenses: Host	$930.00	
Payroll Expenses: Bartender	$1,005.00	
Payroll Expenses: Kitchen Staff	$1,535.63	
Payroll Expenses: Expeditor	$0	
Payroll Expenses: Dishwasher	$875.00	
Payroll Expenses: Social Security	$597.20	
Payroll Expenses: Medicare	$139.68	
Payroll Expenses: Federal Unemployment	$77.06	
Payroll Expenses: State Unemployment	$520.14	
Payroll Expenses: Employee Benefits	$700.00	
Payroll Liabilities: Social Security		$1,194.40
Payroll Liabilities: Medicare		$279.36
Payroll Liabilities: Federal Unemployment		$77.06
Payroll Liabilities: State Unemployment		$520.14
Payroll Liabilities: Federal Income Tax		$746.00
Payroll Liabilities: State Income Tax		$310.94
Payroll Liabilities: Health and Dental		$924.00
Checking Account		$6,986.81
Memo: To record **January 15, 2008 payroll**.		

Click **Save & Close**.

Reports

Report Center

QuickBooks has a variety of payroll-related reports. A detailed list of available reports can be obtained through the **Report Center** icon or by clicking the **Reports** drop-down menu and selecting **Employees & Payroll**. The following sections include some examples of reports that maybe useful to the restaurant operator.

Payroll Summary

Click the **Reports** drop-down menu.

Select **Employees & Payroll**.

Select **Payroll Summary** (see Figure 6-16).

		Amy Jameson			Carlos Garcia			Peter Petrov			TOTAL	
	Hours	Rate	Jan 1 - 15, 08	Hours	Rate	Jan 1 - 15, 08	Hours	Rate	Jan 1 - 15, 08	Hours	Ra...	Jan 1 - 15, 08
Employee Wages, Taxes and Adjustments												
Gross Pay												
Manager			0.00			0.00	80		1,875.00	80		1,875.00
Bartender			0.00	80	12.00	960.00			0.00	80		960.00
Bartender OT			0.00	2.5	18.00	45.00			0.00	2.5		45.00
Kitchen Staff	75.5	13.50	1,019.25			0.00			0.00	75.5		1,019.25
Kitchen Staff OT		20.25	0.00			0.00			0.00			0.00
Reported Cash Tips			0.00			212.00			0.00			212.00
Total Gross Pay	75.5		1,019.25	82.5		1,217.00	80		1,875.00	238		4,111.25
Deductions from Gross Pay												
Extra Withholding			0.00			20.00			0.00			20.00
Total Deductions from Gross Pay			0.00			20.00			0.00			20.00
Adjusted Gross Pay	75.5		1,019.25	82.5		1,237.00	80		1,875.00	238		4,131.25
Taxes Withheld												
Federal Withholding			-54.00			-78.00			-156.00			-288.00
Medicare Employee			-14.78			-17.65			-27.19			-59.62
Social Security Employee			-63.19			-75.45			-116.25			-254.89
NY - Income Tax			-30.10			-42.20			-84.88			-157.18
Total Taxes Withheld			-162.07			-213.30			-384.32			-759.69
Deductions from Net Pay												
Dental Insurance (taxable)			-7.00			-7.00			-7.00			-21.00
Health Insurance (taxable)			-25.00			-25.00			-25.00			-75.00
Reported Cash Tips (offset)			0.00			-212.00			0.00			-212.00
Total Deductions from Net Pay			-32.00			-244.00			-32.00			-308.00

Figure 6-16.

This report provides a detailed list of all the payroll items included in the calculation from gross pay to net pay and a list of the employer taxes and contributions for each individual employee. This report can be used to determine how much overtime an employee earned, list the type of deductions an employee might have, obtain a year-to-date gross pay for the employee, and so on.

Employee Earnings Summary

Click the **Reports** drop-down menu.

Select **Employees & Payroll**.

Select **Employee Earnings Summary** (see Figure 6-17).

	Manager		Bartender		Bartender OT		Kitchen Staff		Kitchen Staff OT		Reported Cash Tips		Federal Withh
Amy Jameson ▶	0.00 ◀		0.00		0.00		1,019.25		0.00		0.00		
Carlos Garcia	0.00		960.00		45.00		0.00		0.00		212.00		
Peter Petrov	1,875.00		0.00		0.00		0.00		0.00		0.00		
TOTAL	1,875.00		960.00		45.00		1,019.25		0.00		212.00		

Aroma Ristorante
Employee Earnings Summary
January 1 - 15, 2008

11:15 AM
04/06/08

Figure 6-17.

This report is similar to the Payroll Summary Report. The information is displayed in a different format. Each column includes a payroll item, and each row includes a different employee. This report could be used to determine earnings for a specific time period and/or job position.

Payroll Transactions by Payee

Click the **Reports** drop-down menu.

Select **Employees & Payroll**.

Select **Payroll Transactions by Payee** (see Figure 6-18).

11:17 AM
04/06/08

Aroma Ristorante
Payroll Transactions by Payee
January 1 - 15, 2008

Date	Name	Num	Type	Memo	Account	Amount
Amy Jameson						
01/15/2008	Amy Jameson		Paycheck		10000 · Checking Account	-825.18
Total Amy Jameson						-825.18
Carlos Garcia						
▶ 01/15/2008	Carlos Garcia		Paycheck		10000 · Checking Account	-779.70 ◀
Total Carlos Garcia						-779.70
Peter Petrov						
01/15/2008	Peter Petrov		Paycheck		10000 · Checking Account	-1,458.68
Total Peter Petrov						-1,458.68
TOTAL						-3,063.56

Figure 6-18.

This report contains a list of all the payments made to each employee and payroll-related payees. It is sorted by payee and can be used to acquire the detail of the individual amounts of each payment and the total number of payments made to a particular employee or other payroll payee.

Payroll Liability Balances

Click the **Reports** drop-down menu.

Select **Employees & Payroll**.

Select **Payroll Liability Balances** (see Figure 6-19).

	BALANCE
Payroll Liabilities	
Federal Withholding	288.00
Medicare Employee	59.62
Social Security Employee	254.89
Federal Unemployment	32.89
Medicare Company	59.62
Social Security Company	254.89
NY - Income Tax	157.18
NY - Unemployment	222.01
Extra Withholding	-20.00
Dental Insurance (taxable)	21.00
Health Insurance (taxable)	75.00
Dental Insurance (company paid)	75.00
Health Insurance (company paid)	225.00
Total Payroll Liabilities	**1,705.10**

Figure 6-19.

This report is a list of all the outstanding payroll-related liabilities, including Social Security and Medicare, federal and state withholdings, federal and state unemployment insurance, and any other payroll liabilities due for the period of time identified. Management's awareness of these liabilities helps to ensure that the appropriate funds are available when the liabilities are due. In most cases, a penalty may be incurred for late payment.

Summarize Payroll Data in Excel

QuickBooks has the capability to export payroll data into Excel Worksheets previously created by QuickBooks. Click the **Reports** drop-down menu, select **Employees & Payroll**, and select **Summarize Payroll Data in Excel**. Once a date range is specified, the payroll data will be exported from QuickBooks and will populate these worksheets (see Figure 6-20).

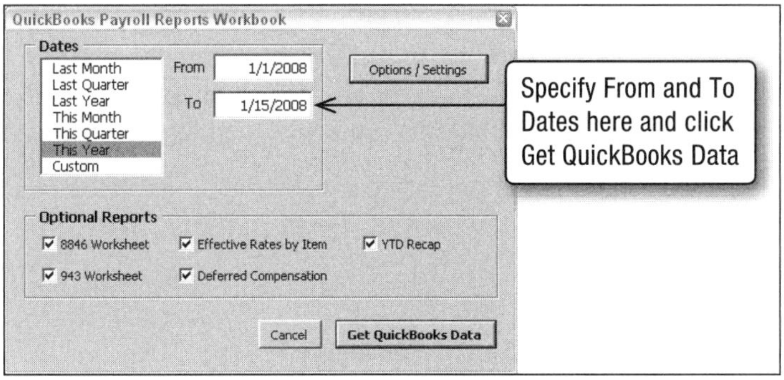

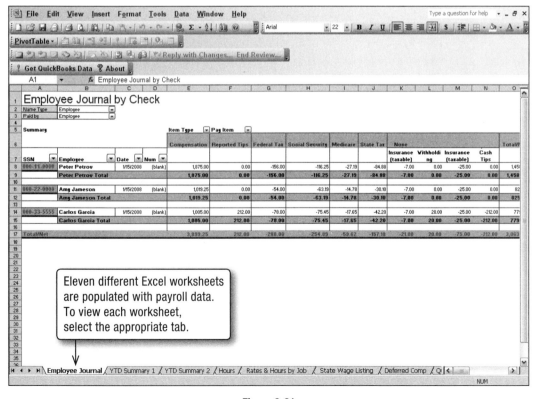

Figure 6-20.

The worksheets use pivot tables, which are interactive tables that summarize large amounts of data. Once a pivot table has been created, a user can click inside the pivot table to access the Pivot Table field list. A user can drag items from the field list into the pivot table to include an item or drag an item out of the pivot table into the field list to remove it. For details on how to use pivot tables, search "pivot tables" in Microsoft Excel Help (see Figure 6-21).

Figure 6-21.

Most of these worksheets contain summarized payroll data that a restaurant operator would find useful, such as Employee Journal by Check, YTD Summaries, and Rates & Hours by Job. These worksheets can be customized by the user to meet the needs of individual establishments.

Information on payroll-related year-end reports, including Forms 941, 940, W-2, W-3, and 1099-MISC, is included in Chapter 10.

Chapter Review Problems

1. Aroma Ristorante has hired the following employees as of January 1, 2008. Using the data in the tables that follows, create an employee file for each of the following new employees.

Personal Info. Tab: Personal

	First Name	Last Name	Social Security	Gender	DOB
1	George	Watson	000-44-5555	Male	3/26/1979
2	Bethany	Stewart	000-99-8000	Female	9/12/1984
3	Julia	Rodriquez	093-33-0003	Female	1/12/1985
4	Ji	Hiromi	094-44-0004	Female	2/20/1990
5	Jason	Robertson	000-11-3333	Male	7/28/1975

Personal Info. Tab: Address and Contact

First Name	Last Name	Street Address	City	State	Zip	Phone
George	Watson	6525 Riverside Drive #898	Capital City	NY	11112	555-444-3333
Bethany	Stewart	8787 North River Drive	Capital City	NY	11112	555-777-2000
Julia	Rodriquez	715 Park Place	Capital City	NY	11112	555-666-3000
Ji	Hiromi	229 North 8th St.	Capital City	NY	11112	555-333-9999
Jason	Robertson	1812 South LaSalle	Capital City	NY	11112	555-555-9966

Payroll and Conpensation Info. Tab: Payroll Info

	First Name	Last Name	Item Name	EARNINGS Hourly/ Annual Rate	Pay Period	Additional Deductions, Company Contributions Health/Dental Company Paid	Health/Dental Taxable
1	George	Watson	Dishwasher Dishwasher OT	$10.00 $15.00	Semimonthly	$75.00/$25.00	$25.00/$7.00
2	Bethany	Stewart	Service & Bus Staff	$8.00	Semimonthly		
3	Julia	Rodriquez	Expeditor	$11.00	Semimonthly		
4	Ji	Hiromi	Host Host OT	$12.00 $18.00	Semimonthly	$75.00/$25.00	$25.00/$7.00
5	Jason	Robertson	Chef	$42,000	Semimonthly	$75.00/$25.00	$25.00/$7.00

Taxes and Employment Info Tab

	First Name	Last Name	Fed/State Status	Fed/State Allowances	State	Hire Date
1	George	Watson	Single	1	NY	1/1/2008
2	Bethany	Stewart	Single	1	NY	1/1/2008
3	Julia	Rodriquez	Single	0	NY	1/15/2008
4	Ji	Hiromi	Single	0	NY	1/1/2008
5	Jason	Robertson	Married	3	NY	1/1/2008

2. Using the table that follows, create paychecks for each employee for the January 1, 2008 – January 15, 2008 payroll.

Payroll for January 1, 2008, to January 15, 2008

	George Watson	Bethany Stewart	Ji Hiromi	Jason Robertson
Earnings				
Regular Hours	80	18.25	77.5	80
Overtime Hours	5			
Other Payroll Items				
Dental Insurance (company paid)	$25		$25	$25
Health Insurance (company paid)	$75		$75	$75
Dental Insurance (taxable)	$7		$7	$7
Health Insurance (taxable)	$25		$25	$25
Reported Paycheck Tips		$86.25		
Extra Withholdings				
Company Summary				
Social Security	$54.25	$14.40	$57.66	$108.50
Medicare	$12.69	$3.37	$13.49	$25.38
Federal Unemployment	$7.00	$1.86	$7.44	$14.00
NY Unemployment	$47.25	$12.54	$50.22	$94.50
Employee Summary				
Federal Withholding	$77.00	$0	$107.00	$117.00
Social Security	$54.25	$14.40	$57.66	$108.50
Medicare	$12.69	$3.37	$13.49	$25.38
NY Income Tax	$23.10	$0	$29.10	$73.46

3. Using the table that follows, create paychecks for each employee for the January 16, 2008–January 31, 2008 payroll.

Payroll for January 16, 2008 to January 31, 2008

	Rosa Gomez	Benjamin Young	Mary Hoffman
Earnings			
Regular Hours	18.5	21.75	80
Overtime Hours			3.25
Other Payroll Items			
Dental Insurance (company paid)			$25
Health Insurance (company paid)			$75
Dental Insurance (taxable)			$7
Health Insurance (taxable)			$25
Reported Paycheck Tips	$138.75		$650
Extra Withholding			$15
Company Summary			
Social Security	$17.78	$18.20	$82.40
Medicare	$4.16	$4.26	$19.27
Federal Unemployment	$2.29	$2.35	$10.63
NY Unemployment	$15.48	$15.86	$71.77
Employee Summary			
Federal Withholding	$17.00	$4.00	$167.00
Social Security	$17.78	$18.20	$82.40
Medicare	$4.16	$4.26	$19.27
NY Income Tax	$0	$0	$54.70

4. Assume that on January 15, 2008 a duplicate paycheck was created for Peter Petrov. What are the necessary steps to correct the error?

5. Tips for Rosa Gomez were not recorded on her paycheck for the pay period of January 16–31, 2008. Her cash tips were $138.75. Make the necessary correction to her paycheck.

You can find additional Review Problems at *www.wiley.com/college/murphy*.

Adjusting Journal Entries

Access the Chapter 7 data file from the CD-ROM that accompanies this book or download the file from the web site.

Chapter Outline

Identifying the Steps of the Accounting Cycle

There are several steps involved in the preparation of financial statements. Initially, a restaurant creates a Chart of Accounts, which is a list of all the accounts that will be used in the business. Every business transaction has an impact on at least two accounts. When a transaction is recorded, the appropriate accounts are increased or decreased depending on the transaction. Transactions are recorded in QuickBooks by using such forms as Sales Receipts and Customer Invoices and by using QuickBooks functions, such as Write Checks or Recording Deposits. Business transactions are also recorded using journal entries. A journal entry is simply a way to record information. Once the transaction is entered, the amount is recorded in the

General Ledger, which is a file or a book that keeps tracks of all the increases and decreases in each account and provides an ending balance of the account at any given time. After all the transactions are entered and posted to the individual accounts in the General Ledger, the restaurant manager may generate a trial balance to review the account balances before proceeding to the next step. A *trial balance* is a list of all the ending balances of every account in the General Ledger and ensures that all accounts with ending balances on the debit side (balances on the left side of the account) are equal to the accounts with ending balances on the credit side (balances on the right side of an account).

After reviewing the trial balance, the next step is to record adjusting journal entries. (See the section on adjusting journal entries later in the chapter.) After the adjusting journal entries are recorded, another trial balance may be generated. This is usually referred to as an adjusted trial balance because it is prepared after the adjusting entries. The adjusted trial balance may also be reviewed by management. Once management is satisfied with the account balances, the final step is to generate financial statements. Not all restaurant operators will follow all the steps each time. Some managers may not prepare a trial balance and may generate financial statements after all the transactions are recorded. If there are any errors, corrections can still be made and new financial statements can be generated.

Preparing a Journal

The Journal is a list of transactions that were recorded for the accounting period. It displays the debit and credit entries for every transaction.

Click the **Reports** drop-down menu.

Select **Accountant & Taxes**.

Select **Journal**.

Select the appropriate date range in the Journal window (see Figure 7-1).

Click **Refresh**.

Use the Dates drop-down list to select predetermined report dates, such as Month-to-Date. Other report dates can be selected by entering a date or date range by clicking on the calendar. QuickBooks supports customized reports, exporting reports to other applications, and e-mailing reports from the report window.

| Modify Report... | Memorize... | Print... | E-mail ▾ | Export... | Hide Header | Refresh |

Dates Custom ⌄ From 01/01/2008 🔳 To 01/31/2008 🔳 Sort By Default ⌄

11:48 AM
04/06/08

Aroma Ristorante
Journal
January 2008

Trans #	Type	Date	Num	Name	Memo	Account	Debit	Credit
▶ 14	Paycheck	01/15/2008	1095	Ji Hiromi		10000 · Checking A...		690.75 ◀
				Ji Hiromi		66030 · Host	930.00	
				Ji Hiromi		66030 · Host	0.00	
				Ji Hiromi		24070 · Health and...		7.00
				Ji Hiromi		24070 · Health and...		25.00
				Ji Hiromi		66080 · Employee ...	25.00	
				Ji Hiromi		24070 · Health and...		25.00
				Ji Hiromi		66080 · Employee ...	75.00	
				Ji Hiromi		24070 · Health and...		75.00
				Ji Hiromi		24050 · Federal Inc...		107.00
				Ji Hiromi		66060 · Social Sec...	57.66	
				Ji Hiromi		24010 · Social Sec...		57.66
				Ji Hiromi		24010 · Social Sec...		57.66
				Ji Hiromi		66065 · Medicare	13.49	
				Ji Hiromi		24020 · Medicare		13.49
				Ji Hiromi		24020 · Medicare		13.49
				Ji Hiromi		66070 · Federal Un...	7.44	
				Ji Hiromi		24030 · Federal Un...		7.44
				Ji Hiromi		24060 · State Inco...		29.10
				Ji Hiromi		66075 · State Unem...	50.22	
				Ji Hiromi		24040 · State Unem...		50.22
							1,158.81	1,158.81
16	Paycheck	01/15/2008	1097	Peter Petrov		10000 · Checking A...		1,458.68
				Peter Petrov		66005 · Manager	1,875.00	
				Peter Petrov		24070 · Health and...		7.00
				Peter Petrov		24070 · Health and...		25.00
				Peter Petrov		66080 · Employee ...	25.00	
				Peter Petrov		24070 · Health and...		25.00
				Peter Petrov		66080 · Employee ...	75.00	
				Peter Petrov		24070 · Health and...		75.00

Figure 7-1.

QUICKBOOKS TIP

QuickBooks can be customized to automatically refresh reports. Click the **Edit** drop-down menu, select **Preferences** from the menu, select the **Reports & Graphs** icon and choose the **My Preferences** tab, select **Refresh Automatically**, and click **OK**.

Preparing a General Ledger

This report shows all the activities that occurred during a specified period of time and provides an account balance for each account listed in the restaurant's Chart of Accounts.

Click the **Reports** drop-down menu.

Select **Accountant & Taxes**.

Select **General Ledger**.

Select the appropriate date range in the General Ledger window (see Figure 7-2).

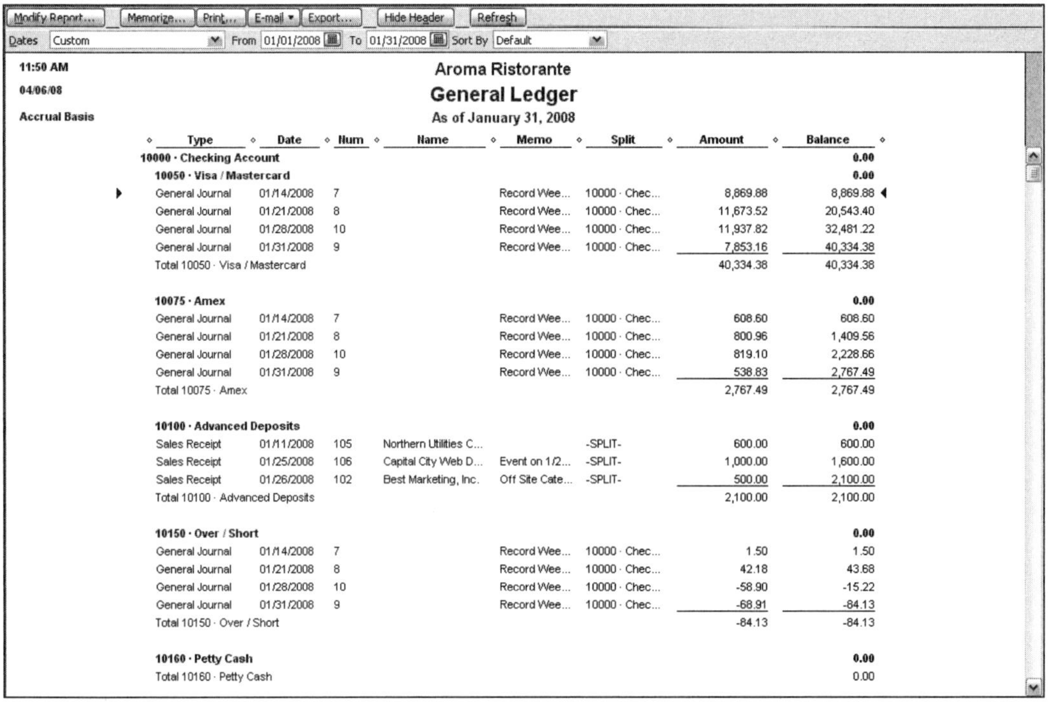

Type	Date	Num	Name	Memo	Split	Amount	Balance
10000 · Checking Account							**0.00**
10050 · Visa / Mastercard							**0.00**
General Journal	01/14/2008	7		Record Wee...	10000 · Chec...	8,869.88	8,869.88
General Journal	01/21/2008	8		Record Wee...	10000 · Chec...	11,673.52	20,543.40
General Journal	01/28/2008	10		Record Wee...	10000 · Chec...	11,937.82	32,481.22
General Journal	01/31/2008	9		Record Wee...	10000 · Chec...	7,853.16	40,334.38
Total 10050 · Visa / Mastercard						40,334.38	40,334.38
10075 · Amex							**0.00**
General Journal	01/14/2008	7		Record Wee...	10000 · Chec...	608.60	608.60
General Journal	01/21/2008	8		Record Wee...	10000 · Chec...	800.96	1,409.56
General Journal	01/28/2008	10		Record Wee...	10000 · Chec...	819.10	2,228.66
General Journal	01/31/2008	9		Record Wee...	10000 · Chec...	538.83	2,767.49
Total 10075 · Amex						2,767.49	2,767.49
10100 · Advanced Deposits							**0.00**
Sales Receipt	01/11/2008	105	Northern Utilities C...		-SPLIT-	600.00	600.00
Sales Receipt	01/25/2008	106	Capital City Web D...	Event on 1/2...	-SPLIT-	1,000.00	1,600.00
Sales Receipt	01/26/2008	102	Best Marketing, Inc.	Off Site Cate...	-SPLIT-	500.00	2,100.00
Total 10100 · Advanced Deposits						2,100.00	2,100.00
10150 · Over / Short							**0.00**
General Journal	01/14/2008	7		Record Wee...	10000 · Chec...	1.50	1.50
General Journal	01/21/2008	8		Record Wee...	10000 · Chec...	42.18	43.68
General Journal	01/28/2008	10		Record Wee...	10000 · Chec...	-58.90	-15.22
General Journal	01/31/2008	9		Record Wee...	10000 · Chec...	-68.91	-84.13
Total 10150 · Over / Short						-84.13	-84.13
10160 · Petty Cash							**0.00**
Total 10160 · Petty Cash							0.00

Figure 7-2.

Click **Refresh**.

Preparing a Trial Balance

A trial balance is prepared prior to recording adjusting journal entries. (See the section on adjusting journal entries later in this chapter.) Another additional trial balance is prepared after the adjusting journal entries have been recorded and prior to the generation of financial statements. The trial balance provides verification of the equality of debits and credits and should be reviewed by management for any blatant abnormalities in the accounts.

Select **Reports** drop-down menu.

Select **Accountant & Taxes**.

Select **Trial Balance**.

Select the appropriate date range in the Trial Balance window (see Figure 7-3).

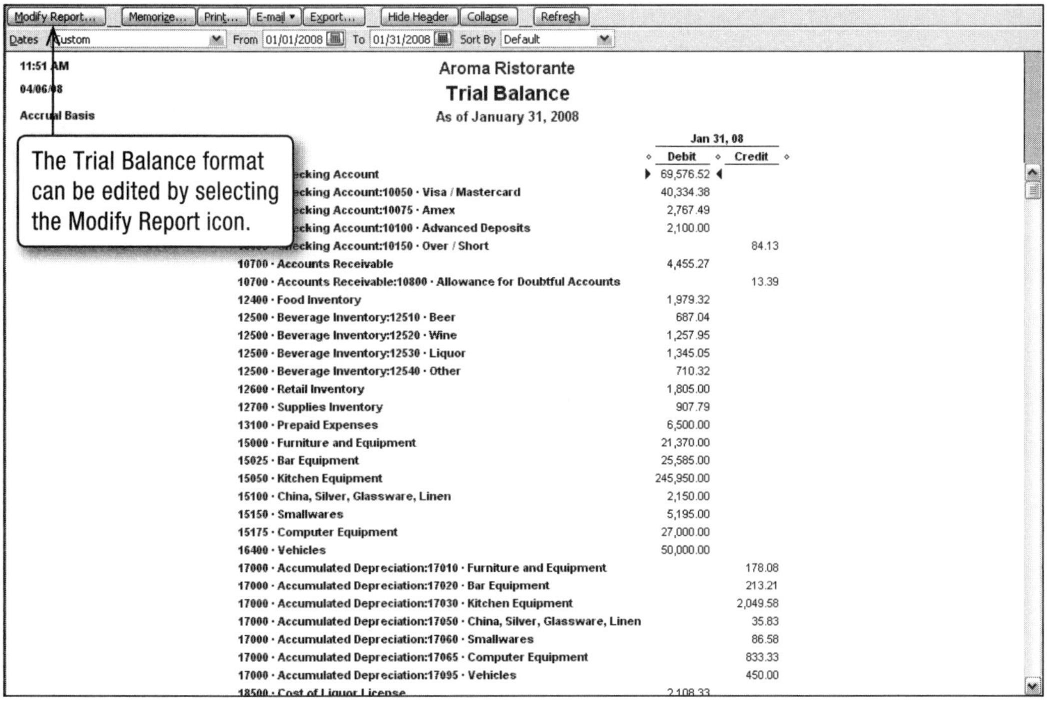

Aroma Ristorante
Trial Balance
As of January 31, 2008

	Jan 31, 08	
	Debit	Credit
ecking Account	69,576.52	
ecking Account:10050 · Visa / Mastercard	40,334.38	
ecking Account:10075 · Amex	2,767.49	
ecking Account:10100 · Advanced Deposits	2,100.00	
ecking Account:10150 · Over / Short		84.13
10700 · Accounts Receivable	4,455.27	
10700 · Accounts Receivable:10800 · Allowance for Doubtful Accounts		13.39
12400 · Food Inventory	1,979.32	
12500 · Beverage Inventory:12510 · Beer	687.04	
12500 · Beverage Inventory:12520 · Wine	1,257.95	
12500 · Beverage Inventory:12530 · Liquor	1,345.05	
12500 · Beverage Inventory:12540 · Other	710.32	
12600 · Retail Inventory	1,805.00	
12700 · Supplies Inventory	907.79	
13100 · Prepaid Expenses	6,500.00	
15000 · Furniture and Equipment	21,370.00	
15025 · Bar Equipment	25,585.00	
15050 · Kitchen Equipment	245,950.00	
15100 · China, Silver, Glassware, Linen	2,150.00	
15150 · Smallwares	5,195.00	
15175 · Computer Equipment	27,000.00	
16400 · Vehicles	50,000.00	
17000 · Accumulated Depreciation:17010 · Furniture and Equipment		178.08
17000 · Accumulated Depreciation:17020 · Bar Equipment		213.21
17000 · Accumulated Depreciation:17030 · Kitchen Equipment		2,049.58
17000 · Accumulated Depreciation:17050 · China, Silver, Glassware, Linen		35.83
17000 · Accumulated Depreciation:17060 · Smallwares		86.58
17000 · Accumulated Depreciation:17065 · Computer Equipment		833.33
17000 · Accumulated Depreciation:17095 · Vehicles		450.00
18500 · Cost of Liquor License	2,108.33	

Figure 7-3.

Click **Refresh**.

Transaction details for a specific account can be displayed by double-clicking on the account in the trial balance.

Recording Adjusting Journal Entries

Using cash basis accounting, business transactions are recorded when cash is received or when cash is disbursed. Accrual basis accounting requires that transactions be recorded in the period of time when the actual revenue (sales) is earned and the expense has been incurred regardless of when the actual cash changes hands. With cash basis accounting, it is possible to manipulate financial data by simply altering the timing of cash receipts and disbursements. Accrual basis accounting may provide a more accurate reporting of business transactions by recording the transaction in the accounting period in which the transaction has actually occurred and is less susceptible to manipulation. Accrual accounting requires the use of adjusting journal entries to ensure that the revenues and expenses are recorded in the correct period of time. Adjusting entries are recorded at the end of the accounting period prior to the preparation of financial statements. An accounting period can be a week, month, quarter, year, or any other time period designated by management. Most often, financial statements are prepared monthly. There are various types of adjusting entries that a restaurant may be required to record. Certain transactions can be recorded only after the passage of time, such as the cost of goods sold, depreciation of long-term assets (fixed assets), rent expense, or insurance expense. Other transactions may not have been recorded at all, such as interest on a bank account that was earned in one accounting period but actually received in another.

Adjusting Journal Entry—Prepaid Expenses

A *prepaid expense* is a good or service that has been paid for in advance before the goods were used or the service was performed. On January 1, 2008, Aroma Ristorante paid $4,500 for six months of insurance premiums. The payment covers the period of January 1 through June 30. When the payment was made, the transaction resulted in an increase in Prepaid Expenses and a decrease in Cash. (DEBIT: Prepaid Expenses, CREDIT: Cash.) Because Aroma Ristorante prepares monthly financial statements, accrual accounting requires that insurance expenses be recorded for each month.

Using the following data, enter the information in the appropriate fields.

DATA: Record the Monthly Adjusting Journal Entry for Prepaid Expenses.

At the beginning of the year, Aroma Ristorante paid $4,500 for its semi-annual insurance premium.

DATE:	1/31/2008
ENTRY NO.:	50
DEBIT ACCOUNT:	63310 Insurance Expense: General Liability Insurance
CREDIT ACCOUNT:	13100 Prepaid Expenses
AMOUNT:	$750
MEMO:	Record monthly insurance expense

Click the **Company** drop-down menu.

Select **Make General Journal Entries**.

Select **Date – Jan 31, 2008**

Select the **Account** drop-down list.

Select **Insurance Expense**.

Tab to the Debit column.

Enter **$750**.

Tab to the Memo column.

Enter **Record monthly insurance expense**.

Use the down-arrow key to access the next line of the Journal. QuickBooks will automatically drop the balance to the Credit column.

Select **Prepaid Expenses** from the Account drop-down list.

Tab to the Memo column.

Enter **Record Monthly Insurance Expense** (see Figure 7-4).

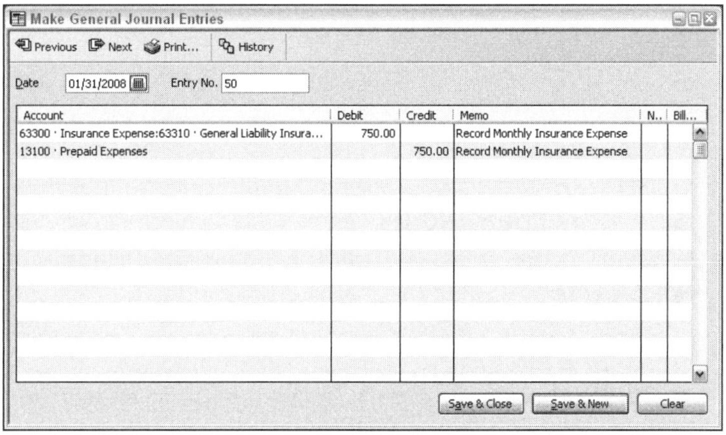

Figure 7-4.

Click **Save & Close**.

QUICKBOOKS TIP

It is good practice to enter a memo on each line of a journal entry. If the memo will be duplicated, use Copy and Paste to reduce data entry.

QUICKBOOKS TIP

Use the QuickBooks calculator to calculate monthly insurance premiums. Press the equal sign (=) in the Debit column, delete 0.00, and enter **$4,500.** Press the slash (/) for division, enter **6,** and press Enter. QuickBooks calculates and enters the amount automatically in the Debit column.

Adjusting Journal Entry—Depreciation Expense

A depreciation expense is recorded for tangible, long-term fixed assets, including buildings, furniture, and equipment, to reflect the normal wear and tear and routine replacement of these assets. Land is never depreciated because it has a continuous useful life. Depreciation expenses can be computed using different methods, such as the straight line method, production method, and double declining balance method—just to name a few. The straight line method calculates depreciation based on the passage of time, and it is the easiest to compute. Using this method, the same amount of depreciation is recorded for every year of the asset's useful life. Aroma Ristorante uses the straight line method to calculate depreciation. Depreciation can be recorded with an adjusting journal entry or by entering the amount in the appropriate account register.

ACCOUNTING TIP

The following is the formula used to calculate depreciation using the straight line method:

Original Cost of the Asset less Salvage Value divided by Life of the Asset.
The salvage value, also referred to as "scrap value" or "residual value," is an estimated value of an asset as of the anticipated date of disposal.

ACCOUNTING TIP

The production method calculates depreciation based on the usage of the asset. The double declining balance method is an accelerated method of depreciation. Large amounts of depreciation are recorded at the beginning of the asset's life and smaller amounts are recorded at the end of the asset's life.

Recording Depreciation Expense Using a Journal Entry

Using the following data, enter the information in the appropriate fields.

DATA: Record the Monthly Adjusting Journal Entry for Depreciation.

Aroma Ristorante must record a $178.08 depreciation expense for Furniture and Equipment and $833.33 for Vehicles for January 2008.

DATE:	1/31/2008
ENTRY NO.:	55
DEBIT ACCOUNT:	62410 Depreciation Expense: Furniture and Equipment
	62495 Depreciation Expense: Vehicle
CREDIT ACCOUNT:	17010 Accumulated Depreciation: Furniture and Equipment
	17095 Accumulated Depreciation: Vehicles
AMOUNT:	$178.08
	$833.33
MEMO:	Record monthly depreciation expense

Recording Depreciation Expense Using the Account Register

Using the following data, enter the information in the appropriate fields.

DATA: Record the Monthly Adjusting Journal Entry for Depreciation.

Using the Account Register, record a $35.83 monthly depreciation expense for China, Silver, Glassware, Linen for January 2008.

DATE:	1/31/2008
REF:	4
ACCOUNT:	62450 Depreciation Expense: China, Silver, Glassware, Linen
MEMO:	Record monthly Depreciation Expense
DECREASE:	$35.83

Click the **Lists** drop-down menu.

Select **Chart of Accounts**.

Double-click on **17050 Accumulated Depreciation: China, Silver, Glassware, Linen**.

Enter the data in the appropriate fields (see Figure 7-5).

⬍ Go to...	🖨 Print...	📝 Edit Transaction	📋 QuickReport						
Date	Ref		Payee			Decrease	✓	Increase	Balance
	Type	Account		Memo					
01/31/2008	39					35.83			-35.83
	GENJRNL	62400 · Depreciation Expense:62450 · China, Silver, Glassware Funds Transfer							
	📖 Ref	Payee			✔	Decrease		Increase	
		Account	✔	Memo					

Figure 7-5.

Click **Record**.

Memorizing Adjusting Journal Entries

Because adjusting entries are recorded frequently, it is advantageous to set them up as memorized transactions. Recording a straight line depreciation expense is an example of a transaction that can be memorized and automatically recorded by QuickBooks. For details on memorized options, see page 80.

After the journal entry has been created and is displayed on the desktop, click the **Edit** drop-down menu.

Select **Memorize General Journal** (see Figure 7-6).

Figure: Memorize Transaction dialog

Name: Depreciation Expense

- ⦿ Remind Me
- ○ Don't Remind Me
- ○ Automatically Enter
- ○ With Transactions in Group

How Often: Never
Next Date: 02/29/2008
Number Remaining:
Days In Advance To Enter: 0
Group Name: <None>

OK   Cancel

> A reminder can be set to prompt a QuickBooks user to generate a memorized transaction.

Figure 7-6.

Enter a name for the Memorized Transaction.

Click **OK**

ACCOUNTING TIP

Different methods of depreciation can be used to prepare financial statements and the tax return. Because depreciation expense directly affects taxable income, we recommend that you consult an accountant or tax specialist to help determine which method of depreciation is appropriate. Once a method is chosen, it should be consistently used over the entire life of the asset.

QUICKBOOKS TIP

QuickBooks has a fixed asset tracking system. The fixed asset list includes the asset's name and number, cost, purchase date, vendor, location, description, serial number, and warranty expiration date. Fixed assets can also be managed using another software application. The detail is maintained in this fixed asset software and only the balances are entered into QuickBooks via a journal entry.

Adjusting Journal Entry—Unearned Revenue

When the restaurant records a refundable deposit received for a service to be performed in the future, this results in an increase in Cash and Unearned Revenue (Sales) (DEBIT: Cash; CREDIT: Unearned Revenue). When the service is performed, the Unearned Revenue and Revenue (Sales) accounts must be adjusted to record the revenue in the correct accounting period. This entry would result in an increase in Revenue/Sales and a decrease in Unearned Revenue accounts (DEBIT: Unearned Revenue; CREDIT: Revenue /Sales). An Advance Deposit–Refundable item was created in the item list and was used to record deposits received prior to the service. This eliminates the need to record a manual adjusting journal entry for unearned revenue (see Chapter 5, page 126).

Adjusting Journal Entry—Salary and Wage Accrual

An entry is required to record the accrual for salary and wages earned during the accounting period but not yet paid as of the end of the accounting period. Because Aroma Ristorante's pay periods are the 15th and the last day of each month, this adjusting journal entry is not required.

Adjusting Journal Entry—Cost of Goods Sold

An entry is not required to adjust the Inventory account and record the related Cost of Goods Sold when using the QuickBooks Inventory feature. This adjustment is made on completion of the physical inventory account by entering the new quantity in the Adjust Quantity/Value on Hand sheet (see Chapter 4). When using another inventory system, an adjusting journal entry must be manually entered into QuickBooks.

Other adjusting entries may include accrued interest on a bank account or investment account, accrued interest on a loan, bad debt expense, and supplies expense.

Chapter Review Problems

Note that some of these problems assume you have completed or at least read previous chapters.

1. After completion of the physical inventory count for supplies, the ending balance of supplies on hand at the end of January 2008 is $907.79.

   a. Generate a trial balance at January 30, 2008, to determine the current balance in the supplies account.

   b. Record the adjusting journal entry for supplies using the appropriate accounts.

2. As of the end of the month, Aroma Ristorante has earned, but has not yet received, $30.00 of interest income on the savings account. Record the necessary adjusting journal entry using the appropriate accounts.

3. Aroma Ristorante borrowed $50,000 from a local bank. The accrued interest for the month is $312.50. Record the necessary journal entry using the appropriate accounts.

4. Use the following information to calculate depreciation for January 2008 using the straight line method. Record the necessary adjusting journal entry.

Asset Name:	Bar Equipment
Original Cost:	$25,585
Salvage Value:	$0
Estimated Life:	10 Years

Asset Name:	Kitchen Equipment
Original Cost:	$245,950
Salvage Value:	$0
Estimated Life:	10 Years

Asset Name:	Smallwares
Original Cost:	$5,195
Salvage Value:	$0
Estimated Life:	5 Years

Asset Name:	Computer Equipment
Original Cost:	$27,000
Salvage Value:	$0
Estimated Life:	5 Years

5. Generate the current A/R Aging Summary Report for January 2008. The estimated percentage uncollectible for each age group is as follows:

0–30 days: 1%

31–60 days: 2%

61–90 days: 5%

Use the report to calculate the amount of bad debt expense for the period, and record the adjusting journal entry using the appropriate accounts.

You can find additional Review Problems at *www.wiley.com/college/murphy.*

Financial Reporting and Analysis

Access the Chapter 8 data file from the CD-ROM that accompanies this book or download the file from the web site.

Chapter Outline

Financial Statements

Preparing the Profit & Loss Statement

Preparing the Balance Sheet

Preparing the Statement of Cash Flows

Preparing the Cash Flow Forecast

Chapter Review Problems

Financial Statements

After all transactions have been entered, financial statements are prepared for the accounting period. There are four basic financial statements: Profit & Loss Statement (also referred to as an Income Statement), Balance Sheet, Statement of Shareholders' Equity, and Statement of Cash Flows. In QuickBooks, the equity section of the Balance Sheet includes the information that is typically found in the Statement of Shareholders' Equity. These statements contain useful and pertinent financial information to assist managers, creditors, investors, auditors, and others, in making informed business decisions.

Managers can use the four financial statements along with other reports to make such various operational decisions as:

Should the business rent or buy equipment?

Should the business borrow additional funds?

How many days a week should the business be open?

Should the business prepare a business plan to reduce expenses and/or increase sales?

External auditors need a complete set of financial statements to prepare the annual audit report. Tax accountants use the information to calculate taxable income, prepare tax returns, and develop a tax plan to minimize the restaurant's tax liability. Creditors use the information for a variety of decisions, including the determination of the extension of credit and the amount of credit and assessment of the restaurant's liquidity.

Preparing the Profit & Loss Statement

A Profit & Loss Statement, also referred to as an Income Statement, is a report that displays sales, expenses, and profit or loss for the accounting period. The statement measures the profitability of the restaurant for a specified time period. It is essential for the restaurant to maintain its profitability in order to continue its existence as a viable business entity. Profits are reinvested in the restaurant and provide the owners with a return on their investment. Profitability is necessary for growth and expansion, and to maintain existing investors while attracting new ones.

Given the small profit margin for restaurants, it is essential for management to track and analyze sales and control expenses. Analysis of the Profit & Loss Statement provides management with information such as the percentage of increase or decrease in sales and expenses from one period to another, the labor cost ratio and the cost of sales ratio, and other important information.

Industry Fact:

In the 2006/2007 Edition of the Restaurant Industry Operations Report, the National Restaurant Association reported a 4 percent profit margin for full service restaurants in the United States.

Prepare the Profit & Loss Statement

Click the **Reports** drop-down menu.

This report can also be accessed through the Report Center.

Select **Company & Financial**.

Select **Profit & Loss Standard**.

Select the appropriate date range (see Figure 8-1).

Modify Report...	Memorize...	Print...	E-mail ▾	Export...	Hide Header	Collapse	Refresh

Dates | Custom ▾ | From 01/01/2008 📅 To 01/31/2008 📅 Columns | Total only ▾ | Sort By Default ▾

10:21 PM		Aroma Ristorante	
04/06/08		**Profit & Loss**	
Accrual Basis		January 2008	

	◦ Jan 08 ◦
Ordinary Income/Expense	
Income	
41400 · Beverage Sales	
41410 · Beer	▶ 2,044 ◀
41420 · Wine	9,367
41430 · Liquor	4,598
41440 · Other	1,022
Total 41400 · Beverage Sales	17,031
42100 · Catering Sales	
42110 · Food	7,389
42120 · Beverage	750
Total 42100 · Catering Sales	8,139
43800 · Food Sales	39,738
43900 · Sales Comps, Discounts & Promo	-1,928
Total Income	62,980
Cost of Goods Sold	
50900 · Food Purchases	14,878
51000 · Beverage Purchases	
51010 · Beer	1,587
51020 · Wine	1,842
51030 · Liquor	2,214
51040 · Other	866
Total 51000 · Beverage Purchases	6,509
51800 · Merchant Account Fees	894
Total COGS	22,281
Gross Profit	40,699

Figure 8-1.

Click **Refresh**.

QUICKBOOKS TIP

QuickBooks can be customized to automatically refresh reports. Click the **Edit** drop-down menu, select **Preferences from the menu,** click the **Reports & Graphs** icon and choose the **My Preferences** tab, select **Refresh Automatically,** and click **OK.**

QUICKBOOKS TIP

Reports can be e-mailed as an Excel document or PDF file. Reports can also be exported from QuickBooks to Microsoft Excel.

For a more detailed version of the Profit & Loss Statement, select **Profit & Loss Detail Report.** This report displays all of the transactions that comprise the individual balance of an account. Details of individual account transactions can also be viewed by double-clicking on a specific account in the Profit & Loss Standard Report.

Photo courtesy
Christine DeWeese

Mike DeWeese

Mike DeWeese, owner/operator of a full-service ale house and grill with over 12 years of food and beverage experience. Former director of franchise operations, former owner of six restaurants, and noted beer expert.

"QuickBooks Online is essential to running a restaurant in a fast paced environment. Real-time data allows us to address issues and problems in an immediate fashion. Food cost can be analyzed daily if necessary, and quarterly reports do not have to be sent to shareholders; they can access the financial data online. QuickBooks Online should be considered as an option for restaurant operators."

Customize the Profit & Loss Statement

Reports can be customized to meet the needs of the individual user. A customized report can be memorized so that you don't have to change the report each time it is generated.

Customizing the Title

Click the **Modify Report** button.

Click the **Header/Footer** tab.

Select **Report Title** and change the title to **Income Statement**.

Click **OK**.

Customizing Fonts and Numbers

Click the **Modify Report** button.

Select the **Fonts & Numbers** tab.

Select the category of what should be changed in the Change Font For window. Click the **Change Font** button and select the appropriate font, font style, and size.

Click **OK**.

Customizing to Display No Cents

Click the **Modify Report** button.

Click the **Fonts & Numbers** tab.

Place a checkmark next to **Without Cents** under Show All Numbers.

Click **OK**.

Customizing a Report to Print in Portrait Orientation and on One Page

Click the **Print** button in the Report window.

Select **Portrait** orientation.

Place a checkmark next to **Fit report to 1 page(s) wide** (see Figure 8-2).

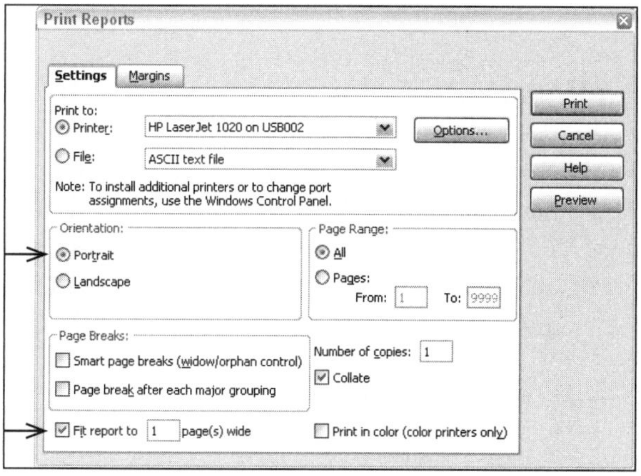

Figure 8-2.

ACCOUNTING TIP

The accepted practice in financial report preparation is to round to the nearest dollar and print the statement in portrait orientation.

Memorize Profit & Loss Statement

When a report has been modified, including changing the date range, QuickBooks prompts the user to memorize the report. If the report has been customized and will be used again, it should be memorized (see Figure 8-3).

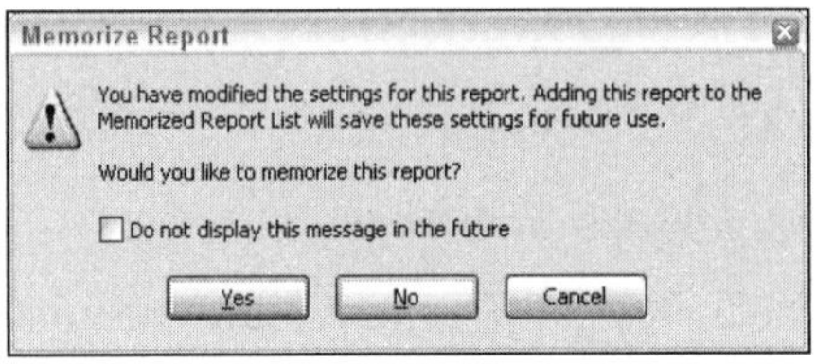

Figure 8-3.

QuickBooks automatically places the name of the report in the name box. The name can be changed.

To retrieve the memorized report, click the **Reports** drop-down menu and select **Memorized Reports** to display all reports in the list.

Exporting Reports to Excel

QuickBooks reports can be exported into an Excel spreadsheet. This feature allows management to take advantage of the various Excel functions and features. This significantly enhances management's ability to manipulate, reorganize, and analyze the information in a manner that best serves the specific and unique needs of the individual restaurant.

Generate the report to be exported.

Click the **Export** button.

In the Export Report window, select a **New Excel workbook**.

Click the **Export** button.

The Profit & Loss YTD Comparison Report

This report displays the comparison of the Profit & Loss Statement for a specified period of time. It can be modified to add additional columns to display changes in dollar amounts and percentages. This report is generated by clicking the **Reports** drop-down menu, selecting **Company & Financial,** and selecting **Profit & Loss YTD Comparison**.

QUICKBOOKS TIP

To modify this report to include changes in dollar amounts and percentages, follow these steps:

Click the **Modify Report** button.

Click the **Display** tab.

Select either **Previous Period** or **Previous Year.**

At Add subcolumns for, place a checkmark next to **$ Change** and **% Change.**

Photo courtesy of the Culinary Institute of America.

Susan Wysocki

Susan Wysocki is Chef Proprietor of a bakery and café with over 20 years food and beverage experience.

"QuickBooks allows me to track catering invoices, receive payments, process payroll, and generate financial reports and graphs and year-end forms, including W-2s and 941 and state tax forms. The software is easy to use and allows me to perform these tasks on my own, which decreases my accounting expenses. Using QuickBooks allows me to account for all disbursements; immediately recognize when expenses are out of line; and use reports to analyze labor costs, cost of sales, and profitability."

Profit & Loss Prev Year Comparison Report

The Profit & Loss Prev Year Comparison report is useful for further analysis of the restaurant's profitability. This report shows the changes in dollar amounts and percentages from one period to another. The report is generated by clicking the **Reports** drop-down menu, selecting **Company & Financial,** and selecting **Profit & Loss Prev Year Comparison**.

Exporting reports to Excel can facilitate the use of various analytical tools, such as horizontal and vertical analysis (also known as common-size statements) and ratio analysis. *Horizontal analysis* of a financial statement shows the changes in dollar amount and percentages from one period to another. A *common-size statement* shows each section of the financial statement expressed as a percentage of a total amount in the statement. *Ratio analysis* is a tool used to access a company's financial performance by evaluating relationships between components of the financial statements.

Preparing the Balance Sheet

A Balance Sheet is a report that displays the assets, liabilities, and equity of a business as of a specific date. It informs management and others of such information as the balance of the Cash account, the total amount of debt owed by the restaurant, the net value of the restaurant's fixed assets, the amount of allowances for receivables, and the amount of equity the stockholders have in the restaurant. The Balance Sheet shows the financial position of the restaurant at a specified point in time. It can be used to determine the liquidity of the restaurant by calculating *working capital* (current assets minus current liabilities) and the *current ratio* (current assets divided by current liabilities).

The Balance Sheet Summary is a general overview of the Balance Sheet. It displays only the account balance for each account type, whereas the Balance Sheet Standard provides more detail by displaying the balance of all of the individual accounts that make up each account type. A Balance Sheet Prev Year Comparison report is also available. This provides a horizontal analysis of the Balance Sheet from one period to another. This allows management to see the change in the financial position of the restaurant from one period to the next. It indicates whether the restaurant's assets and liabilities increased or decreased and in which specific area these changes occurred. Management should determine the underlying causes for these changes. A change may have occurred simply because of a recording error, or it may be indicative of some other problem that requires management's attention. The Net Worth Graph provides a visual display of the change in the restaurant's net worth for the specified period of time.

Prepare the Balance Sheet

Click the **Reports** drop-down menu.

🗒️
Report Center

This report can also be accessed through the Report Center.

Select **Company & Financial.**

Select **Balance Sheet Standard.**

Select the appropriate date (see Figure 8-4).

Aroma Ristorante
Balance Sheet
As of January 31, 2008

	◦ Jan 31, 08 ◦
ASSETS	
Current Assets	
Checking/Savings	
10000 · Checking Account	
10050 · Visa / Mastercard	▶ 40,334 ◀
10075 · Amex	2,767
10100 · Advanced Deposits	2,100
10150 · Over / Short	-84
10000 · Checking Account - Other	68,577
Total 10000 · Checking Account	113,694
10500 · Savings Account	1,000
Total Checking/Savings	114,694
Accounts Receivable	
10700 · Accounts Receivable	
10800 · Allowance for Doubtful Accounts	-13
10700 · Accounts Receivable - Other	4,455
Total 10700 · Accounts Receivable	4,442
Total Accounts Receivable	4,442
Other Current Assets	
12050 · Interest Receivable	30
12400 · Food Inventory	1,979
12500 · Beverage Inventory	
12510 · Beer	687
12520 · Wine	1,258
12530 · Liquor	1,345
12540 · Other	710
Total 12500 · Beverage Inventory	4,000

Figure 8-4.

Click **Refresh.**

Preparing the Statement of Cash Flows

The Profit & Loss Statement measures a restaurant's profitability but does not provide information about the flow of cash. Under accrual basis accounting, transactions are recorded when revenue is earned and when expenses are incurred, not when cash is received or disbursed. The Balance Sheet shows only the cash on hand at a specified point in time. Neither statement provides information about where the restaurant's cash comes from and what the cash is being used for. This information is obtained from the Statement of Cash Flows.

The Statement of Cash Flows is a report that shows the net cash receipts and net cash disbursements during the accounting period. The report categorizes cash inflows and outflows into one of three activities: operating, investing, and financing. *Operating* activities include the daily activities required to run the business, such as paying bills, selling goods or rendering services, and paying employees. *Investing* activities include the purchase of and payments for business assets, such as land, building, and equipment. *Financing* activities include cash received from investors and loans and cash used to pay off debt.

From this report, management and external users can obtain the following information:

- Has the restaurant purchased any additional fixed assets?
- What is the total amount of cash disbursed for these assets?
- Is the restaurant generating cash from operations or is it obtaining cash from borrowings?
- How much cash was paid to investors?
- How much cash was used to repay existing loans?

When preparing the Statement of Cash Flows, QuickBooks allows the user to alter the operating, investing, and financing activity classification of accounts. Balance Sheet accounts can be classified but cannot be removed from the statement. Income and expense accounts that track non-cash transactions may be added or removed from the report. To use this feature, click the **Report Center** icon, click **Preferences**, select **Reports & Graphs,** click **Company Preferences** tab, and click the **Classify Cash** button.

Prepare the Statement of Cash Flows

Click the **Reports** drop-down menu.

Report Center

This report can also be accessed through the Report Center.

Select **Company & Financial**.

Select **Statement of Cash Flows**.

Select the appropriate date (see Figure 8-5).

Aroma Ristorante

Statement of Cash Flows

January 2008

	Jan 08
OPERATING ACTIVITIES	
Net Income	-12,683
Adjustments to reconcile Net Income	
to net cash provided by operations:	
10700 · Accounts Receivable	-4,455
10700 · Accounts Receivable:10800 · Allowance for Doubtful Accounts	13
12050 · Interest Receivable	-30
12400 · Food Inventory	-1,979
12500 · Beverage Inventory:12510 · Beer	-687
12500 · Beverage Inventory:12520 · Wine	-1,258
12500 · Beverage Inventory:12530 · Liquor	-1,345
12500 · Beverage Inventory:12540 · Other	-710
12600 · Retail Inventory	-1,805
12700 · Supplies Inventory	-908
13100 · Prepaid Expenses	-6,500
20000 · Accounts Payable	6,634
21000 · Interest Payable	313
24000 · Payroll Liabilities:24010 · Social Security	2,712
24000 · Payroll Liabilities:24020 · Medicare	634
24000 · Payroll Liabilities:24030 · Federal Unemployment	175
24000 · Payroll Liabilities:24040 · State Unemployment	1,181
24000 · Payroll Liabilities:24050 · Federal Income Tax	1,813
24000 · Payroll Liabilities:24060 · State Income Tax	726
24000 · Payroll Liabilities:24070 · Health and Dental	1,980
25200 · Gift Certificates Outstanding	700
25300 · Gift Certificates Redeemed	-100
25500 · Sales Tax Payable	5,286
27000 · Unearned Revenue	500
Net cash provided by Operating Activities	-9,794
INVESTING ACTIVITIES	

Figure 8-5.

Click **Refresh**.

Preparing the Cash Flow Forecast

Cash includes all currency and coins on hand, including petty cash, cash in the bank, and cash equivalents. Cash equivalents are short-term investments, such as Certificate of Deposits, that can easily be converted into cash normally within a three month period.

Whereas the Statement of Cash Flows provides information about the restaurant's past performance, this report provides information concerning the restaurant's future. Management should be concerned with the current and future cash position of the restaurant. It is vital information that is useful for effective planning and growth of the restaurant. With this information, management can identify periods when, after meeting all current obligations, excess cash is available to purchase additional investments and other assets. Management can also determine when the restaurant needs to borrow additional funds in order to meet it obligations.

The Cash Flow Forecast report shows the restaurant's cash inflows, outflows, and current cash position for a specified time period. This report uses existing information recorded in the restaurant's Cash, Accounts Receivable, and Accounts Payable accounts. In order to use this report effectively, all cash accounts must be classified as a "Bank" account type in the chart of accounts (see Chapter 3). The report assumes that customer receivables are received when due. If this is not the case, the due dates can be altered by entering the number of days past due in the report's Delay Receipts field.

Prepare the Cash Flow Forecast

Click the **Reports** drop-down menu.

Select **Company & Financial**.

Select **Cash Flow Forecast**.

Select the appropriate date (see Figure 8-6).

Aroma Ristorante
Cash Flow Forecast
January 2008

	Accnts Receivable	Accnts Payable	Bank Accnts	Net Inflows	Proj Balance
Beginning Balance	0	0	0		0
Jan 1 - 5, 08	0	0	416,953	416,953	416,953
Week of Jan 6, 08	0	0	-16,228	-16,228	400,725
Week of Jan 13, 08	0	0	-2,084	-2,084	398,641
Week of Jan 20, 08	1,517	0	10,268	11,785	410,426
Jan 27 - 31, 08	2,368	0	-294,215	-291,848	118,579
Jan 08	3,884	0	114,694	118,579	
Ending Balance	3,884	0	114,694		118,579

Figure 8-6.

Click **Refresh**.

This report can also be accessed through the Report Center.

Cash Flow Projector

The Cash Flow Forecast report considers cash flows based on customer receivables and the restaurant's payables. A restaurant may expect cash receipts from other sources, such as investors and loans, and can anticipate other future expenditures. The Cash Flow Projector is a step-by-step guide that allows management to develop a six-week projection of cash inflows and outflows using existing information in combination with additional information, provided by management, regarding anticipated cash inflows and outflows from other sources. To access this feature, click the **Company** drop-down menu, select **Planning & Budgeting**, and select **Cash Flow Projector**. Specific information about this feature can be obtained by selecting **Learn More** in the Cash Flow Projector window.

Chapter Review Problems

1. Generate the Balance Sheet Standard report at January 31, 2008. Using the information from this statement, compute the following and comment on the results. (See Glossary for Ratios.)

   Working Capital

   Current Ratio

   Quick Ratio

   Debt to Equity

2. Generate the Profit & Loss Standard Statement for the month of January 2008. Using the information from this statement, compute the following and comment on the results. (See Glossary for Ratios.)

   Cost of Sales Ratio

   Labor Cost Ratio

   Total Profit Margin

3. Generate the Profit & Loss Standard Statement for the month of January 2008. Prepare a common-size Profit & Loss Statement and comment on any significant findings.

4. Generate the Balance Sheet Standard at January 31, 2008. Prepare a common-size Balance Sheet and comment on any significant findings.

5. Generate the Cash Flow Forecast for the month of February 2008. Should management be concerned about the restaurant's cash position for this time period?

You can find additional Review Problems at *www.wiley.com/college/murphy.*

Budgeting

Access the Chapter 9 data file from the CD-ROM that accompanies this book or download the file from the web site.

Chapter Outline

Preparing an Operating Budget

Reports

Chapter Review Problems

Preparing an Operating Budget

An *operating budget* is a formal plan developed by management that projects the expected future sales and expenses of an organization for a specified time period. The budget process for a restaurant must take into consideration various external and internal factors. External factors include the overall state of the economy, inflation, consumer confidence, and industry trends. Internal factors include the restaurant's direct competitors, location, customer base, access to the labor pool, availability of suppliers, and financial performance in previous years. During the budgeting process, management establishes the goals and objectives of the organization and plans for the future by forecasting anticipated sales and expenses. A budget can be used as part of the internal controls procedures of the restaurant. By comparing actual amounts to budget amounts and investigating the variances, management can determine the underlining cause of any discrepancies and take the necessary steps to correct the problem. This process can improve the reliability of accounting records as well as the efficiency of the restaurant's operations.

QUICKBOOKS TIP

QuickBooks allows a user to create a budget using Profit & Loss Accounts and Balance Sheet Accounts. An account must exist in the Chart of Accounts to be viewed in the budget.

Budgets are most often used to forecast revenue and expense accounts. Budgets can be created from scratch, using data from the previous year or from the previous year's budget. QuickBooks can create a budget by customer, job, or class if the class tracking feature has been enabled. Budgeted amounts can be altered at any time.

Preparing a Budget from Scratch

Click the **Company** drop-down menu.

Select **Planning & Budgeting**.

Select **Set Up Budgets**.

Select the appropriate date, in the Create New Budget window.

Select **Profit & Loss** budget type.

Click **Next**.

Select **No additional criteria** at the Additional Profit & Loss Budget Criteria prompt.

Click **Next**.

Select **Create budget from scratch** at the Choose how you want to create a budget prompt.

Click **Finish**.

Input budget data (see Figure 9-1).

| Budget | | | | | | | | | | | | | | |
| FY2008 - Profit & Loss by Account ▾ | | | | | | | | | | | Create New Budget | | | |

Account	Annual T...	Jan08	Feb08	Mar08	Apr08	May08	Jun08	Jul08	Aug08	Sep08	Oct08	Nov08	Dec08
41400 · Beverage Sales													
41410 · Beer	6,617.00	1,914.00	2,178.00	2,525.00									
41420 · Wine	30,329.00	8,773.00	9,984.00	11,572.00									
41430 · Liquor	14,889.00	4,307.00	4,901.00	5,681.00									
41440 · Other	3,308.00	957.00	1,089.00	1,262.00									
42100 · Catering Sales													
42110 · Food	9,360.00	2,160.00	3,600.00	3,600.00									
42120 · Beverage	3,640.00	840.00	1,400.00	1,400.00									
43800 · Food Sales	157,981.00	44,082.00	50,225.00	63,674.00									
43900 · Sales Comps, Discounts & Promo	-4,355.00	-1,136.00	-1,578.00	-1,641.00									
50000 · Cost of Goods Sold													
50900 · Food Purchases	54,718.00	15,445.00	17,978.00	21,295.00									
51000 · Beverage Purchases													
51010 · Beer	2,150.00	643.00	698.00	809.00									
51020 · Wine	9,853.00	2,946.00	3,200.00	3,707.00									
51030 · Liquor	4,837.00	1,446.00	1,571.00	1,820.00									
51040 · Other	1,074.00	321.00	349.00	404.00									
51800 · Merchant Account Fees	7,996.00	2,086.00	2,897.00	3,013.00									
60000 · Advertising and Promotion	3,176.00	1,176.00	2,000.00										
60200 · Automobile Expense	300.00	100.00	100.00	100.00									
60400 · Bank Service Charges													
60500 · Bad Debt Expense	180.00	50.00	60.00	70.00									
61000 · Business Licenses and Permits	510.00	170.00	170.00	170.00									
61200 · Cash Drawer Payouts													
61400 · Charitable Contributions													
61700 · Computer and Internet Expenses	570.00	190.00	190.00	190.00									
62000 · Continuing Education													

| Copy Across | Adjust Row Amounts | Clear | | | | | | Save | OK | Cancel | Help |

Figure 9-1.

Click **Save**.

Click **OK**.

QUICKBOOKS TIP
When entering fixed monthly budgeted amounts, enter the amount in the first month and click the **Copy Across** button to populate each month in the year.

Reports

Several budget reports are available, and all budget reports can be obtained by clicking the **Reports** drop-down menu, selecting **Budgets**, and selecting the desired budget report.

Report Center

This report can also be accessed through the Report Center.

Profit & Loss Budget Overview

This report displays a summary of the budget for the period selected. Each figure displayed is the amount budgeted for a specific income or expense account. Double-click on an amount to view the transactions related to the account. Once the budget is created, management can use this report to review the budget when necessary and determine if any adjustments are required. It can be distributed to all managers to assist them in making the appropriate decisions in order to adhere to the established budgeted amounts.

Click the **Reports** drop-down menu.

Select **Budgets**.

Select **Budget Overview**.

Select **FY2008 – Profit & Loss by Account** at the Select the budget to use when generating the budget report prompt.

Click **Next**.

Select **Account by Month** at the Select a report layout for the budget report prompt.

Click **Next**.

Click **Finish**.

Select the appropriate date (see Figure 9-2).

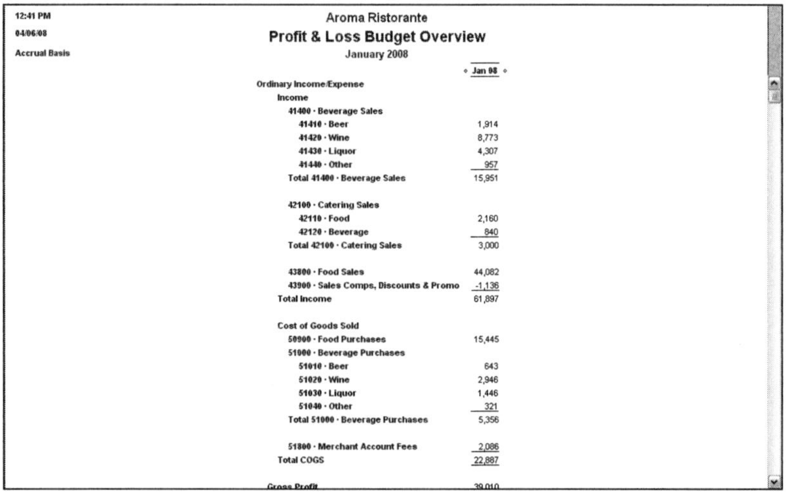

Figure 9-2.

Click **Refresh**.

Profit & Loss Budget vs. Actual

This report compares budgeted and actual amounts for the period selected. All differences are shown in dollar amounts and percentages. By reviewing this report, management can determine whether the company is operating within the budget. Adherence to a budget provides assurance that the restaurant is on track in meeting its established goals and objectives. Management may even be rewarded for consistently staying within the budget. Differences from the budgeted amounts can identify problems and/or if any adjustments to the budget are required based on a change in the restaurant's assumptions used to prepare the budget or its operating environment. Each month management should analyze any differences between budgeted and actual amounts to determine the cause and take the necessary corrective action.

Click the **Reports** drop-down menu.

Select **Budgets**.

Select **Budget vs. Actual**.

Select **FY2008 – Profit & Loss by Account** at the Select the budget to use when generating the budget report prompt.

Click **Next**.

Select **Account by Month** at the Select a report layout for the budget report prompt.

Click **Next**.

Click **Finish**.

Select the appropriate date (see Figure 9-3).

	Jan 08	Budget	$ Over Budget	% of Budget
Ordinary Income/Expense				
Income				
41400 · Beverage Sales				
41410 · Beer	▶ 2,044	◀ 1,914	130	107%
41420 · Wine	9,367	8,773	594	107%
41430 · Liquor	4,598	4,307	291	107%
41440 · Other	1,022	957	65	107%
Total 41400 · Beverage Sales	17,031	15,951	1,080	107%
42100 · Catering Sales				
42110 · Food	7,389	2,160	5,229	342%
42120 · Beverage	750	840	-90	89%
Total 42100 · Catering Sales	8,139	3,000	5,139	271%
43800 · Food Sales	39,738	44,082	-4,344	90%
43900 · Sales, Comps, Discounts & Promo	-1,928	-1,136	-792	170%
Total Income	62,980	61,897	1,083	102%
Cost of Goods Sold				
50900 · Food Purchases	14,878	15,445	-567	96%
51000 · Beverage Purchases				
51010 · Beer	1,587	643	944	247%
51020 · Wine	1,842	2,946	-1,104	63%
51030 · Liquor	2,214	1,446	768	153%
51040 · Other	866	321	545	270%
Total 51000 · Beverage Purchases	6,509	5,356	1,153	122%
51800 · Merchant Account Fees	894	2,086	-1,192	43%
Total COGS	22,281	22,887	-606	97%
Gross Profit	40,699	39,010		

Aroma Ristorante
Profit & Loss Budget vs. Actual
January 2008

11:24 AM
10/06/08
Accrual Basis

A negative amount means the restaurant was under budget, and a positive number means the operation was over budget.

Figure 9-3.

Click **Refresh**.

Profit & Loss Budget Performance

This report compares the actual income and expenses to what the restaurant budgeted during the specified time period.

Click the **Reports** drop-down menu.

Select **Budgets**.

Select **Profit & Loss Budget Performance**.

Select **FY2008 – Profit & Loss by Account** at the Select the budget to use when generating the budget report prompt.

Click **Next**.

Select **Account by Month** at the Select a report layout for the budget report prompt.

Click **Next**.

Click **Finish**.

Select the appropriate date (see Figure 9-4).

		Jan 08	Budget	Jan 08	YTD Budget	Annual Budget
Ordinary Income/Expense						
Income						
41400 · Beverage Sales						
41410 · Beer		2,044	1,914	2,044	1,914	6,617
41420 · Wine		9,367	8,773	9,367	8,773	30,329
41430 · Liquor		4,598	4,307	4,598	4,307	14,889
41440 · Other		1,022	957	1,022	957	3,308
Total 41400 · Beverage Sales		17,031	15,951	17,031	15,951	55,143
42100 · Catering Sales						
42110 · Food		7,389	2,160	7,389	2,160	9,360
42120 · Beverage		750	840	750	840	3,640
Total 42100 · Catering Sales		8,139	3,000	8,139	3,000	13,000
43800 · Food Sales		39,738	44,082	39,738	44,082	157,981
43900 · Sales Comps, Discounts & Promo		-1,928	-1,136	-1,928	-1,136	-4,355
Total Income		62,980	61,897	62,980	61,897	221,769
Cost of Goods Sold						
50900 · Food Purchases		14,878	15,445	14,878	15,445	54,718
51000 · Beverage Purchases						
51010 · Beer		1,587	643	1,587	643	2,150
51020 · Wine		1,842	2,946	1,842	2,946	9,853
51030 · Liquor		2,214	1,446	2,214	1,446	4,837
51040 · Other		866	321	866	321	1,074
Total 51000 · Beverage Purchases		6,509	5,356	6,509	5,356	17,914
51800 · Merchant Account Fees		894	2,086	894	2,086	7,996
Total COGS		22,281	22,887	22,281	22,887	80,628
Gross Profit		40,699	39,010	40,699	39,010	141,141

Figure 9-4.

Click **Refresh**.

Budget vs. Actual Graph

The graph displays the comparison between the actual amounts and the budgeted amounts. The graph in the top half of the window displays the difference between the actual net income and the budgeted net income for a specific month. The graph in the lower half of the window displays the variances in the income and expense accounts. Five income and expense accounts can be viewed at a time. The next five accounts will be displayed by clicking the **Next Group** button.

Click the **Reports** drop-down menu.

Select **Budgets**.

Select **Budget vs. Actual Graph**.

Select the appropriate date (see Figure 9-5).

Click **OK**.

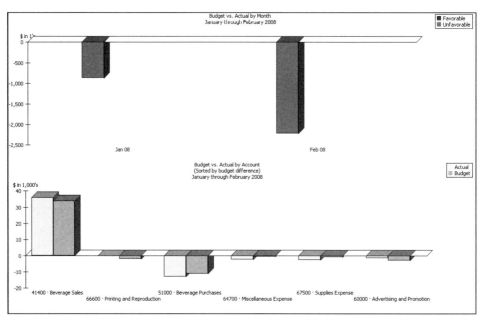

Figure 9-5.

Chapter Review Problems

1. Use the information in Figure 9-6 to develop the budget for Aroma Ristorante for January 2008. Create a budget in QuickBooks and generate the Profit & Loss Budget Overview report.

2. Generate the Profit & Loss Budget vs. Actual report for Aroma Ristorante for January 2008. Comment on any significant differences.

3. In your hometown, what factors should be taken into consideration if you were creating a budget for a local restaurant?

You can find additional Review Problems at *www.wiley.com/college/murphy.*

**Aroma Ristorante Profit & Loss Budget Overview
January 2008**

	Jan 08
Ordinary Income/Expense	
Income	
41400 · Beverage Sales	
41410 · Beer	1,914
41420 · Wine	8,773
41430 · Liquor	4,307
41440 · Other	957
Total 41400 · Beverage Sales	15,951
42100 · Catering Sales	
42110 · Food	2,160
42120 · Beverage	840
Total 42100 · Catering Sales	3,000
43800 · Food Sales	44,082
43900 · Sales Comps, Discounts & Promo	−1,136
Total Income	61,897
Cost of Goods Sold	
50900 · Food Purchases	15,445
51000 · Beverage Purchases	
51010 · Beer	643
51020 · Wine	2,946
51030 · Liquor	1,446
51040 · Other	321
Total 51000 · Beverage Purchases	5,356
51800 · Merchant Account Fees	2,086
Total COGS	22,887
Gross Profit	39,010
Expense	
60000 · Advertising and Promotion	1,176
60200 · Automobile Expense	100
60500 · Bad Debt Expense	50
61000 · Business Licenses and Permits	170
61700 · Computer and Internet Expenses	190
62400 · Depreciation Expense	
62410 · Furniture and Equipment	400
62420 · Bar Equipment	490
62430 · Kitchen Equipment	4,500

Figure 9-6.

Aroma Ristorante Profit & Loss Budget Overview
January 2008

	Jan 08
62450 · China, Silver, Glassware, Linen	90
62460 · Smallwares	190
62465 · Computer Equipment	1,840
62495 · Vehicle	990
Total 62400 · Depreciation Expense	8,500
62500 · Dues and Subscriptions	124
63300 · Insurance Expense	950
63550 · Kitchen Utensils and Tableware	2,600
64000 · Linen and Dry Cleaning Expense	320
64200 · Maintenance Fee	200
64700 · Miscellaneous Expense	100
64800 · Music and Entertainment	390
64900 · Office Supplies	175
66000 · Payroll Expenses	21,500
66500 · Postage and Delivery	20
66600 · Printing and Reproduction	1,400
67100 · Rent Expense	9,000
67200 · Repairs and Maintenance	170
67300 · Start-Up Costs	1,000
67500 · Supplies Expense	450
68100 · Telephone Expense	150
68600 · Utilities	1,800
Total Expense	50,535
Net Ordinary Income	−11,525
Other Income/Expense	
Other Income	
70010 · Retail Income	400
70200 · Interest Income	360
Total Other Income	760
Other Expense	
80300 · Interest Expense	1,000
80600 · Retail Expense	40
Total Other Expense	1,040
Net Other Income	−280
Net Income	−11,805

Figure 9-6.   (continued)

Year-End Procedures and Reporting

Chapter Outline

Payroll Tax Forms

Payroll involves the processing of employees' paychecks and filing various tax forms. As mentioned earlier, because payroll can be extremely time-consuming and because employers face potential penalties if forms are not filed correctly and in a timely fashion, restaurant operators may opt to outsource payroll. If outsourced, most payroll companies will process the restaurant's payroll and file all the necessary forms. If the restaurant decides to process payroll in-house, using data from the files, QuickBooks allows the user to complete the required payroll tax returns and other payroll-related documents, such as Form W-2: Wage and Tax Statement and Form 1099 MISC: Miscellaneous Income.

QUICKBOOKS TIP
Refer to the QuickBooks Help feature for additional information and instructions on how to complete these tax forms.

Form 941: Employer's Quarterly Federal Tax Return

Employers are required to file the Form 941 tax return. The return is used to report the amount of Social Security, Medicare, and federal income tax withheld and deposited for all employees. Generally, employers deposit these withholdings semiweekly and the Form 941 is filed on a quarterly basis. The tax return is due on the last business day of the month following the end of the quarter (see Figure 10-1).

ACCOUNTING TIP
Refer to Internal Revenue Service Publication 15 (Circular E), Employer's Tax Guide, and *IRS.gov* for additional information and preparation instructions for tax forms (*www.irs .gov/pub/irs-pdf/p15.pdf*).

Form 940: Employer's Annual Federal Unemployment (FUTA) Tax Return

The Form 940 is an annual tax return used to report the restaurant's federal unemployment (FUTA) tax liability for the year. The federal unemployment system is funded by the unemployment tax collected from the employers. These funds are used to provide unemployment payments to individuals who have lost their jobs. Federal funds are disbursed to states that in turn make disbursements to individuals. The federal unemployment tax is borne only by the employer. The tax return is due on January 31 of the following year. Generally, federal unemployment tax deposits are made each quarter to the appropriate authorities (see Figure 10-2).

Form **941 for 2008:** Employer's QUARTERLY Federal Tax Return		950108
(Rev. January 2008)	Department of the Treasury — Internal Revenue Service	OMB No. 1545-0029

(EIN)
Employer identification number ☐☐ – ☐☐☐☐☐☐☐

Name *(not your trade name)* _____

Trade name *(if any)* _____

Address _____
    Number   Street   Suite or room number

    City   State   ZIP code

Report for this Quarter of 2008
(Check one.)

☐ **1:** January, February, March
☐ **2:** April, May, June
☐ **3:** July, August, September
☐ **4:** October, November, December

Read the separate instructions before you fill out this form. Please type or print within the boxes.

Part 1: Answer these questions for this quarter.

1 Number of employees who received wages, tips, or other compensation for the pay period including: *Mar. 12* (Quarter 1), *June 12* (Quarter 2), *Sept. 12* (Quarter 3), *Dec. 12* (Quarter 4) **1** �▢

2 Wages, tips, and other compensation . . . . **2** ▢

3 Total income tax withheld from wages, tips, and other compensation . . . . . . **3** ▢

4 If no wages, tips, and other compensation are subject to social security or Medicare tax . ☐ Check and go to line 6.

5 Taxable social security and Medicare wages and tips:

	Column 1		Column 2
5a Taxable social security wages	▢	× .124 =	▢
5b Taxable social security tips	▢	× .124 =	▢
5c Taxable Medicare wages & tips	▢	× .029 =	▢

5d Total social security and Medicare taxes (*Column 2*, lines 5a + 5b + 5c = line 5d) . **5d** ▢

6 Total taxes before adjustments (lines 3 + 5d = line 6) . . . . **6** ▢

7 **TAX ADJUSTMENTS** (read the instructions for line 7 before completing lines 7a through 7g):

7a Current quarter's fractions of cents . . . . ▢

7b Current quarter's sick pay . . . . ▢

7c Current quarter's adjustments for tips and group-term life insurance ▢

7d Current year's income tax withholding (attach Form 941c) . . ▢

7e Prior quarters' social security and Medicare taxes (attach Form 941c) ▢

7f Special additions to federal income tax (attach Form 941c) . . ▢

7g Special additions to social security and Medicare (attach Form 941c) ▢

7h **TOTAL ADJUSTMENTS** (combine all amounts: lines 7a through 7g) . . . **7h** ▢

8 Total taxes after adjustments (combine lines 6 and 7h) . . . . . . **8** ▢

9 Advance earned income credit (EIC) payments made to employees . . . . **9** ▢

10 Total taxes after adjustment for advance EIC (line 8 – line 9 = line 10) . . . . **10** ▢

11 Total deposits for this quarter, including overpayment applied from a prior quarter . . **11** ▢

12 **Balance due** (If line 10 is more than line 11, write the difference here.) . . . . . **12** ▢
For information on how to pay, see the instructions.

13 **Overpayment** (If line 11 is more than line 10, write the difference here.) ▢ Check one ☐ Apply to next return. ☐ Send a refund.

▶ You **MUST** fill out both pages of this form and **SIGN** it.   Next ➡

For Privacy Act and Paperwork Reduction Act Notice, see the back of the Payment Voucher.   Cat. No. 17001Z   Form **941** (Rev. 1-2008)

Figure 10-1.

Courtesy of the U.S. Department of Treasury, Internal Revenue Service.

950208

Name *(not your trade name)*	Employer identification number (EIN)

Part 2: Tell us about your deposit schedule and tax liability for this quarter.

If you are unsure about whether you are a monthly schedule depositor or a semiweekly schedule depositor, see *Pub. 15 (Circular E)*, section 11.

14 ☐☐ Write the state abbreviation for the state where you made your deposits OR write "MU" if you made your deposits in *multiple* states.

15 Check one: ☐ Line 10 is less than $2,500. Go to Part 3.

☐ You were a monthly schedule depositor for the entire quarter. Fill out your tax liability for each month. Then go to Part 3.

Tax liability: Month 1 ☐ .

Month 2 ☐ .

Month 3 ☐ .

Total liability for quarter ☐ . Total must equal line 10.

☐ You were a semiweekly schedule depositor for any part of this quarter. Fill out *Schedule B (Form 941): Report of Tax Liability for Semiweekly Schedule Depositors,* and attach it to this form.

Part 3: Tell us about your business. If a question does NOT apply to your business, leave it blank.

16 If your business has closed or you stopped paying wages . . . . ☐ Check here, and

enter the final date you paid wages ☐ / / .

17 If you are a seasonal employer and you do not have to file a return for every quarter of the year . . ☐ Check here.

Part 4: May we speak with your third-party designee?

Do you want to allow an employee, a paid tax preparer, or another person to discuss this return with the IRS? See the instructions for details.

☐ Yes. Designee's name and phone number ☐ ( ) –

Select a 5-digit Personal Identification Number (PIN) to use when talking to IRS. ☐☐☐☐☐

☐ No.

Part 5: Sign here. You MUST fill out both pages of this form and SIGN it.

Under penalties of perjury, I declare that I have examined this return, including accompanying schedules and statements, and to the best of my knowledge and belief, it is true, correct, and complete.

X **Sign your name here** ☐

Print your name here ☐

Print your title here ☐

Date ☐ / /

Best daytime phone ( ) –

Part 6: For paid preparers only (optional)

Paid Preparer's Signature			
Firm's name (or yours if self-employed)			
Address		EIN	
		ZIP code	
Date	/ / Phone ( ) –	SSN/PTIN	

☐ Check if you are self-employed.

Figure 10-1. (continued)

Form **940 for 2008:** Employer's Annual Federal Unemployment (FUTA) Tax Return   850108

Department of the Treasury — Internal Revenue Service

OMB No. 1545-0028

(EIN)
Employer identification number ☐☐ – ☐☐☐☐☐☐☐

Name (not your trade name)

Trade name (if any)

Address

Number   Street   Suite or room number

City   State   ZIP code

Type of Return
(Check all that apply.)

☐ **a.** Amended
☐ **b.** Successor employer
☐ **c.** No payments to employees in 2008
☐ **d.** Final: Business closed or stopped paying wages

Read the separate instructions before you fill out this form. Please type or print within the boxes.

Part 1: Tell us about your return. If any line does NOT apply, leave it blank.

1   If you were required to pay your state unemployment tax in ...

    1a One state only, write the state abbreviation . . . . **1a** ☐☐
    - OR -
    1b More than one state (You are a multi-state employer) . . . . **1b** ☐ Check here. Fill out Schedule A.
        Skip line 2 for 2008 and go to line 3.
2   If you paid wages in a state that is subject to **CREDIT REDUCTION** . . . . **2** ☐ Check here. Fill out Schedule A (Form 940), Part 2.

Part 2: Determine your FUTA tax before adjustments for 2008. If any line does NOT apply, leave it blank.

3   Total payments to all employees . . . . **3** [.]

4   Payments exempt from FUTA tax . . . . **4** [.]

    Check all that apply: **4a** ☐ Fringe benefits   **4c** ☐ Retirement/Pension   **4e** ☐ Other
                     4b ☐ Group-term life insurance   **4d** ☐ Dependent care

5   Total of payments made to each employee in excess of
    $7,000 . . . . **5** [.]

6   Subtotal (line 4 + line 5 = line 6) . . . . **6** [.]

7   Total taxable FUTA wages (line 3 – line 6 = line 7) . . . . **7** [.]

8   FUTA tax before adjustments (line 7 × .008 = line 8) . . . . **8** [.]

Part 3: Determine your adjustments. If any line does NOT apply, leave it blank.

9   If ALL of the taxable FUTA wages you paid were excluded from state unemployment tax,
    multiply line 7 by .054 (line 7 × .054 = line 9). Then go to line 12 . . . . **9** [   ]
10   If SOME of the taxable FUTA wages you paid were excluded from state unemployment tax,
    OR you paid ANY state unemployment tax late (after the due date for filing Form 940), fill out
    the worksheet in the instructions. Enter the amount from line 7 of the worksheet onto line 10 . **10** [   ]
          Skip line 11 for 2008 and go to line 12.
11   If credit reduction applies, enter the amount from line 3 of Schedule A (Form 940) **11**

Part 4: Determine your FUTA tax and balance due or overpayment for 2008. If any line does NOT apply, leave it blank.

12   Total FUTA tax after adjustments (lines 8 + 9 + 10 + 11 = line 12) . . . . **12** [.]

13   FUTA tax deposited for the year, including any payment applied from a prior year . . . . **13** [.]
14   Balance due (If line 12 is more than line 13, enter the difference on line 14.)
    ● If line 14 is more than $500, you must deposit your tax.
    ● If line 14 is $500 or less, you may pay with this return. For more information on how to pay, see
    the separate instructions . . . . **14** [.]

15   Overpayment (If line 13 is more than line 12, enter the difference on line 15 and check a box
    below.) . . . . **15** [.]

                             Check one: ☐ Apply to next return.
    ▶ You **MUST** fill out both pages of this form and **SIGN** it.   ☐ Send a refund.

Next ➡

For Privacy Act and Paperwork Reduction Act Notice, see the back of Form 940-V, Payment Voucher.   Cat. No. 11234O   Form **940** (2008)

Figure 10-2.

Courtesy of the U.S. Department of Treasury, Internal Revenue Service.

850208

Name (not your trade name)	Employer identification number (EIN)

Part 5: Report your FUTA tax liability by quarter only if line 12 is more than $500. If not, go to Part 6.

16 Report the amount of your FUTA tax liability for each quarter; do NOT enter the amount you deposited. If you had no liability for a quarter, leave the line blank.

16a **1st quarter** (January 1 – March 31) . . . . 16a [.]

16b **2nd quarter** (April 1 – June 30) . . . . 16b [.]

16c **3rd quarter** (July 1 – September 30) . . . . 16c [.]

16d **4th quarter** (October 1 – December 31) . . . . 16d [.]

17 **Total tax liability for the year** (lines 16a + 16b + 16c + 16d = line 17) 17 [.]   Total must equal line 12.

Part 6: May we speak with your third-party designee?

Do you want to allow an employee, a paid tax preparer, or another person to discuss this return with the IRS? See the instructions for details.

☐ **Yes.** Designee's name and phone number [   ]   ( ) –

Select a 5-digit Personal Identification Number (PIN) to use when talking to IRS ☐ ☐ ☐ ☐ ☐

☐ **No.**

Part 7: Sign here. You MUST fill out both pages of this form and SIGN it.

Under penalties of perjury, I declare that I have examined this return, including accompanying schedules and statements, and to the best of my knowledge and belief, it is true, correct, and complete, and that no part of any payment made to a state unemployment fund claimed as a credit was, or is to be, deducted from the payments made to employees. Declaration of preparer (other than taxpayer) is based on all information of which preparer has any knowledge.

✗ Sign your name here [   ]

Print your name here [   ]
Print your title here [   ]

Date [/   /   ]

Best daytime phone ( ) –

Paid preparer's use only Check if you are self-employed . . . ☐

Preparer's name	[ ]	Preparer's SSN/PTIN	[ ]
Preparer's signature	[ ]	Date	[/ /]
Firm's name (or yours if self-employed)	[ ]	EIN	[ ]
Address	[ ]	Phone	( ) –
City	[ ] State [ ]	ZIP code	[ ]

Page **2**   Form **940** (2008)

Figure 10-2. (continued)

Form W-2: Wage and Tax Statement and Form W-3: Transmittal of Wage and Tax Statements

For each employee, the employer is required to complete Form W-2 at the end of the year. This form reports an employee's wages and withholdings for the year and must be completed before January 31 of the next year. A copy is submitted to federal, state, and local authorities. Three copies are given to the employee and the restaurant keeps a copy for its own records. In addition, the employer must complete and submit Form W-3: Transmittal of Wage and Tax Statements to the federal government. This form is a summary of all the W-2 forms submitted to the federal government (see Figure 10-3).

ATTENTION:

Caution — Change to the 2008 Form W-2

If you downloaded the 2008 Form W-2 before March 8, 2008, please note the following correction.

On page 10, under Due dates, the first two sentences should read, "Furnish Copies B, C, and 2 to the employee generally by February 2, 2009. File Copy A with the SSA by March 2, 2009."

This form is provided for informational purposes only. Copy A appears in red, similar to the official IRS form. Do *not* file copy A with the SSA. The official printed version of this IRS form is scannable, but the online version of it, printed from this web site, is not. A penalty of $50 per information return may be imposed for filing forms that cannot be scanned.

To order official IRS forms, call 1-800-TAX-FORM (1-800-829-3676) or order information returns and employer returns online, and we'll mail you the scannable forms and other products.

You may file Forms W-2 and W-3 electronically on the SSA's web site at Employer Reporting Instructions & Information. You can create fill-in versions of Forms W-2 and W-3 for filing with the SSA. You may also print out copies for filing with state or local governments, for distribution to your employees, and for your records. See IRS Publications 1141, 1167, 1179 and other IRS resources for information about printing these tax forms.

Courtesy of the U.S. Department of Treasury, Internal Revenue Service

22222	a Employee's social security number		
	OMB No. 1545-0008		

b Employer identification number (EIN)		1 Wages, tips, other compensation	2 Federal income tax withheld
c Employer's name, address, and ZIP code		3 Social security wages	4 Social security tax withheld
		5 Medicare wages and tips	6 Medicare tax withheld
		7 Social security tips	8 Allocated tips
d Control number		9 Advance EIC payment	10 Dependent care benefits
e Employee's first name and initial Last name Suff.		11 Nonqualified plans	12a
		13 Statutory employee Retirement plan Third-party sick pay	12b
		14 Other	12c
			12d
f Employee's address and ZIP code			

15 State Employer's state ID number	16 State wages, tips, etc.	17 State income tax	18 Local wages, tips, etc.	19 Local income tax	20 Locality name

Form W-2 Wage and Tax Statement   **2008**   Department of the Treasury—Internal Revenue Service

Copy 1—For State, City, or Local Tax Department

Figure 10-3.

Form 1099-MISC: Miscellaneous Income and Form 1096: Annual Summary and Transmittal of US Information Return

Restaurants are required to complete the Form 1099-MISC for all independent contractors paid $600 or more for services rendered in the calendar year. This form is used to report all payments received by an independent contractor. Generally, independent contractors are self-employed individuals, such as plumbers and electricians, who are not considered employees of the restaurant. They are not directly supervised by management and do not receive any employee benefits. The restaurant is not required to withhold any payroll taxes from their payments. Form 1099 MISC must be completed and submitted to the independent contractor before January 31 of the following year. The independent contractor receives copies and the restaurant retains a copy for its records. The Form 1099 function must be established (see Chapter 3, page 53) and the independent contractor must be identified as a Form 1099 vendor in the vendor record. Form 1096:

Annual Summary and Transmittal of US Information Returns must also be completed and submitted to the government. This form is a summary of the information on the Form 1099-MISC (see Figure 10-4).

ATTENTION:

This form is provided for informational purposes only. Copy A appears in red, similar to the official IRS form. Do *not* file copy A with the IRS. The official printed version of this IRS form is scannable, but the online version of it, printed from this web site, is not. A penalty of $50 per information return may be imposed for filing forms that cannot be scanned.

To order official IRS forms, call 1-800-TAX-FORM (1-800-829-3676) or order information returns and employer returns online, and we'll mail you the scannable forms and other products.

See IRS Publications 1141, 1167, 1179, and other IRS resources for information about printing these tax forms.

Courtesy of the U.S. Department of Treasury, Internal Revenue Service.

9595	☐ VOID	☐ CORRECTED			
PAYER'S name, street address, city, state, ZIP code, and telephone no.		**1** Rents $	OMB No. 1545-0115	**2008** Form **1099-MISC**	Miscellaneous Income
		2 Royalties $			
		3 Other income $	**4** Federal income tax withheld $		Copy A For Internal Revenue Service Center
PAYER'S federal identification number	RECIPIENT'S identification number	**5** Fishing boat proceeds $	**6** Medical and health care payments $		File with Form 1096.
RECIPIENT'S name		**7** Nonemployee compensation $	**8** Substitute payments in lieu of dividends or interest $		For Privacy Act and Paperwork Reduction Act
Street address (including apt. no.)		**9** Payer made direct sales of $5,000 or more of consumer products to a buyer (recipient) for resale ▶ ☐	**10** Crop insurance proceeds $		Notice, see the 2008 General Instructions for
City, state, and ZIP code		**11**	**12**		Forms 1099, 1098, 5498, and W-2G.
Account number (see instructions)	2nd TIN not. ☐	**13** Excess golden parachute payments $	**14** Gross proceeds paid to an attorney $		
15a Section 409A deferrals $	**15b** Section 409A income $	**16** State tax withheld $	**17** State/Payer's state no.	**18** State income $ $	

Form **1099-MISC**   Cat. No. 14425J   Department of the Treasury - Internal Revenue Service

Do Not Cut or Separate Forms on This Page — Do Not Cut or Separate Forms on This Page

Figure 10-4.

The Closing Process

The end of the accounting cycle involves recording closing journal entries to zero out the balances of temporary accounts, such as income and expense accounts that are only used for a period of time, and transfer the net income for the accounting period to Owner's Equity on the Balance Sheet. By establishing a period end date, QuickBooks automatically performs this function and closing journal entries are not required. At the end of the business year, a year-end audit of the restaurant's financial statements, by an independent accounting firm, is recommended. Some lenders may require an audit. Additional audit adjustments may be required for the auditors to successfully complete their report. Subsequent to the completion of the audit, management can decide whether or not to close the financial records for the period. The financial records are not required to be closed. Closing the financial records for the period prevents entering data in a prior accounting period and altering the prior year's audited financial statements. If the records are closed, the previous year's data is still available. Once the files are closed, access to financial records can be restricted by establishing a password and only individuals with access to the closing date and the password can change the records. Selecting a password is optional. Advantages to not closing financial records include easy access to all financial data and the ability to create detailed annual comparison reports.

To create a password and close the financial records for the period, follow these steps:

Click the **Edit** drop-down menu.

Select **Preferences**.

Select **Accounting**.

Select **Company Preferences**.

Click the **Set Date/Password** button in the closing date field.

Enter the **Closing Date** and **Closing Date Password** in the appropriate fields.

Click **OK**.

Chapter Review Problems

1. What is the purpose of Form W-2?

2. What is the purpose of Form 1099-MISC?

3. If an employee has worked at a restaurant for only one day, is the employer still required to prepare Form W-2 for the employee?

4. Under which circumstances would you recommend closing the financial records for the period?

You can find additional Review Problems at *www.wiley.com/college/murphy*.

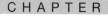

Other Restaurant Functions

Access the Chapter 11 data file from the CD-ROM that accompanies this book or download the file from the web site.

Chapter Outline

Managing Fixed Assets

QuickBooks has a fixed asset management feature that allows managers to keep track of the restaurant's fixed assets—their costs, description, date of purchase, and other information. Fixed assets are tangible assets with a long life span. They include such assets as buildings, furniture, equipment, and so on. To use this function, the asset must be entered in QuickBooks as a fixed asset item.

Create a Fixed Asset Item

Click the **Lists** drop-down menu.

Select **Fixed Asset Item** list.

Select **Item**.

Select **New**.

Using the following data, enter the information in the appropriate fields.

DATA: Create a Fixed Asset Item.	
TYPE:	Fixed Asset
ASSET NAME/NUMBER:	Pizza Oven
ASSET ACCOUNT:	15050 Kitchen Equipment
PURCHASE DESCRIPTION:	Pizza Oven
ITEM IS:	New
DATE:	January 1, 2008
COST:	$8,200
VENDOR/PAYEE:	Restaurant Equipment, Inc.
ASSET DESCRIPTION:	Pizza Oven
SERIAL NUMBER:	9998-65-45
WARRANTY EXPIRES:	1/1/2011

Click **OK**.

A manager can generate a list of all the fixed assets owned by the restaurant. The list includes the asset's name/number, purchase date and description, account, and cost. Managers can utilize this list to create an asset depreciation schedule. This is important information considering depreciation expense directly affects the restaurant's profits.

Generate a Fixed Asset List

Click the **Reports** drop-down menu.

Select **List**.

Select **Fixed Asset Listing** (see Figure 11-1).

Aroma Ristorante
Fixed Asset Listing

Item	Purchase Date	Purchase Description	Account	Cost
20 QT Mixer	01/01/2008	20 QT Mixer	15050 · Kitchen Equipment	4,500.00
40 G Kettle	01/01/2008	40 G kettle	15050 · Kitchen Equipment	6,000.00
Bar Stools 15 @ $99 Each	01/01/2008	Bar Stools 15 @ $99 Each	15025 · Bar Equipment	1,485.00
Bar with Back Display	01/01/2008	Bar with Back Display	15025 · Bar Equipment	5,000.00
Beer Refrigerator	01/01/2008	Beer Refrigerator	15025 · Bar Equipment	1,900.00
Butcher Block Table	01/01/2008	Butcher Block Table	15050 · Kitchen Equipment	2,800.00
Can Wash/Mop Sink	01/01/2008	Can Wash/Mop Sink	15050 · Kitchen Equipment	1,200.00
Catering Van	01/01/2008	Catering Van (including transport equipment)	16400 · Vehicles	50,000.00
Chair - 125 Wooden	01/01/2008	Chair - 125 Wooden @$85 Each	15000 · Furniture and Equipment	11,050.00
Coffee Maker	01/01/2008	Coffee Maker	15050 · Kitchen Equipment	1,800.00
Cooking Suite	01/01/2008	Cooking Suite	15050 · Kitchen Equipment	62,000.00
Cooking Suite with Salamander	01/01/2008	Cooking Suite with Salamander	15050 · Kitchen Equipment	40,000.00
Counter	01/01/2008	Counter	15050 · Kitchen Equipment	1,450.00
Counter with Sink	01/01/2008	Counter with Sink	15050 · Kitchen Equipment	4,700.00
Dessert Counter and Sink	01/01/2008	Dessert Counter and Sink	15050 · Kitchen Equipment	15,000.00
Dishwasher	01/01/2008	Dishwasher	15050 · Kitchen Equipment	7,000.00
Double Deck Convection Oven	01/01/2008	Double Deck Convection Oven	15050 · Kitchen Equipment	2,500.00
Double Deck Oven Steamer	01/01/2008	Double Deck Oven Steamer	15050 · Kitchen Equipment	10,000.00
Draft System, Lines and Taps	01/01/2008	Draft System, Lines and Taps	15025 · Bar Equipment	3,500.00
Espresso Machine	01/01/2008	Espresso Machine	15050 · Kitchen Equipment	1,600.00
Flatware - 21 Boxes	03/10/2008	Flatware - 21 Boxes	15100 · China, Silver, Glassware, Linen	1,050.00
Grande Manger Counter	01/01/2008	Grande Manger Counter	15050 · Kitchen Equipment	3,500.00
Hot Food Counter and Sink	01/01/2008	Hot Food Counter and Sink	15050 · Kitchen Equipment	4,200.00
Ice Chest	01/01/2008	Ice Chest	15050 · Kitchen Equipment	1,000.00
Ice Machine	01/01/2008	Ice Machine	15050 · Kitchen Equipment	4,500.00
Lobby Chairs - 6 @$250 Each	03/07/2008	Lobby Chairs - 6 @$250 Each	15000 · Furniture and Equipment	1,500.00
Lockers	01/01/2008	Lockers	15050 · Kitchen Equipment	1,300.00
Low Boy	01/01/2008	Low Boy	15050 · Kitchen Equipment	3,200.00
Margarita Machine	03/17/2008	Margarita Machine	15025 · Bar Equipment	2,500.00
Mobile Pan Racks	01/01/2008	Mobile Pan Racks	15050 · Kitchen Equipment	2,100.00
Pasta Machine	01/01/2008	Pasta Machine	15050 · Kitchen Equipment	4,500.00
Pizza Counter	01/01/2008	Pizza Counter	15050 · Kitchen Equipment	1,950.00

Figure 11-1.

Recording the Stock Issuance

Aroma Ristorante is a start-up restaurant that began its operations on January 1, 2008. The restaurant is a privately held corporation with a single stockholder. The initial stock issuance was recorded on January 1, 2008. This transaction resulted in an increase in assets and owner's equity (DEBIT: Cash; CREDIT: Capital Stock).

On January 1, 2008, Aroma Ristorante recorded the stock issuance using the following steps:

Click the **Banking** drop-down menu.

Select **Make Deposits**.

At the Make Deposits window, the following information was entered (see Figure 11-2).

Stock Issuance	
Deposit To:	10000 Checking Account
Date:	January 1, 2008
Received From:	Mrs. Sally Shareholder
From Account:	30100 Capital Stock
Memo:	Record Initial Stock Issuance
Check No.:	100
Pmt Method:	Check
Amount:	$450,000

Click **Save & Close**.

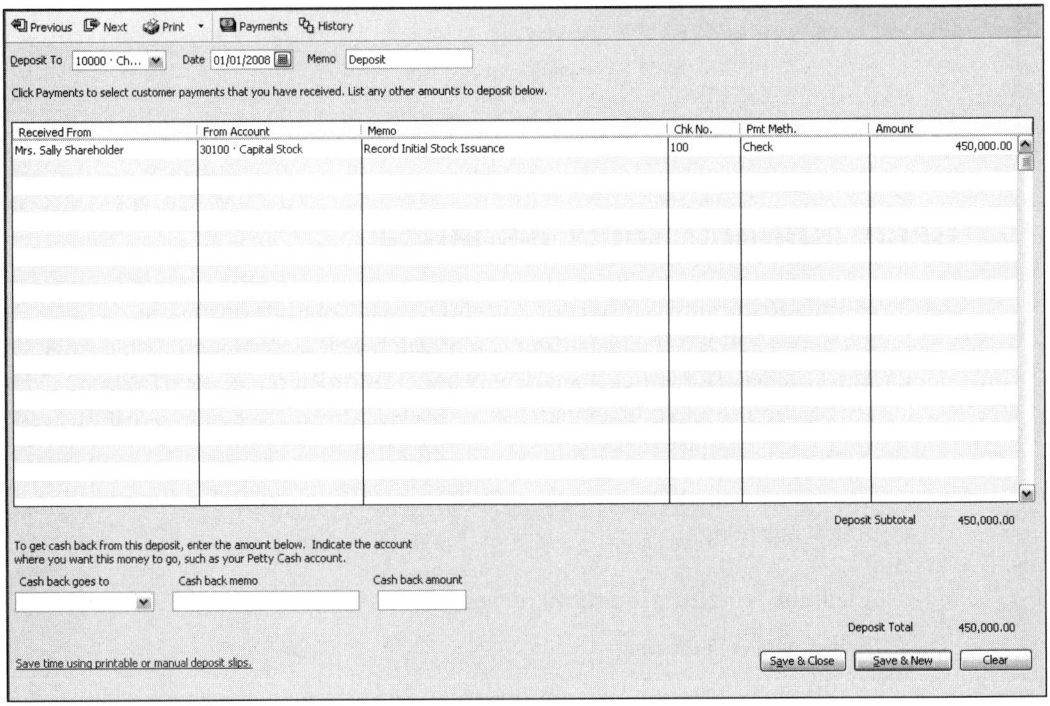

Figure 11-2.

Recording the Dividend Distribution

Profits from a corporation can be retained in the corporation or can be distributed to the shareholders. When earnings are distributed to the shareholders, the result is a decrease in assets and owner's equity (DEBIT: Dividend Paid; CREDIT: Cash). On January 31, 2008, Aroma Ristorante distributed $1,000 to Mrs. Sally Shareholder using the following steps:

Click the **Banking** drop-down menu.

Select **Write Checks**.

In the Write Checks window, the following information was entered (see Figure 11-3).

Bank Account:	10000 Checking Account
Pay to the Order of:	Mrs. Sally Shareholder
Check No.	205
Date:	January 31, 2008
Amount:	$1,000
Memo:	Distribute Dividend to Shareholder
Account:	30200 Dividends Paid

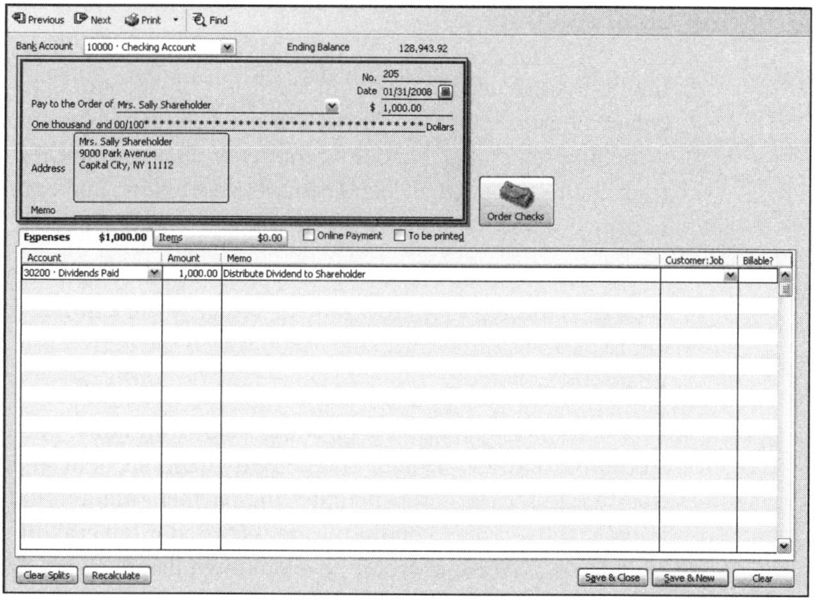

Figure 11-3.

Click **Save & Close**.

Establishing a Petty Cash Fund

A petty cash account is maintained for situations where miscellaneous and unexpected purchases are required. Because easily available cash on hand is susceptible to theft, it is important to maintain good internal control over petty cash and account for all expenditures. The cash should be secured with limited access.

A specified amount of cash is put into the petty cash fund. When the cash is disbursed for expenditures, the expenditures are recorded in the appropriate accounts and the fund is replenished. All expenditures should be approved by management and supported with receipts or other supporting documentation.

ACCOUNTING TIP

The accounting theory of objective evidence requires business transactions to be supported by such documents as canceled checks, receipts, invoices, and other documents that verify the transaction.

Petty Cash Account

If a Petty Cash account is not in the Chart of Accounts, the first step is to create a new account for Petty Cash by clicking the **Company** drop-down menu and selecting **Chart of Accounts** or clicking the **Chart of Accounts** icon from the Home page. Select **Account**, select **New**, and enter the appropriate information (see Chapter 3).

To transfer the funds from the Checking account to the Petty Cash account, click the **Banking** drop-down menu, select **Write Checks**, and write a check out to cash from the Checking account into the Petty Cash account (see Chapter 4).

To record the expenditures, click the **Lists** drop-down menu, select **Chart of Accounts**, and double-click on the **Petty Cash** account to open the Account Register. Enter the date, and enter the payment amount in the Payment field. Usually petty cash expenditures are recorded in several different accounts. If so, select the **Account** from the drop-down list, click the **Splits** button at the bottom of the window, enter the amounts in the appropriate accounts, and click **Record**. The Petty Cash account is replenished by writing out a check to cash for an amount equal to the total expenditures.

Writing-Off Accounts Receivable

On occasion, the customer may refuse to pay or is unable to pay an outstanding invoice. The restaurant manager must determine how to proceed. When deciding whether or not to write-off a customer's receivable or when to write it off, the manager must consider the cost versus the benefit of the decision. After all attempts to collect have failed, it may be necessary to write-off the customer's receivable to Bad Debt Expense.

Click the **Customers** drop-down menu.

Select **Receive Payments**.

Select the customer's name from the Received From drop-down list.

Select **10700 Accounts Receivable** from the A/R Account drop-down list.

Leave the amount field at $0.00, and enter the appropriate date.

Click the **Discount & Credits** button.

Select **60500 Bad Debt Expense** from the Discount Account drop-down list.

Enter the amount for the appropriate invoice in the Amount of Discount field.

Click **Done**.

Click **Save & Close**.

QUICKBOOKS TIP

The Bad Debt expense account will automatically appear in the Discount Account field if it was previously created as a Discount Item type in the Item list.

When a customer invoice is created for a taxable item, the result is an increase in Food Sales for the amount of the items sold, an increase in Sales Tax Payable for the sales tax amount, and an increase in Accounts Receivable for the total amount of the Customer Invoice (DEBIT: Accounts Receivable;

CREDIT: Food Sales; CREDIT: Sales Tax Payable). When the Customer Invoice is written off to Bad Debt Expense using the steps outlined previously, the result is a decrease in Accounts Receivable and an increase in Bad Debt Expense for the total amount of the invoice (DEBIT: Bad Debt Expense; CREDIT: Accounts Receivable). The sales tax amount is recorded in the Bad Debt Expense account and the sales tax liability still remains in the Sales Tax Payable account. A journal entry is required to remove the sales tax amount from both accounts (DEBIT: Sales Tax Payable; CREDIT: Bad Debt Expense).

Recording Gift Certificate (Gift Card) Transactions

A gift certificate or gift card is purchased for a specified amount at one point in time, giving someone or some entity the right to receive the good or service for the purchased value at another point in time. The purchase of a gift certificate (gift card) creates a liability because the service has yet to be rendered. Based on the revenue principle, the revenue (sale) cannot be recorded until the goods have been delivered or the service has been performed; therefore, the revenue is recognized when the gift certificate (gift card) is redeemed. At the time of purchase, the cash account and a liability account are increased (DEBIT: Cash; CREDIT: Gift Certificate Outstanding). Upon redemption, the sales account increases and a liability account is decreased (DEBIT: Gift Certificate Redeemed; CREDIT: Sales).

Many software solutions are available to assist in managing the gift card process. Aroma Ristorante utilizes software from its point-of-sale provider that assists in managing gift card sales and redemptions. These transactions are recorded in QuickBooks using a journal entry (see Chapter 5, page 113). If this software is not being used, gift certificates can be recorded in QuickBooks using customer invoices.

HELPFUL TIP

Although one liability account can be used to record the purchase and redemption of gift certificates (gift cards), two different liability accounts should be created to allow management to clearly distinguish between the total amount of gift certificates (gift cards) purchased and the total amount of gift certificates (gift cards) redeemed at any given time. When the gift certificate (gift card) expires, the outstanding balance should be removed from the liability account and recorded as a sale.

Recording Gift Certificates Using Customer Invoices

Gift Certificate Outstanding (Other Charge, nontaxable item), Gift Certificate Redeemed (Other Charge, taxable item), and Gift Certificate Payment should be created in the Item List (see Chapter 3). These items are used in order to increase the Gift Certificate Outstanding account when the certificate is purchased and decrease the Gift Certificate Redeemed liability account when the certificate is redeemed. The Gift Certificate Payment item is classified as a Payment Item and is associated with the Checking account. It is used to record the increase in the cash at the time the gift certificate is purchased.

Gift Certificate Purchases

Click the **Customer Center** icon and click the **New Transactions** icon, or click the **Customer** drop-down menu.

Select **Invoices** from the drop-down list.

Select the **Customer Name** from the Customer Job drop-down list.

Enter the appropriate date.

On the first line of the invoice, select the **Gift Certificate Outstanding** item from the Item list.

Enter the amount in the amount field.

Enter the description.

On the second line of the invoice, select the **Gift Certificate Payment** item, and enter the same amount as a negative number in the amount field.

(Note: Check to make sure the total invoice amount is zero.)

Click **Save & Close**.

Gift Certificate Redemptions

Using the preceding steps, create a Customer Invoice and enter the customer name, date, and invoice number.

On the first line of the invoice, select the item from the Item drop-down list and enter the quantity.

On the next line of the Customer Invoice, select the **Gift Certificate Redeemed** item from the Item drop-down list, and enter the amount as a negative number.

Click **Save & Close**.

If the amount of the purchase, using the gift certificate, is more than the total amount of the Customer Invoice, the customer should pay the difference. If the purchase amount is less than the value of the gift certificate, the customer can be paid out with cash. If the manager decides not to disburse cash, the customer should be given an updated Customer Invoice from QuickBooks displaying the available balance. This will allow the customer to redeem the remaining amount at a later time. The unredeemed amount will remain in the liability account until it is redeemed or the certificate expires.

Recording Sales Tax Payments

In certain states and localities, restaurants are required to collect and pay sales tax. Sales tax payments are paid on a regular basis to the appropriate agency. Once the sales tax feature has been enabled through the EasyStep Interview or Sales Tax: Company Preferences (see Chapter 2) and a sales tax item and vendor have been created, QuickBooks will track sales tax transactions.

Click the **Vendors** drop-down menu.

Select **Sales Tax**.

Select **Pay Sales Tax**.

Select **10000 Checking Account** from the Pay From Account drop-down list.

Enter the appropriate dates for Check Date and the Show sales tax due through.

Verify or change the check number.

Click **Pay All Tax**.

Click **OK**.

QUICKBOOKS TIP

To avoid record keeping errors, do not record sales tax payments using the Write Checks or Pay Bills window.

Preparing the Bank Reconciliation

All bank accounts should be reconciled on a monthly basis to make sure all transactions have been recorded and to make any necessary adjustments to the accounts. Bank reconciliations allow the restaurant operator to account for all cash-related transactions and can be a valuable tool in detecting fraudulent transactions. You should print and retain a copy of the monthly bank reconciliation report and submit a copy to the auditors at the end of the year.

Click the **Banking** drop-down menu.

Select **Reconcile**.

Enter the data in the appropriate fields (see Figure 11-4).

Account:	Enter 10000 Checking Account.
Statement Date:	Enter the date on the bank statement.
Ending balance:	Enter the balance on the bank statement.
Service Charge:	Enter service charge from bank statement.
Date:	Enter the last day of the month.
Account:	Enter 60400 Bank Service Charges.
Interest Earned:	Enter interest earned from the bank statement.
Date:	Enter the last day of the month.
Account:	Enter 70200 Interest Income.

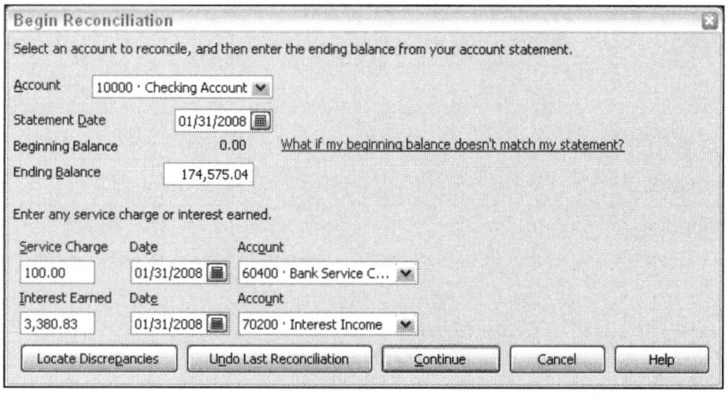

Figure 11-4.

Click **Continue**.

Place a checkmark next to all checks and deposits except for the outstanding checks and deposits that have not yet cleared the bank.

Click **Reconcile Now**.

Click **Print** to print the report at the Select Reconciliation Report window.

Chapter Review Problems

1. Identify the steps to record a Sales Tax payment in QuickBooks.

2. Assume that CMR Consulting Group filed for bankruptcy and it is unable to pay its outstanding invoice to Aroma Ristorante. What steps are required to write off the accounts receivable? How would you handle the sales tax associated with the invoice?

3. Using the information that follows, prepare the bank reconciliation for the month of February 2008. The restaurant received its monthly bank statement dated March 5, 2008.

   The following information is based on the review of the monthly bank statement:

Bank Statement Balance:		$136,093.66
Outstanding Checks:		
Date	Payee	Amount
2/29/2008	ABC Security, Inc.	$50.00
2/29/2008	Capital City Utilities, Inc.	$4,100.00
2/29/2008	STK Waste Removal, Inc.	$350.00
Deposits Not Recorded by the Bank:		
Date	Deposit Amount	
2/29/2008	$3,510.91	
Interest Earned:		$3,937.27
Bank Service Charge:		$75.00

You can find additional Review Problems at *www.wiley.com/college/murphy.*

Comprehensive Project

Access the Chapter 12 data file from the CD-ROM that accompanies this book or download the file from the web site.

This project reinforces QuickBooks functions, accounting principles, and analysis of financial statements. You will select one of the two options that follow to complete this project.

You will generate transactions for Aroma Ristorante simulating a one-month period of time using QuickBooks software. Transactions will be outlined per week, with week five being a partial week. These transactions should be recorded in QuickBooks using the steps outlined in the chapters of this book. After five weeks of transactions are recorded in QuickBooks, you will prepare financial statements, analyze the statements, and make recommendations based on your findings.

Comprehensive Project Objectives

- Perform tasks within the software that have been previously identified in this book such as
    - Creating vendor, customer, and item lists
    - Creating employee records and payroll
    - Using purchase orders, and entering and paying bills
    - Writing checks
    - Receiving payments
    - Creating monthly budget
    - Creating catering invoices
    - Creating month end inventory adjustments
    - Completing bank reconciliation
    - Recording monthly journal entries
    - Recording Adjusting journal entries
    - Generating financial statements and reports

- Identify and correct errors that have been made in the QuickBooks Company file
- Calculate and analyze ratios as a performance measure
- Make recommendations based on performance measures

Note: Refer to Aroma Ristorante's Company Profile in Chapter 1. These facts and characteristics are going to apply to both Option A and Option B.

Option A

Using the data file named Chapter 12. QBW, you will generate transactions for Aroma Ristorante, which operates in Capital City, New York. The operation opened its doors on January 1, 2008, and has been operating for two months. You will generate transactions for the month of March 2008, using the transactions outlined later in this chapter. At the end of March, the restaurant will have been operating for a full quarter. You will prepare and analyze financial statements for January, February, and March 2008 as well as the First Quarter, 2008. You will make recommendations based on the analysis of the restaurant's performance over this period of time.

Option B

Aroma Ristorante is opening its second location on March 1, 2008, in your hometown. You will create a new company file for the operation and will generate transactions for the restaurant simulating a one-month period of time. You will generate transactions for the month of March 2008 using the transactions outlined later in this chapter, and/or transactions will be provided by the instructor. On March 31, 2008, the operation will have been open for a full month. You will prepare and analyze financials for the month. You will make recommendations based on the restaurant's performance for this period of time.

All other information needed to complete the EasyStep Interview is located in Chapter 2.

After the Company Interview is complete, you should create the Chart of Accounts for a Table Service Restaurant located on page 60. The company's preferences should be identified as well (see page 21). You should also create lists, including an Item List, Employee List, Customer List, and Vendor List. These lists are provided by the instructor. Sample lists are available at *www.wiley.com/college/murphy*.

To simplify the company file set up, you can use the data file named Chapter 12B. QBW for this option. The EasyStep Interview, payroll set up, and initial lists have been created for this location in Hometown, NY.

RESTAURANT PROFILE FOR LOCATION 2 IN YOUR HOMETOWN (FOR EASYSTEP INTERVIEW)

Company Name:	Aroma Ristorante
Legal Name:	Aroma Ristorante
Tax ID Number:	88-8888888
Street Address:	99 North Avenue
City:	Your Hometown
State:	Your State
Zip:	XXXXX
Phone Number:	333-444-5555
Fax Number:	333-444-5000
Type:	Northern Italian
Hours of Operation:	Lunch and dinner served daily, Tuesday through Sunday, 11:00 a.m.–11:00 p.m. (kitchen closes at 10:00 p.m.)
Number of Seats:	156
Number of Employees:	15
Projected Check Average:	Lunch $17.50
	Dinner $30.00
Projected Weekly Covers	650
Services Provided:	Lunch and dinner menu, full service bar, wine list, take-out, off-site catering
Retail Items Sold:	Cookbooks and specialty food items, etc.
Projected Food vs. Beverage Sales:	70%, 30%
Type of Business Organization:	Corporation (Privately Held)
Operating Cycle:	Calendar Year
Business Start Date:	March 1, 2008
Employee Benefits:	Health and dental benefits start upon employment for full-time employees. Both the company and employee contribute. No retirement benefits are offered. Sick and vacation paid time off begins at 90 days of employment for full-time employees. Payroll tax calculations include tip income, and tips are disbursed daily and are not included in employee paychecks.

Transactions for Week One: March 1–March 7, 2008

March 1

1. Enter March 2008 budget figures into QuickBooks. The budget is the FY2008 – Profit & Loss by Account (see Figure 12-1).

2. Write a check to PE Real Estate for $9,500 for monthly Rent Expense for March, 2008. Use the Write Checks feature and choose the 67100 Rent Expense account to record the rent.

41410 Beverage Sales: Beer	$2,525		62465 Depreciation Expense: Computer Equipment	$1,840
41420 Beverage Sales: Wine	$11,572		62495 Depreciation Expense: Vehicle	$990
41430 Beverage Sales: Liquor	$5,681		62500 Dues and Subscriptions	$50
41440 Beverage Sales: Other	$1,262		63300 Insurance Expense	$950
42110 Catering Sales: Food	$3,600		63550 Kitchen Utensils and Tableware	$0
42120 Catering Sales: Beverage	$1,400		64000 Linen and Dry Cleaning Expense	$320
43800 Food Sales	$63,674			
43900 Sales Comps, Discounts & Promo	$(1,641)		64200 Maintenance Fee	$200
50900 Food Purchases	$21,295		64300 Meals and Entertainment	$0
51010 Beverage Purchases: Beer	$809		64700 Miscellaneous Expense	$500
51020 Beverage Purchases: Wine	$3,707		64800 Music and Entertainment	$390
51030 Beverage Purchases: Liquor	$1,820		64900 Office Supplies	$200
51040 Beverage Purchases: Other	$404		66000 Payroll Expenses	$27,828
51800 Merchant Account Fees	$3,013		66500 Postage and Delivery	$20
60200 Automobile Expense	$100		66600 Printing and Reproduction	$800
60500 Bad Debt Expense	$70		67100 Rent Expense	$9,000
61000 Business Licenses and Permits	$170		67200 Repairs and Maintenance	$170
61700 Computer and Internet Expenses	$190		67300 Start-Up Costs	$0
62410 Depreciation Expense: Furniture and Equipment	$400		67500 Supplies Expense	$700
			68100 Telephone Expense	$150
62420 Depreciation Expense: Bar Equipment	$490		68600 Utilities	$2,000
62430 Depreciation Expense: Kitchen Equipment	$4,500		70010 Retail Income	$500
			70200 Interest Income	$450
62450 Depreciation Expense: China, Silver, Glassware, Linen	$90		80300 Interest Expense	$1,000
62460 Depreciation Expense: Smallwares	$190		80600 Retail Expense	$50

Figure 12-1.

3. Using the following data, record a stock issuance on March 1, 2008. (See page 217, Recording the Stock Issuance.)

Deposit To:	10000 Checking Account
Date:	March 1, 2008
Received From:	Mrs. Sally Shareholder
From Account:	30100 Capital Stock
Memo:	Record Stock Issuance
Check No.:	101
Pmt Meth.:	Check
Amount:	$5,000

March 3

4. Create a Purchase Order for the items that follow. The order should be placed with Capital City Liquor, Wine, and Beer for delivery on March 5. Use PO No.151 (see Figure 12-2).

Item	Qty	Rate ($)	Amount ($)
Beer – Lager Bottle, Case	3	23.52	70.56
Beer – Porter Bottle, Case	2	29.28	58.56
Beer – Ale Bottle, Case	3	24.48	73.44
Cabernet, Case	3	120.25	360.75
Chardonnay, Case	2	98.64	197.28
Chianti, Case	3	102.00	306.00
Pinot Gris, Case	1	89.56	89.56
Keg – Domestic	1	65.00	65.00
Keg – Import Dark	1	103.00	103.00
Keg – Lite Domestic	1	62.00	62.00
Rum – BTL	12	10.95	131.40
Liquor Premium – BTL	12	16.50	198.00
Gin Premium – BTL	6	19.25	115.50
Gin Well – BTL	12	11.95	143.40
Vodka Premium – BTL	12	20.10	241.20
Vodka Well - BTL	12	11.25	135.00

Figure 12-2.

5. Record weekly sales via a journal entry.

Account	Debit ($)	Credit ($)
10000 Checking Account	1,995.66	
10050 Checking Account: Visa/MasterCard	3,551.33	
10075 Checking Account: Amex	78.00	
51800 Merchant Account Fees	78.72	
43900 Sales Comps, Discounts & Promo	74.98	
66080 Payroll Expenses: Employee Benefits	49.98	
25300 Gift Certificates Redeemed		
10150 Checking Account: Over Short		209.50
25200 Gift Certificates Outstanding		150.00
43800 Food Sales		3,648.80
41410 Beverage Sales: Beer		175.44
41420 Beverage Sales: Wine		674.78
41430 Beverage Sales: Liquor		418.36
41440 Beverage Sales: Other		80.97
70010 Retail Income		54.00
25500 Sales Tax Payable		416.82

March 4

6. Vegetable and fruit delivery arrives. Write a check for $84.00 to Freshest Produce, Inc. Use the Write Checks feature and choose the 50900 Food Purchases account to record the transaction.

7. A catering delivery is made to Capital City Web Design, Inc. Create Customer Invoice No.107 for the following off-site catering job. The Customer Invoice total is $402.69, and the payment terms are Due on receipt.

Quantity	Item	Price Per Item ($)
1	Coffee – Decaf	14.00
1	Coffee – Regular	14.00
8	Iced Tea	5.00

Quantity	Item	Price Per Item ($)
1	Caesar Salad Small	25.00
1	Tomato/Mozzarella Salad Small	30.00
1	Ravioli Large	100.00
1	Veal Medallions Small	100.00
1	Tiramisu	49.00

March 5

8. Capital City Liquor, Wine, and Beer made its delivery, which included the bill (No. 97521). The bill amount is $2,350.65. Receive the inventory and turn PO No. 151 into a bill. Payment terms are Net 15.

March 6

9. Create a Purchase Order to Quality Food Vendor for the items that follow. Use PO No. 152. The delivery is expected on March 7 (see Figure 12-3).

Item	Qty	Rate ($)	Amount ($)
Angel Hair Pasta	6	14.55	87.30
Asparagus Green lb	15	2.53	37.95
Baby Arugula lb	10	4.52	45.20
Balsamic Vinegar Bottle	6	7.49	44.94
Boneless Prosciutto	25	70.55	1,763.75
Butter – Unsalted lb	24	1.85	44.40
Capers – Small 32 oz jar	36	5.15	185.40
Chicken Breast Bnlss/Sknlss lb	50	3.81	190.50
Cranberry Juice gal	6	2.50	15.00
Eggs Large	12	2.86	34.32
Flour, W 50 lb	3	16.05	48.15
Garlic Fresh lb	12	.91	10.92
Herb Oregano oz	36	.39	14.04
Mahi Mahi Fillet lb	25	6.65	166.25
Milk – Heavy Cream qt	24	2.32	55.68

Figure 12-3.

Item	Qty	Rate ($)	Amount ($)
Milk gal	6	3.14	18.84
Mozzarella Cheese lb	12	2.34	28.08
OJ gal	6	3.90	23.40
Olive Oil, Extra Virgin	1	23.70	23.70
Parmesan Shredded 5# Bag	5	17.28	86.40
Parmesan Wheel	3	7.17	21.51
Pecorino Cheese lb	2	6.09	12.18
Pesto 64 oz	3	17.50	52.50
Pork Tenderloin	5	36.00	180.00
Ricotta P/Skim 15 oz	6	3.92	23.52
Romaine, Baby Case	2	9.22	18.44
Romano Cheese	1	83.45	83.45
Sea Salt 200g Bag	10	3.58	35.80
Shrimp 16–20/lb	10	6.13	61.30
Spaghetti, Pasta Case	2	13.25	26.50
Tilapia Fillet/lb	10	4.08	40.80
Tomato Crushed #10 Can	6	3.45	20.70
Tomato It Plum #10 Can	10	3.40	34.00
Veal Loin lb	10	8.75	87.50
Veal Top Cutlet lb	10	15.68	156.80
Ziti Pasta, Case	1	15.35	15.35
Aluminum Foil Rolls	2	19.00	38.00
Detergent, Case	1	60.00	60.00
Facial Tissue	1	55.00	55.00
Foil Wrap Sheets	1	36.15	36.15
Napkins – Dinner White	1	35.00	35.00
Polish	1	18.50	18.50
Surface Cleaner gal	2	8.00	16.00
Toilet Tissue	1	18.00	18.00

Figure 12-3. (continued)

March 7

10. Quality Food Vendor made its delivery, which included the bill (No. 27836). The bill amount is $4,071.22. Receive inventory and turn PO No. 152 into a bill. Payment terms are Due on receipt.

11. Create a Purchase Order for new lobby chairs. Order six chairs. The chairs are $250 each, totaling $1,500. The order should be placed with Restaurant Furniture Direct. Use PO No. 153. Prior to creating the Purchase Order, create a new record named "Lobby Chairs" for this asset in the Fixed Asset Item List.

12. Aroma Ristorante received a bill from Best Linen Service, Inc. Enter this bill into QuickBooks. Use the Enter Bills function and choose the 64000 Linen and Dry Cleaning Expense account to record the bill (see Figure 12-4).

Invoice

Best Linen Service, Inc.

59 Worthwent Street
Your Hometown, Your State XXXXX or Capital City, NY 10001

Date:	March 7, 2008
Invoice #:	27519
Customer ID:	1022

To: Aroma Ristorante

                  Capital City, NY 11100 or Your Hometown, Your State XXXXX

Salesperson	Job	Payment Terms		Due Date
Jeffery Tillman		Due upon receipt		Upon Receipt

Qty	Description	Unit Price	Line Total
	Weekly Linen Rental		$ 175.00

Subtotal	$	175.00
Sales Tax		
Total	**$**	**175.00**

Make all checks payable to Best Linen Service, Inc.
Thank you for your business!

Figure 12-4.

13. Pay the following bill to Quality Food Vendor. Use the Pay Bills function to record the payment.

Invoice No. 27836	Quality Food Vendor	$4,071.22

Transactions for Week Two: March 8–March 14, 2008

March 10

14. Bankers Association of Capital City booked an off-site Catering Event for 5/3/2008. Create a Sales Receipt for a $500 non-refundable advance deposit from this customer. The check is number 2956.

15. Create a Purchase Order for 21 boxes of flatware. Each box of flatware costs $50, totaling $1,050. The order should be placed with Glass and Silver Source Corp. Use PO No. 128. Prior to creating the Purchase Order, create a new record, named "Flatware," for this asset in the Fixed Asset Item List.

16. Record weekly sales via a journal entry.

Account	Debit ($)	Credit ($)
10000 Checking Account	4,821.65	
10500 Checking Account: Visa/MasterCard	11,062.31	
10075 Checking Account: Amex	759.03	
51800 Merchant Account Fees	245.22	
43900 Sales Comps, Discounts & Promo	233.55	
66080 Payroll Expenses: Employee Benefits	155.70	
25300 Gift Certificates Redeemed	150.00	
10150 Checking Account: Over Short		196.54
25200 Gift Certificates Outstanding		250.00
43800 Food Sales		11,365.92
41410 Beverage Sales: Beer		546.50
41420 Beverage Sales: Wine		2,101.92
41430 Beverage Sales: Liquor		1,303.19
41440 Beverage Sales: Other		252.23
70010 Retail Income		117.00
25500 Sales Tax Payable		1,294.16

March 11

17. Write a check to Bargain Office Supplies for $126.95. Office supplies purchased include copy paper, toner, folders, envelopes, and pens. Use the Write Checks feature and choose the 64900 Office Supplies Expense account to record the transaction.

March 13

18. Six lobby chairs from Restaurant Furniture Direct were received with the bill included (No. 00219561). The bill amount is $1,500. Turn PO No. 153 into a bill. Payment terms are Net 15.

19. Flatware from Glass and Silver Source Corp. was received with the bill included (No. 56329824). The bill amount is $1,050. Turn PO No. 128 into a bill. Payment terms are 2% 10 Net 30.

20. Create a Purchase Order to Quality Food Vendor for the items that follow. Use PO No. 155. The delivery is expected on March 14 (see Figure 12-5).

Item	Qty	Rate ($)	Amount ($)
Angel Hair Pasta	5	14.55	72.75
Asparagus Green lb	10	2.53	25.30
Baby Arugula lb	5	4.52	22.60
Balsamic Vinegar Bottle	6	7.49	44.94
Boneless Prosciutto	10	70.55	705.50
Butter – Unsalted lb	5	1.85	9.25
Capers – Small 32 oz jar	6	5.15	30.90
Chicken Breast Bnlss/Sknlss lb	20	3.81	76.20
Cranberry Juice gal	24	2.50	60.00
Eggs Large	3	2.86	8.58
Flour, W 50 lb	2	16.05	32.10
Garlic Fresh lb	10	.91	9.10
Herb Oregano oz	32	.39	12.48
Mahi Mahi Fillet lb	25	6.65	166.25
Milk – Heavy Cream qt	24	2.32	55.68
Milk gal	15	3.14	47.10
Mozzarella Cheese lb	10	2.34	23.40

Figure 12-5.

Item	Qty	Rate ($)	Amount ($)
OJ gal	24	3.90	93.60
Olive Oil, Extra Virgin	2	23.70	47.40
Parmesan Shredded 5# Bag	5	17.28	86.40
Parmesan Wheel	3	7.17	21.51
Pecorino Cheese lb	3	6.09	18.27
Pesto 64 oz	12	17.50	210.00
Pork Tenderloin	8	36.00	288.00
Ricotta P/Skim 15 oz	6	3.92	23.52
Romaine, Baby, Case	5	9.22	46.10
Romano Cheese	5	83.45	417.25
Sea Salt 200g Bag	10	3.58	35.80
Shrimp 16–20/lb	60	6.13	367.80
Spaghetti, Pasta Case	6	13.25	79.50
Tilapia Fillet lb	50	4.08	204.00
Tomato Crushed #10 Can	24	3.45	82.80
Tomato lt Plum #10 Can	24	3.40	81.60
Veal Loin lb	50	8.75	437.50
Veal Top Cutlet lb	50	15.68	784.00
Ziti Pasta, Case	5	15.35	76.75
Paper Towel	1	24.85	24.85
Sanitizing Tablets	3	24.00	72.00
Steel Wool Heavy Weight	1	9.00	9.00

Figure 12-5.   (continued)

21. Write a check to the U.S. Postal Service for postage and delivery for the amount of $97.47. Use the Write Checks feature and choose the 66500 Postage and Delivery Expense account to record the transaction.

March 14

22. Vegetable and fruit delivery arrives. Write a check for $107.00 to Freshest Produce, Inc. Use the Write Checks feature and choose the 50900 Food Purchases account to record the transaction.

23. Quality Food Vendor made its delivery, which included the bill (No. 28610). The bill amount is $4,909.78. Receive inventory and turn PO No. 155 into a bill. Payment terms are Due on receipt.

24. Aroma Ristorante received a bill from Best Linen Service, Inc. (see Figure 12-6). Enter this bill into QuickBooks. Use the Enter Bills function and choose the 64000 Linen and Dry Cleaning Expense account to record the bill.

Invoice

Best Linen Service, Inc.

59 Worthwent Street
Your Hometown, Your State XXXXX or Capital City, NY 10001

Date:	March 14, 2008
Invoice #:	27999
Customer ID:	1022

To: Aroma Ristorante

Capital City, NY 11100 or Your Hometown, Your State XXXXX

Salesperson	Job	Payment Terms	Due Date
Jeffery Tillman		Due upon receipt	Upon Receipt

Qty	Description	Unit Price	Line Total
	Weekly Linen Rental		$ 175.00
		Subtotal	$ 175.00
		Sales Tax	
		Total	**$ 175.00**

Make all checks payable to Best Linen Service, Inc.
Thank you for your business!

Figure 12-6.

25. Aroma Ristorane received a bill from Cool Waves Satellite, Inc. (see Figure 12-7). Enter this bill into QuickBooks. Use the Enter Bills function and choose the 64800 Music and Entertainment Expense account to record the bill.

COOL WAVES SATELLITE, INC.

INVOICE

PO Box 2275
Hometown, PA 66666

INVOICE NO.	86523456
DATE	March 14, 2008

TO   Aroma Ristorante
                Capital City, NY 11100 or Your Hometown, Your State XXXXX

PAYMENT TERMS	DUE DATE
1% 10 Net 30	April 13,2008

Service	DESCRIPTION		LINE TOTAL
3/7/2008 – 4/7/2008	Satellite Radio Service		$ 30.00
		SUBTOTAL	$ 30.00
		SALES TAX	
		TOTAL	$ **30.00**

Figure 12-7.

26. Pay the following bills to Glass and Silver Source Corp., Quality Food Vendor, and Bob's Snow Removal. Use the Pay Bills function to record the payments.

Glass and Silver Source Corp.	Invoice No. 56329824	$1,050.00
Quality Food Vendor	Invoice No. 28610	$4,909.78
Bob's Snow Removal	Invoice No. 829	$1,100.00

Transactions for Week Three: March 15–March 21, 2008

March 15

27. Record payroll for March 1 – March 15 using the information that follows (see Figures 12-8 and 12-9).

28. Aroma Ristorante needs to get ready for St. Patrick's Day! Create a Purchase Order to Capital City Liquor, Wine, and Beer for the items that follow. Use PO No. 157 and request a March 17th delivery (see Figure 12-10).

29. Aroma Ristorante received a bill from ATC Phone and Cable Company (see Figure 12-11). Enter this bill into QuickBooks. Use the Enter Bills function and choose the 68100 Telephone Expense and 64800 Music and Entertainment Expense accounts to record the bill.

30. Aroma Ristorante received a bill from ABC Security, Inc. (see Figure 12-12). Enter this bill into QuickBooks. Use the Enter Bills function and choose the 64200 Maintenance Fee Expense account to record the bill.

March 16

31. Aroma Ristorante received a bill from Capital City News and Guide for an advertisement (see Figure 12-13). Enter this bill into QuickBooks. Use the Enter Bills function and choose the 60000 Advertising and Promotion Expense account to record the bill.

March 17

32. Aroma Ristorante would like to order a margarita machine. Create a Purchase Order to Restaurant World, Inc. The cost of the margarita machine is $2,500. Use PO No. 156. Prior to creating the Purchase Order, create a new record named "Margarita Machine" for this asset in the Fixed Asset Item List.

33. Capital City Liquor, Wine, and Beer made their delivery with the bill (No. 99002). The bill amount is $3,020.21. Receive inventory and turn PO No. 157 into a bill. Payment terms are Net 15.

March 1–March 15 Payperiod

First Name	Last Name	Position	Filing Status	Allowances	Salary or Hourly Rate	Regular Hours Worked 3/1/2008–3/15/2008	OT Hours Worked 3/1/2008–3/15/2008	Regular Hours Pay	OT Hours Pay
Peter	Petrov	Manager	Married	2	$45,000	80	N/A	$1,875.00	
Ji	Hiromi	Host	Single	0	$12.00	79	0	$948.00	
Carlos	Garcia	Bartender	Married	1	$12.00	79.5	0	$954.00	
Rosa	Gomez	Service & Bus Staff	Single	0	$8.00	18.5	0	$148.00	
Mary	Hoffman	Service & Bus Staff	Single	0	$8.00	80	2	$640.00	$24.00
Betthany	Stewart	Service & Bus Staff	Single	1	$8.00	22.75	0	$182.00	
Jason	Robertson	Chef	Married	3	$42,000	80	N/A	$1,750.00	
Amy	Jameson	Kitchen Staff	Married	1	$13.50	76.75	0	$1,036.13	
Deborah	Smith	Kitchen Staff	Single	0	$13.50	75	0	$1,012.50	
Amy	Yang	Kitchen Staff	Married	3	$13.50	16.5	0	$222.75	
Benjamin	Young	Kitchen Staff	Single	1	$13.50	21.75	0	$293.63	
Julia	Rodriquez	Expeditor	Single	0	$11.00	65	0	$715.00	
George	Watson	Dishwasher	Single	1	$10.00	79	0	$790.00	

Figure 12-8.

Tips	Total Gross Pay	Federal Income Tax	State Income Tax	Social Security 6.2%	Medicare 1.45%	Health (Employee)	Dental (Employee)	Extra Withholding	Net Pay	Net Pay No Tips
	$1,875.00	$156.00	$84.88	$116.25	$27.19	$25.00	$7.00	$0.00	$1,458.68	$1,458.68
	$948.00	$110.00	$30.30	$58.78	$13.75	$25.00	$7.00	$0.00	$703.18	$703.18
$645.94	$1,599.94	$135.00	$68.89	$99.20	$23.20	$25.00	$7.00	$20.00	$1,221.65	$575.71
$159.75	$307.75	$19.00	$0.80	$19.08	$4.46			$0.00	$264.41	$104.66
$678.95	$1,342.95	$170.00	$56.00	$83.26	$19.47	$25.00	$7.00	$15.00	$967.21	$288.26
$210.25	$392.25	$14.00	$2.30	$24.32	$5.69			$0.00	$345.94	$135.69
	$1,750.00	$117.00	$73.46	$108.50	$25.38	$25.00	$7.00	$0.00	$1,393.67	$1,393.67
	$1,036.13	$56.00	$31.30	$64.24	$15.02	$25.00	$7.00	$0.00	$837.56	$837.56
	$1,012.50	$119.00	$33.80	$62.78	$14.68	$25.00	$7.00	$0.00	$750.24	$750.24
	$222.75	$0.00	$0.00	$13.81	$3.23			$0.00	$205.71	$205.71
	$293.63	$4.00	$0.00	$18.20	$4.26			$0.00	$267.16	$267.16
	$715.00	$74.00	$17.20	$44.33	$10.37			$0.00	$569.10	$569.10
	$790.00	$65.00	$18.90	$48.98	$11.46	$25.00	$7.00	$0.00	$613.67	$613.67

March 1–March 15 Pay Period—Employer Payroll Taxes

First Name	Last Name	Total Gross Pay	Social Security 6.2%	Medicare 1.45%	FUI .008%	SUI .054%	Health (Company)	Dental (Company)
Peter	Petrov	$1,875.00	$116.25	$27.19	$15.00	$101.25	$75.00	$25.00
Ji	Hiromi	$948.00	$58.78	$13.75	$7.58	$51.19	$75.00	$25.00
Carlos	Garcia	$1,599.94	$99.20	$23.20	$12.80	$86.40	$75.00	$25.00
Rosa	Gomez	$307.75	$19.08	$4.46	$2.46	$16.62		
Mary	Hoffman	$1,342.95	$83.26	$19.47	$10.74	$72.52	$75.00	$25.00
Betthany	Stewart	$392.25	$24.32	$5.69	$3.14	$21.18		
Jason	Robertson	$1,750.00	$108.50	$25.38	$14.00	$94.50	$75.00	$25.00
Amy	Jameson	$1,036.13	$64.24	$15.02	$8.29	$55.95	$75.00	$25.00
Deborah	Smith	$1,012.50	$62.78	$14.68	$8.10	$54.68	$75.00	$25.00
Amy	Yang	$222.75	$13.81	$3.23	$1.78	$12.03		
Benjamin	Young	$293.63	$18.20	$4.26	$2.35	$15.86		
Julia	Rodriquez	$715.00	$44.33	$10.37	$5.72	$38.61		
George	Watson	$790.00	$48.98	$11.46	$6.32	$42.66	$75.00	$25.00

Figure 12-9.

Item	Qty	Rate	Amount
Beer – Lager Bottle, Case	3	23.52	70.56
Beer – Porter Bottle, Case	2	29.28	58.56
Beer – Ale Bottle, Case	2	24.48	48.96
Cabernet, Case	5	120.25	601.25
Chardonnay, Case	3	98.64	295.92
Chianti, Case	4	102.00	408.00
Pinot Gris, Case	1	89.56	89.56
Keg – Domestic	1	65.00	65.00
Keg – Import Dark	1	103.00	103.00
Keg – Lite Domestic	1	62.00	62.00
Rum – BTL	18	10.95	197.10
Liquor Premium – BTL	12	16.50	198.00
Gin Premium – BTL	12	19.25	231.00
Gin Well – BTL	18	11.95	215.10
Vodka Premium – BTL	12	20.10	241.20
Vodka Well – BTL	12	11.25	135.00

Figure 12-10.

ATC Phone and Cable Company   INVOICE

PO Box 5600   **DATE:**   March 15, 2008
Capital City, NY 11113   **INVOICE #**   865093
888-800-8888   *2%10 Net 30*

Bill To:
Aroma Ristorante
Capital City, NY 11100 or Your Hometown, Your State XXXXX

DESCRIPTION	AMOUNT
Phone Service Business Line	$ 195.00
Cable TV Service including Sports Pack	150.00
TOTAL	$ 345.00

Make all checks payable to **ATC Phone and Cable Company**
If you have any questions concerning this invoice, contact Customer Service 999-800-8888

THANK YOU FOR YOUR BUSINESS!

Figure 12-11.

INVOICE

ABC Security, Inc.

222 Spring Street
Capital City, NY 11112 or Your Hometown, Your State XXXXX

INVOICE NO.   2154833
DATE   March 15, 2008

TO   Aroma Ristorante
            5000 Capital Park
            Capital City, NY 11100 or Your Hometown, Your State XXXXX

PAYMENT TERMS	DUE DATE
Net 15	3/30/08

DESCRIPTION		UNIT PRICE	LINE TOTAL
Security System Fee for 3/15/2008–4/15/2008		$ 50.00	$ 50.00
SUBTOTAL	$ 50.00		
SALES TAX			
TOTAL	$ **50.00**		

Make all checks payable to ABC Security, Inc.
THANK YOU FOR YOUR BUSINESS!

Figure 12-12.

Capital City News and Guide INVOICE

PO Box 990   **DATE:**   March 16, 2008
Capital City, NY 11112   **INVOICE #**   54229732
                                                              1%10 Net 30

Bill To:
Aroma Ristorante
Capital City, NY 11100 or Your Hometown, Your State XXXXX

DESCRIPTION	AMOUNT
Monthly 1/2 Page Advertisement in Capital City News and Guide	$ 350.00
TOTAL	$ 350.00

Make all checks payable to Capital City News and Guide
If you have any questions concerning this invoice, contact Customer Service 999-555-5200

THANK YOU FOR YOUR BUSINESS!

Figure 12-13.

34. Mary Hoffman lost her paycheck from the previous pay period (March 1 through March 15, 2008). Void the original paycheck and reissue a new paycheck. (See page 146.)

35. Record the weekly sales via a journal entry.

Account	Debit ($)	Credit ($)
10000 Checking Account	4,286.58	
10050 Checking Account: Visa/MasterCard	9,601.55	
10075 Checking Account: Amex	658.80	
51800 Merchant Account Fees	212.84	
43900 Sales Comps, Discounts & Promo	202.71	
66080 Payroll Expenses: Employee Benefits	135.14	
25300 Gift Certificates Redeemed		
10150 Checking Account: Over Short		209.70
25200 Gift Certificates Outstanding		125.00
43800 Food Sales		9,865.07
41410 Beverage Sales: Beer		474.33
41420 Beverage Sales: Wine		1,824.36
41430 Beverage Sales: Liquor		1,131.11
41440 Beverage Sales: Other		218.92
70010 Retail Income		124.00
25500 Sales Tax Payable		1,125.13

March 18

36. A new customer, Smith, Brothers, and Associates, requests an estimate for an off-site catering job on March 25. Create a new Customer record and an Estimate.

Customer Information:		
Smith, Peterson, and Associates		
James Smith		
6767 Capital City Drive		
Capital City, NY 11114		
555-333-0000		
Estimate Information:		
1	Caesar Salad Large	$50.00
1	Tomato/Mozzarella Salad Small	$30.00
1	Penne Large	$80.00
1	Rosemary Chicken Large	$120.00
6	Iced Tea	@ $5.00 Each

37. Create a Purchase Order to Capital City Beverages, Inc., for the items that follow. Use PO No. 150. The delivery is expected on March 19.

Quantity	Item	Amount
2	Diet Soda–Box	@$46.00 Each
2	Soda–Box	@$46.00 Each
3	Club Soda	@$12.00 Each

March 19

38. The margarita machine is delivered with the bill (No. 002659883). The bill is $2,500 from Restaurant World, Inc. Turn PO No. 156 into a bill. Payment terms are Net 15.

39. Capital City Beverages, Inc. made its delivery with the bill (#65329). The bill is for $220.00. Receive inventory and turn PO No. 150 into a bill. Payment terms are Net 15.

March 20

40. Create a Purchase Order to Quality Food Vendor for the items that follow. Use PO No. 159. The delivery is expected on March 21 (see Figure 12-14).

Item	Qty	Rate ($)	Amount ($)
Angel Hair Pasta	2	14.55	29.10
Asparagus Green lb	15	2.53	37.95
Baby Arugula lb	10	4.52	45.20
Balsamic Vinegar Bottle	6	7.49	44.94
Boneless Prosciutto	15	70.55	1,058.25
Butter – Unsalted lb	12	1.85	22.20
Capers – Small 32 oz jar	12	5.15	61.80
Chicken Breast Bnlss/Sknlss lb	25	3.81	95.25
Cranberry Juice gal	6	2.50	15.00
Eggs Large	12	2.86	34.32
Flour, W 50 lb	3	16.05	48.15
Garlic Fresh lb	20	.91	18.20
Herb Oregano oz	36	.39	14.04
Mahi Mahi Fillet lb	20	6.65	133.00

Figure 12-14.

Item	Qty	Rate ($)	Amount ($)
Milk – Heavy Cream qt	24	2.32	55.68
Milk gal	12	3.14	37.68
Mozzarella Cheese lb	25	2.34	58.50
OJ gal	12	3.90	46.80
Olive Oil, Extra Virgin	2	23.70	47.40
Parmesan Shredded 5# Bag	5	17.28	86.40
Parmesan Wheel	2	7.17	14.34
Pecorino Cheese lb	5	6.09	30.45
Pesto 64 oz	12	17.50	210.00
Pork Tenderloin	10	36.00	360.00
Ricotta P/Skim 15 oz	12	3.92	47.04
Romaine, Baby, Case	5	9.22	46.10
Romano Cheese	1	83.45	83.45
Sea Salt 200 Bag	20	3.58	71.60
Shrimp 16–20/lb	10	6.13	61.30
Spaghetti, Case	3	13.25	39.75
Tilapia Fillet lb	10	4.08	40.80
Tomato Crushed #10 Can	12	3.45	41.40
Tomato It Plum #10 Can	12	3.40	40.80
Veal Loin lb	1	8.75	8.75
Veal Top Cutlet lb	10	15.68	156.80
Ziti Pasta, Case	2	15.35	30.70
Detergent, Case	3	60.00	180.00
Detergent, Glass, Case	2	34.00	68.00
Foam Containers	1	26.75	26.75
Foil Wrap Sheets	1	36.15	36.15
Napkins – Dinner White	2	35.00	70.00
Sanitizing Tablets	2	24.00	48.00
Sponge with Scrubber	1	4.00	4.00
Surface Cleaner gal	2	8.00	16.00
Toilet Tissue	1	18.00	18.00

Figure 12-14.   (continued)

March 21

41. A vegetable and fruit delivery arrives. Write a check for $72.00 to Freshest Produce, Inc. Use the Write Checks feature and choose the 50900 Food Purchases account to record the transaction.

42. Quality Food Vendor made its delivery, which included the bill (No. 29618). The bill amount is $3740.04. Receive inventory and turn PO No. 159 into a bill. Payment terms are Due on receipt.

43. Aroma Ristorante received a bill from Best Linen Service, Inc. Enter this bill into QuickBooks. Use the Enter Bills function and choose the 64000 Linen and Dry Cleaning Expense account to record the bill (see Figure 12-15).

Invoice

Best Linen Service, Inc.
59 Worthwent Street
Your Hometown, Your State XXXXX or Capital City, NY 10001

Date:	March 21, 2008
Invoice #:	28297
Customer ID:	1022

To:
Aroma Ristorante
Capital City, NY 11100 or Your Hometown, Your State XXXXX

Salesperson	Job	Payment Terms		Due Date
Jeffery Tillman		Due upon receipt		Upon Receipt

Qty	Description	Unit Price	Line Total
	Weekly Linen Rental		$ 175.00
		Subtotal	$ 175.00
		Sales Tax	
		Total	$ 175.00

Make all checks payable to Best Linen Service, Inc.
Thank you for your business!

Figure 12-15.

44. Pay the bills to the vendors listed here. Use Pay Bills to record the payments.

ABC Security, Inc.	Invoice No. 2154833	$50.00
Best Linen Service, Inc.	Invoice No. 28297 and No. 38961	$350.00
Capital City Utilities, Inc.	Invoice No. 00367211	$3,850.00
Lightning Speed Internet Service	Invoice No. 182790	$56.00
STK Waste Removal, Inc.	Invoice No. 8713169	$350.00
Restaurant Furniture Direct	Invoice No. 00219561	$1,500.00
Restaurant World, Inc.	Invoice No. 002659883	$2,500.00
Capital City Liquor, Wine, and Beer	Invoice No. 97521	$2,350.65

Transactions for Week Four: March 22–March 28, 2008

March 22

45. Create a Customer Invoice No. 104 using the information below to CMR Consulting Group for an off-site catering job. The amount of the invoice is $270.63. Payment terms are Due on receipt.

Quantity	Item	Amount
1	Caesar Salad Large	$50.00
1	Penne Large	$80.00
1	Rosemary Chicken Large	$120.00

March 24

46. Record weekly sales via a journal entry.

Account	Debit ($)	Credit ($)
10000 Checking Account	3,892.09	
10050 Checking Account: Visa/Mastercard	8,688.63	
10075 Checking Account: Amex	596.16	
51800 Merchant Account Fees	192.61	
43900 Sales Comps, Discounts & Promo	183.43	
66080 Payroll Expenses: Employee Benefits	122.29	
25300 Gift Certificates Redeemed		
Account	**Debit ($)**	**Credit ($)**
10150 Checking Account: Over Short		188.92

25200 Gift Certificates Outstanding	150.00
43800 Food Sales	8,927.10
41410 Beverage Sales: Beer	429.23
41420 Beverage Sales: Wine	1,650.90
41430 Beverage Sales: Liquor	1,023.56
41440 Beverage Sales: Other	198.11
70010 Retail Income	91.00
25500 Sales Tax Payable	1,016.39

March 25

47. A catering delivery is made today. Turn the Smith, Brothers, and Associate's Estimate into a Customer Invoice (No. 110). The invoice amount of $335.58. Payment terms are Due on receipt.

Quantity	Item	Amount
1	Caesar Salad Large	$50.00
1	Tomato/Mozzarella Salad Small	$30.00
1	Penne Large	$80.00
1	Rosemary Chicken Large	$120.00
6	Iced Tea Pitchers	@ $5.00 Each

March 26

48. A check from CMR Consulting Group is received in the mail. The check (No. 100275) is for the amount of $270.63. Record the Customer Payment in QuickBooks. The payment should be applied to CMR Consulting Group's invoice No. 104.

March 27

49. Best Marketing, Inc., books an off-site catering event for March 29. Using the information shown in Figure 12-16, create an Estimate and a Sales Receipt for the $1,000 non-refundable advance deposit received (check No. 100275).

50. Write a check to the U.S. Postal Service for postage and delivery for the amount of $58.65. Use the Write Checks feature and choose the 66500 Postage and Delivery Expense account to record the transaction.

Quantity	Item	Description	Amount ($)
3	Caesar Salad Large	Caesar Salad Full Pan	50.00
2	Tomato/Mozzarella Sala…	Tomato/Mozzarella Salad Full Pan	60.00
2	Penne Large	Penne Full Pan	80.00
2	Ravioli Large	Four Cheese Ravioli Full Pan	100.00
3	Rosemary Chicken Large	Rosemany Chicken Full Pan	120.00
2	Veal Medallions Large	Veal Medallions Full Pan	200.00
2	Coffee – Decaf	Coffee Urn – Decaf	14.00
2	Coffee – Regular	Coffee Urn – Regular	14.00
15	Red Wine	Bottle House Chianti	15.00
7	White Wine	Bottle House White	12.00
6	Cheesecake	Cheesecake Full Cake	39.00
2	Tiramisu	Tiramisu Full Cake	49.00
1	Service Fee		200.00

Figure 12-16.

51. Create a Purchase Order to Quality Food Vendor for the items that follow. Use PO No. 160. The delivery is expected on March 28 (see Figure 12-17).

March 28

52. Freshest Produce, Inc. makes a delivery. Products include vegetables and fruit. Write a check for $119.00. Use the Write Checks feature and choose the 50900 Food Purchases account to record the transaction.

Item	Qty	Rate ($)	Amount ($)
Angel Hair Pasta	6	14.55	87.30
Asparagus Green lb	10	2.53	25.30
Baby Arugula lb	10	4.52	45.20
Balsamic Vinegar Bottle	6	7.49	449.4
Boneless Prosciutto	2	70.55	141.10
Butter – Unsalted lb	20	1.85	37.00
Capers – Small 32 oz jar	12	5.15	61.80
Chicken Breast Bnlss/Sknlss lb	50	3.81	190.50
Cranberry Juice gal	6	2.50	15.00
Eggs Large	12	2.86	34.32
Flour, W 50 lb	4	16.05	64.20
Garlic Fresh lb	25	.91	22.75

Figure 12-17.

Item	Qty	Rate ($)	Amount ($)
Herb Oregano oz	36	.39	14.04
Mahi Mahi Fillet lb	25	6.65	166.25
Milk – Heavy Cream qt	12	2.32	27.84
Milk gal	6	3.14	18.84
Mozzarella Cheese lb	20	2.34	46.80
OJ gal	3	3.90	11.70
Olive Oil, Extra Virgin	4	23.70	94.80
Parmesan Shredded 5# Bag	15	17.28	259.20
Parmesan Wheel	1	7.17	7.17
Pecorino Cheese lb	10	6.09	60.90
Pesto 64 oz	12	17.50	210.00
Pork Tenderloin	2	36.00	72.00
Ricotta P/Skim 15 oz	6	3.92	23.52
Romaine, Baby, Case	5	9.22	46.10
Romano Cheese	1	83.45	83.45
Sea Salt 2002g Bag	2	3.58	7.16
Shrimp 16–20/lb	10	6.13	61.30
Spaghetti, Case	6	13.25	79.50
Tilapia Fillet lb	25	4.08	102.00
Tomato Crushed #10 Can	12	3.45	41.40
Tomato It Plum #10 Can	6	3.40	20.40
Veal Loin lb	25	8.75	218.75
Veal Top Cutlet lb	25	15.68	392.00
Ziti Pasta, Case	1	15.35	15.35
Aluminum Foil Rolls	1	19.00	19.00
Detergent, Case	1	60.00	60.00
Foam Containers	1	26.75	26.75
Facial Tissue	1	55.00	55.00
Foil Wrap Sheets	1	36.15	36.15
Napkins – Dinner White	1	35.00	35.00
Polish	1	18.50	18.50
Sanitizing Tablets	1	24.00	24.00
Sponge Cleaner/Sanitizer	1	20.00	20.00
Sponge with Scrubber	1	4.00	4.00
Toilet Tissue	1	18.00	18.00

Figure 12-17.   (continued)

53. Quality Food Vendor made its delivery, which included the bill (No. 29999) for $3,166.28. Receive inventory and turn PO No. 160 into a bill. Payment terms are Due on receipt.

54. Pay the following bill to Quality Food Vendor. Use Pay Bills function to record the payment.

Quality Food Vendor	Invoice No. 29999	$3,166.28

Transactions for Week Five: March 29–March 31, 2008

March 29

55. Two new employees are hired. Their personal information, payroll and compensation information, and employment information are as follows.

Name	Maria Alvarez
Street Address	6523 School House Road
City	Your Hometown or Capital City
State	Your State or New York
Zip Code	XXXXX or 11112
Phone Number	XXX-XXX-XXXX or 555-999-9876
Social Security Number	000-55-2222
Position	Service & Bus Staff
Rate of Pay	$8.00 per Hour
Overtime Rate	$12.00 per Hour
Pay Period	Semimonthly
Federal and State Filing Status	Single
Federal and State Allowances	0
Dental Insurance (company paid)	$25 per paycheck
Health Insurance (company paid)	$75 per paycheck
Dental Insurance (taxable)	$7 per paycheck
Health Insurance (taxable)	$25 per paycheck
Hire Date	4/1/2008

Name	Martin Coleman
Street Address	22 D Street
City	Your Hometown or Capital City
State	Your State or New York
Zip Code	XXXXX or 11112
Phone Number	XXX-XXX-XXXX or 555-666-2626
Social Security Number	999-88-3322
Position	Kitchen Staff
Rate of Pay	$13.50 per Hour
Overtime Rate	$20.25 per Hour
Pay Period	Semimonthly
Federal and State Filing Status	Single
Federal and State Allowances	1
Dental Insurance (company paid)	$25 per paycheck
Health Insurance (company paid)	$75 per paycheck
Dental Insurance (taxable)	$7 per paycheck
Health Insurance (taxable)	$25 per paycheck
Hire Date	4/1/2008

56. A Catering Delivery is made today. Turn the Best Marketing Inc.'s Estimate into a Customer Invoice (No. 108). The invoice amount is $2,475.68. Payment terms are Due on receipt. Remember to apply their advance deposit of $1,000 to the invoice (see Figure 12-18).

Quantity	Item	Description	Amount ($)
3	Caesar Salad Large	Caesar Salad Full Pan	50.00
2	Tomato/Mozzarella Sala...	Tomato/Mozzarella Salad Full Pan	60.00
2	Penne Large	Penne Full Pan	80.00
2	Ravioli Large	Four Cheese ravioli Full Pan	100.00
3	Rosemary Chicken Large	Rosemary Chicken Full Pan	120.00
2	Veal Medallions Large	Veal Medallions Full Pan	200.00
2	Coffee – Decaf	Coffee Urn – Decaf	14.00
2	Coffee – Regular	Coffee Urn – Regular	14.00
15	Red Wine	Bottle House Chianti	15.00
7	White Wine	Bottle House White	12.00
6	Cheesecake	Cheesecake Full Cake	39.00
2	Tiramisu	Tiramisu Full Pan	49.00
1	Service Fee		200.00

Figure 12-18.

March 31

57. Using the following data, record a dividend distribution on March 31, 2008.

Bank Account:	10000 Checking Account
Pay to the Order of:	Mrs. Sally Shareholder
No.	207
Date:	March 31, 2008
Amount:	$1,000
Memo:	Distribute Dividend to Shareholder
Account:	30200 Dividends Paid

58. Aroma Ristorante received a bill from Lightning Speed Internet Service (see Figure 12-19). Enter this bill into QuickBooks. Use the Enter Bills function and choose the 61700 Computer and Internet Expenses account to record the bill.

Invoice

3/31/2008

Lightning Speed Internet Service
PO Box 6767
Capital City, NY 11150

Payment Terms:
2% 10 Net 3

To: Aroma Ristorante,
5000 Capital Park, Capital City, NY 11100
or Your Hometown, Your State, XXXXX

Internet Service for March 2008	**$56.00**
Total Due	**$56.00**

Thank you for your business!

Figure 12-19.

INVOICE Bob's Snow Removal PO Box 2632 Capital City, NY 12222		3/31/2008 Invoice 961
3/5/2008	Snow Removal	150.00
3/5/2008	Snow Removal	150.00
3/6/2008	Snow Removal	150.00
3/10/2008	Snow Removal	150.00
3/11/2008	Salt Only	55.00
Total Due: **$655.00** **Make Checks** **Payable to Bob's** **Snow Removal**		

Figure 12-20.

59. Write a check to Main Street Auto for $395.25 for gas, oil, repairs, and maintenance on the catering van for 3/1/2008–3/31/2008. Use the Write Checks feature and choose the 60200 Automobile Expense account to record the transaction.

60. Amy Jameson is working her last shift on March 31, 2008. In this employee's record, record the release date of 4/1/2008.

61. Aroma Ristorante received a bill from Bob's Snow Removal (see Figure 12-20). Enter this bill into QuickBooks. Use the Enter Bills function and choose the 64700 Miscellaneous Expense Account to record the bill.

62. Record weekly sales via a journal entry.

Account	Debit ($)	Credit ($)
10000 Checking Account	4,251.01	
10050 Checking Account: Visa/Mastercard	10,206.01	
10075 Checking Account: Amex	700.27	
51800 Merchant Account Fees	226.24	
43900 Sales Comps, Discounts & Promo	215.47	
66080 Payroll Expenses: Employee Benefits	143.65	
25300 Gift Certificates Redeemed	200.00	

Account	Debit ($)	Credit ($)
10150 Checking Account: Over Short		176.12
25200 Gift Certificates Outstanding		100.00
43800 Food Sales		10,486.11
41410 Beverage Sales: Beer		504.20
41420 Beverage Sales: Wine		1,939.21
41430 Beverage Sales: Liquor		1,202.31
41440 Beverage Sales: Other		232.71
70010 Retail Income		108.00
25500 Sales Tax Payable		1,193.99

63. Aroma Ristorante received a bill from Capital City Utilities, Inc. (see Figure 12-21). Enter this bill into QuickBooks. Use the Enter Bills function and choose the 68600 Utilities Expense account to record the bill.

Capital City Utilities, Inc.   INVOICE

PO Box 1900   **DATE:**   March 31, 2008
Capital City, NY 11012   **INVOICE #**   497586
                                                               2% 10 Net 30

Bill To:
Aroma Ristorante
Capital City, NY 11100 or Your Hometown, Your State XXXXX

DESCRIPTION		AMOUNT
Gas, Electric and Water for 3/1/3008-3/31/2008	$	3,450.00
	TOTAL $	3,450.00

Make all checks payable to Capital City Utilities, Inc.
If you have any questions concerning this invoice, contact Customer Service 555-555-3333

THANK YOU FOR YOUR BUSINESS!

Figure 12-21.

64. Aroma Ristorante received a bill from Restaurant Equipment, Inc. (see Figure 12-22). Enter this bill into QuickBooks. Use the Enter Bills function and choose the 64200 Maintenance Fee Expense account to record the bill.

65. Aroma Ristorante received a bill from Best Point of Sale Company (see Figure 12-23). Enter this bill into QuickBooks. Use the Enter Bills function and choose the 61700 Computer and Internet Expenses account to record the bill.

66. Aroma Ristorante received a bill from STK Waste Removal, Inc. (see Figure 12-24). Enter this bill into QuickBooks. Use the Enter Bills function and choose the 68600 Utilities Expense account to record the bill.

Invoice

3/31/2008

Restaurant Equipment, Inc
5454 Arlington Avenue
Capital City, NY 11113

Payment Terms:
Net 15

To: Aroma Ristorante,
5000 Capital Park, Capital City, NY 11100
or Your Hometown, Your State, XXXXX

Monthly Service Contract for March 2008	**$120.00**
Total Due	**$120.00**

Your Prompt Payment is Appreciated.

Figure 12-22.

Best Point of Sale Company   INVOICE

INVOICE NO.   18267
DATE   March 31, 2008

1549 Capital City Drive
Capital City, NY 11112

TO   Aroma Ristorante
                Capital City, NY 11100 or Your Hometown, Your State XXXXX

Account	JOB	PAYMENT TERMS	DUE DATE
23652		Net 15	4/15/08

DESCRIPTION	UNIT PRICE	LINE TOTAL
Point of Sale Monthly Maintenance Contract for March 2008	$ 200.00	$ 200.00
SUBTOTAL	$	200.00
SALES TAX		
TOTAL	$	**200.00**

Thank you for your business.

Figure 12-23.

```
INVOICE #34098


STK WASTE REMOVAL, INC.
8427 HWY 55
HOMETOWN, NY 17777



TO: AROMA RISTORANTE
CAPITAL CITY, NY 11100 OR YOUR HOMETOWN, YOUR STATE XXXXX
```

3/31/2008	Terms: 2%10 net 30
Waste Removal Service for March 2008	$350.00
TOTAL DUE	$350.00

Figure 12-24.

67. Write a check to Capital City Gazette for $20.00 for a monthly newspaper subscription fee. Use the Write Checks feature and choose the 62500 Dues and Subscriptions Expense account to record the transaction.

68. Record the payroll for March 16–March 31 using the information that follows (see Figures 12-25 and 12-26).

March 16–March 31 Pay period

First Name	Last Name	Position	Filing Status	Allowances	Salary or Hourly Rate	Regular Hours Worked 3/16/2008– 3/31/2008	OT Hours Worked 3/16/2008– 3/31/2008	Regular Hours Pay	OT Hours Pay
Peter	Petrov	Manager	Married	2	$45,000	80	N/A	$1,875.00	
Ji	Hiromi	Host	Single	0	$12.00	79	0	$948.00	
Carlos	Garcia	Bartender	Married	1	$12.00	79.5	0	$954.00	
Rosa	Gomez	Service & Bus Staff	Single	0	$8.00	18.5	0	$148.00	
Mary	Hoffman	Service & Bus Staff	Single	0	$8.00	80	6	$640.00	$72.00
Betthany	Stewart	Service & Bus Staff	Single	1	$8.00	22.75	0	$182.00	
Jason	Robertson	Chef	Married	3	$42,000	80	N/A	$1,750.00	
Amy	Jameson	Kitchen Staff	Married	1	$13.50	76.75	0	$1,036.13	
Deborah	Smith	Kitchen Staff	Single	0	$13.50	75	0	$1,012.50	
Amy	Yang	Kitchen Staff	Married	3	$13.50	16.5	0	$222.75	
Benjamin	Young	Kitchen Staff	Single	1	$13.50	21.75	0	$293.63	
Julia	Rodriquez	Expeditor	Single	0	$11.00	65	0	$715.00	
George	Watson	Dishwasher	Single	1	$10.00	79	0	$790.00	

Figure 12-25.

Tips	Total Gross Pay	Federal Income Tax	State Income Tax	Social Security 6.2%	Medicare 1.45%	Health (Employee)	Dental (Employee)	Extra Withholding	Net Pay	Net Pay No Tips
	$1,875.00	$156.00	$84.88	$116.25	$27.19	$25.00	$7.00	$0.00	$1,458.68	$1,458.68
	$948.00	$110.00	$30.30	$58.78	$13.75	$25.00	$7.00	$0.00	$703.18	$703.18
$765.25	$1,719.25	$153.00	$77.04	$106.59	$24.93	$25.00	$7.00	$20.00	$1,305.69	$540.44
$185.45	$333.45	$22.00	$1.60	$20.67	$4.84			$0.00	$284.34	$98.89
$745.55	$1,457.55	$164.00	$63.38	$90.37	$21.13	$25.00	$7.00	$15.00	$1,071.67	$326.12
$287.50	$469.50	$21.00	$5.50	$29.11	$6.81			$0.00	$407.08	$119.58
	$1,750.00	$117.00	$73.46	$108.50	$25.38	$25.00	$7.00	$0.00	$1,393.67	$1,393.67
	$1,036.13	$56.00	$31.30	$64.24	$15.02	$25.00	$7.00	$0.00	$837.56	$837.56
	$1,012.50	$119.00	$33.80	$62.78	$14.68	$25.00	$7.00	$0.00	$750.24	$750.24
	$222.75	$0.00	$0.00	$13.81	$3.23			$0.00	$205.71	$205.71
	$293.63	$4.00	$0.00	$18.20	$4.26			$0.00	$267.16	$267.16
	$715.00	$74.00	$17.20	$44.33	$10.37			$0.00	$569.10	$569.10
	$790.00	$65.00	$18.90	$48.98	$11.46	$25.00	$7.00	$0.00	$613.67	$613.67

March 16–March 31 Pay period–Employer Payroll Taxes

First Name	Last Name	Total Gross Pay	Social Security 6.2%	Medicare 1.45%	FUI .008%	SUI .054%	Health (Company)	Dental (Company)
Peter	Petrov	$1,875.00	$116.25	$27.19	$15.00	$101.25	$75.00	$25.00
Ji	Hiromi	$948.00	$58.78	$13.75	$7.58	$51.19	$75.00	$25.00
Carlos	Garcia	$1,719.25	$106.59	$24.93	$13.75	$92.84	$75.00	$25.00
Rosa	Gomez	$333.45	$20.67	$4.84	$2.67	$18.01		
Mary	Hoffman	$1,457.55	$90.37	$21.13	$11.66	$78.71	$75.00	$25.00
Betthany	Stewart	$469.50	$29.11	$6.81	$3.76	$25.35		
Jason	Robertson	$1,750.00	$108.50	$25.38	$14.00	$94.50	$75.00	$25.00
Amy	Jameson	$1,036.13	$64.24	$15.02	$8.29	$55.95	$75.00	$25.00
Deborah	Smith	$1,012.50	$62.78	$14.68	$8.10	$54.68	$75.00	$25.00
Amy	Yang	$222.75	$13.81	$3.23	$1.78	$12.03		
Benjamin	Young	$293.63	$18.20	$4.26	$2.35	$15.86		
Julia	Rodriquez	$715.00	$44.33	$10.37	$5.72	$38.61		
George	Watson	$790.00	$48.98	$11.46	$6.32	$42.66	$75.00	$25.00

Figure 12-26.

69. Physical inventory was taken today. Make the appropriate adjustments to the inventory accounts in QuickBooks. Use Adjust Quantity on Hand.

The Food Inventory is shown in Figure 12-27.

Item	Quantity On Hand	Physical Count as of 3/31/2008	Month-End Adjustment
Angel Hair Pasta	22	6	16
Asparagus Green lb	54	10	44
Baby Arugula lb	37	10	27
Balsamic Vinegar Bottle	33	8	25
Boneless Prosciutto	87	6	81
Butter – Unsalted lb	76	12	64

Figure 12-27.

Item	Quantity On Hand	Physical Count as of 3/31/2008	Month-End Adjustment
Capers – Small 32 oz jar	90	90	0
Chicken Breast Bnlss/Sknlss lb	195	20	175
Coffee Decaf, Case	3	1	2
Coffee High Test Roast, Case	2	1	1
Eggs Large	49	5	44
Espresso Pack, Decaf	1	1	0
Espresso Pack, Regular	2	1	1
Flour, W 50 lb	17	3	14
Garlic Fresh lb	79	10	69
Herb Oregano oz	190	36	154
Mahi Mahi Fillet lb	120	15	105
Mozzarella Cheese lb	91	15	76
Olive Oil, Extra Virgin, Case	13	4	9
Parmesan Shredded 5# Bag	40	9	31
Parmesan Wheel	11	3	8
Pecorino Cheese Lb	23	10	13
Pesto 64 oz	63	13	50
Pork Tenderloin	30	8	22
Ricotta P/Skim 15oz	35	15	20
Romaine, Baby, Case	20	6	14
Romano Cheese	12	4	8
Sea Salt 200g Bag	52	20	32
Shrimp 16–20/lb	115	25	90
Spaghetti, Case	23	6	17
Tilapia Fillet lb	115	20	95
Tomato Crushed #10 Can	59	23	36
Tomato It Plum #10 Can	64	24	40
Veal Loin lb	96	33	63
Veal Top Cutlet lb	115	38	77
Ziti Pasta, Case	17	5	12

Figure 12-27. (continued)

The Beer Inventory is shown in Figure 12-28.

The Wine Inventory is shown in Figure 12-29.

The Liquor Inventory is shown in Figure 12-30.

Item	Quantity On Hand	Physical Count as of 3/31/2008	Month-End Adjustment
Beer – Lager Bottle, Case	16	7	9
Beer – Porter Bottle, Case	11	3	8
Beer – Ale Bottle, Case	16	8	8
Keg – Domestic	5	2	3
Keg – Import Dark	4	1	3
Keg – Lite Domestic	3	2	1

Figure 12-28.

Item	Quantity On Hand	Physical Count as of 3/31/2008	Month-End Adjustment
Cabernet, Case	12	6	6
Chardonnay, Case	8	7	1
Chianti, Case	14	8	6
Merlot, Case	1	1	0
Pinot Gris, Case	5	4	1

Figure 12-29.

Item	Quantity On Hand	Physical Count as of 3/31/2008	Month-End Adjustment
Gin Premium – BTL	37	18	19
Gin Well – BTL	46	14	32
Liquor Premium – BTL	32	16	16
Rum – BTL	39	16	23
Vodka Premium – BTL	48	22	26
Vodka Well – BTL	37	19	18

Figure 12-30.

The Other Beverage Inventory is shown in Figure 12-31.

The Retail Inventory is shown in Figure 12-32.

70. Pay the quarterly sales tax liability in QuickBooks. Do not use Write Checks. (See "Record Sales Tax Payment," page 224).

Item	Quantity On Hand	Physical Count as of 3/31/2008	Month-End Adjustment
Club Soda	15	12	3
Cranberry Juice gal	54	25	29
Diet Soda – Box	10	8	2
Milk – Heavy Cream qt	99	25	74
Milk Gallon	51	9	42
Soda – Box	7	6	1

Figure 12-31.

Item	Quantity On Hand	Physical Count as of 3/31/2008	Month-End Adjustment
Aged Balsamic Large 250ml	23	23	0
Aged Balsamic Small 100ml	23	23	0
Aroma Cookbook	21	19	2
Dipping Oil Set	9	8	1
Mushroom Truffle Cream	0	0	0
Oil/Balsamic Set	22	21	1
Olive Oil 750ml	24	24	0
Olive Oil Extra Virgin 17 oz	0	0	0
Pasta Sauce Sampler	21	20	1

Figure 12-32.

Record the following month-end adjusting journal entries (problems 71 through 78):

71. At the beginning of the year, Aroma Ristorante purchased an insurance policy for $4,500. The policy covers the period from January 1 through June 30. The payment was recorded in the prepaid expenses account on January 1. No additional purchases were made. Prepare the adjusting journal entry for March to record the monthly insurance expense.

72. At the beginning of the year, Aroma Ristorante paid $3,000 for advertisements that will run monthly for one year. The payment was recorded in the prepaid expenses account on January 1 and no additional purchases were made. Prepare the adjusting journal entry for March to record the monthly advertising and marketing expense.

73. At the beginning of the year, Aroma Ristorante paid $2,200 for a liquor license that covers the next 24 months. The payment was recorded in the prepaid expenses account on January 1 and no additional purchases were made. Prepare the adjusting journal entry for March to record the monthly business license and permit expense.

74. Prior to the adjusting journal entry for March, the supplies inventory account balance was $3,228.12. At the end of the month, $1,979.19 of supplies remained in the supplies inventory. Prepare the adjusting journal entry for March to record supplies expense.

75. Accrued interest expense for the month of March is $312.50. Prepare the adjusting entry for March to record interest expense.

76. As of the end of the month, Aroma Ristorante has earned, but has not yet received, $32.00 of interest income on the savings account. Record the necessary adjusting journal entry using the appropriate accounts.

77. Record the monthly depreciation expense using the following information.

Furniture and Equipment	$ 190.58
Bar Equipment	$ 234.04
Kitchen Equipment	$ 2,049.58
China, Silver, Glassware, Linen	$ 52.98
Smallwares	$ 86.58
Computer Equipment	$ 450.00
Vehicles	$ 833.33

78. The Bad Debt Expense for the month of March is $174.05. Record the adjusting journal entry.

79. Use the following information to prepare the bank reconciliation for the month of March 2008. The restaurant received its monthly bank statement dated April 5, 2008.

The following information is based on the review of the monthly bank statement:

Bank Statement Balance:		$138,407.99
Outstanding Checks:		
Date	Payee	Amount
3/31/2008	Main Street Auto	$395.25
3/31/2008	Capital City Gazette	$20.00
3/31/2008	Mrs. Sally Shareholder	$1,000.00
Deposits Not Recorded by the Bank:		
Date		Amount
3/31/2008		$4,251.01
Interest Earned:		$4,131.02
Bank Service Charge:		$75.00

Reports

After completion of all transactions for March 2008, generate the following reports. (For Option B, only generate the appropriate reports for March.)

January Profit & Loss (Standard)

February Profit & Loss (Standard)

March Profit & Loss (Standard)

January 1–March 31 Profit & Loss (Standard)

January Balance Sheet (Standard)

February Balance Sheet (Standard)

March Balance Sheet (Standard)

Profit & Loss Budget vs. Actual Report, January 1–March 31

Sales by Item Summary Report, January 1–March 31

Cash Flow Forecast Report, January 1–March 31

10150 Checking Account: Over/Short Transactions by Account Report from January 1–March 31

Inventory Valuation Summary Report, March 31

Sales by Customer Summary Report, January 1–March 31

Collections Report, March 31

Chapter Review Problems

1. Based on the Balance Sheets and Profit & Loss Statements for January, February, and March, calculate the following liquidity measures for each month. Comment on the results. (See Glossary for Ratios.)
   a. Current Ratio
   b. Quick Ratio
   c. Working Capital

2. Based on the Balance Sheets and Profit & Loss for January, February, and March, calculate the following profitability measures for each month. Comment on the results. (See Glossary for Ratios.)
   a. Gross Profit Margin
   b. Total Cost of Sales Ratio
   c. Cost of Sales Ratio for Food
   d. Cost of Sales Ratio for Beverage
   e. Labor Cost Ratio
   f. Total Profit Margin
   g. Debt to Equity

3. Based on the Balance Sheets and Profit & Loss for January, February, and March, calculate the following profitability measures for February and March. Comment on the results. (See Glossary for Ratios.)
   a. Return on Assets
   b. Return on Equity
   c. Accounts Receivable Turnover
   d. Average Collection Period
   e. Inventory Turnover
   f. Asset Turnover

4. Assuming the industry standards are as follows, compare the ratios computed in problem 2 to the industry standards and comment on the results.

Industry Standard	
Cost of Sales Ratio–Food & Beverage	32%
Gross Profit Ratio	68%
Labor Cost Ratio	34%
Total Profit Margin	4%

5. Prepare a horizontal analysis of the comparative Profit & Loss Statements for February and March. Comment on the results.

6. Prepare a horizontal analysis of the comparative Balance Sheets for February and March. Comment on the results.

7. Based on the Inventory Valuation Summary report for March 31 and on the year-to-date retail income from the January 1–March 31 Profit & Loss Statement, determine if the current retail inventory levels are appropriate. (Refer to Figure 12-32, earlier in this chapter.).

8. Double-click on **10150 Checking Account: Over/Short** on the Balance Sheet at March 31 and generate the Transactions by Account Report for this account for January 1–March 31. Per review of this report, comment on the amounts recorded each week. What action would you recommend to improve the internal controls for cash?

9. Review the Cash Flow Forecast report for January 1–March 31. Based on the report, determine if the restaurant's cash management procedures are adequate. If necessary, what action would you recommend to management for improvement?

10. Review the Sales by Item Summary report for January 1–March 31. Make some suggestions you might make for future purchases and sales.

11. Review the Sales by Customer Summary report for January 1–March 31 and the Collections Report for March 31. Who are the top customers? Are they really top customers?

12. Generate the Profit & Loss Budget vs. Actual Report for January 1–March 31. Evaluate the restaurant's performance in comparison to budgeted amounts. Comment on your findings and suggest recommendations for management. Based on the first quarter, what would you project for the remainder of the year?

You can find additional Review Problems at *www.wiley.com/college/murphy.*

Glossary

Accounts Payable Liabilities owed to a creditor or creditors for the purchase of goods or services.

Accounts Receivable The amount due from customers from the sale of goods and services on credit.

Accounts Receivable Turnover = Net Credit Sales divided by Average Accounts Receivable. It is the number of times an organization turns over its receivables.

Accrual Basis Accounting Accounting type where revenue is recorded when it is earned and expenses are recorded when they have been incurred.

Administrator A person who manages a multi-user computer system.

Asset An owned item that has value.

Asset Turnover = Sales divided by Average Total Assets. It is a measure of an organization's ability to utilize its assets to generate sales.

Average Collection Period = 365 divided by Accounts Receivable Turnover. This identifies the average number of days it takes to convert receivables into cash.

Backup File An additional file copied to a storage device in case of failure. QuickBooks Backup Files (.QBB) are compressed files. (See *Compressed File.*) Backup Files must be restored.

Balance Sheet A tabulated summary of assets, liabilities, and owners' equity for an entity or an individual on a specific date.

Cash Basis Accounting Accounting type where business transactions are recorded when cash is received and when cash is disbursed.

Chart of Accounts A list of all accounts in the general ledger. Accounts can be identified by a specific reference number.

Common-Size Statement Sections of a statement are expressed as a percentage of a total amount in the statement.

Company Preferences Customization of a QuickBooks file to meet the needs of a business.

Compressed File A file where the size of data has been reduced in order to save storage space or to improve transmission.

Corrupt File A file that has been damaged and may be unrecoverable.

Cost of Sales Ratio = Cost of Goods Sold divided by Sales. It is the percentage of sales used to cover cost of goods sold.

Credit The right side of the general ledger account.

Current Asset Assets that will be used within one year or business cycle.

Current Liability Debts or obligations that are due within one year or business cycle.

Current Ratio = Current Assets divided by Current Liabilities. It is a measure of an organization's ability to pay its short-term debt.

Customer Center A QuickBooks module that allows access to customer information and transactions.

Data Integrity Validity of data (example: free of errors and software viruses).

Debit The left side of the general ledger account.

Debt to Equity = Total Liabilities divided by Total Equity. It measures the portion of assets financed by creditors and owners.

Desktop Screen display of a software program that uses graphics. QuickBooks main desktop is accessed by clicking the Home icon.

Dividend A distribution of company assets to its shareholders.

Drop-Down List A field that only shows one choice but reveals the rest of the list when the user clicks the arrow.

Drop-Down Menu A menu of items located at the top of the desktop that reveals options when a user clicks on it.

EasyStep Interview A series of questions that are used to create and customize a new QuickBooks company file.

Employee Center A QuickBooks module that allows access to employee information and transactions.

Field A specified area to input information.

File Corruption See *Corrupted File*.

File Extensions The suffix at the end of a filename denoting what type of file it is.

Financial Statements Documents used to communicate financial information to users. The documents are the Balance Sheet, Income Statement, Statement of Owner's Equity, and Statement of Cash Flows.

Flash Drive A small portable device used to store data that serves as a portable, durable drive.

General Ledger A file that includes all of the accounts in a company's chart of accounts and the account balance for each account.

Gross Profit = Sales minus Cost of Goods Sold.

Gross Profit Margin = Gross Profit divided by Sales. It is the percentage of sales remaining after the cost of goods sold has been deducted.

Hard Drive A device that reads and writes data to a disk; typically the main storage device of a computer.

Horizontal Analysis Shows changes in total dollar amounts and percentages from one period to another.

Icon A small image that represents a file, folder, or program on the desktop.

Income Statement A financial statement (also called a profit and loss statement) showing revenue, expenses, and net profit for a given period.

Internal Control Policies and procedures established by management to ensure compliance with laws and regulations, reliability of accounting records, protection of assets and efficiency of operations.

Intuit Company that developed QuickBooks, Quicken, and TurboTax software.

Inventory Turnover = The Cost of Goods Sold divided by Average Inventory. It measures how often the inventory is being used.

Invoice An itemized bill for goods or services that may contain payment terms.

Labor Cost Ratio = Total Labor Cost divided by Sales. It is the percentage of sales used to cover all labor costs.

Liability A debt or obligation due to an entity.

Liquidity The ability to pay short-term bills when they are due.

Long-Term Liability Debts and obligations that are due in more than one year or business cycle.

Owner's Equity = Total Assets minus Liabilities. It is the net worth of the business.

Password A secret combination of letters and/or numbers used to gain access to information.

Quick Ratio = Cash plus Short-Term Investments plus Accounts Receivables divided by Current Liabilities. It is a measure of an organization's ability to pay its short-term debt. It is more stringent than the current ratio.

QuickBooks Backup File .QBB An additional compressed file that is created for use when a working QuickBooks file is compromised. Backup files should be stored in a different location separate from the working file. Backup files must be restored using the QuickBooks application prior to use.

QuickBooks Working File .QBW A QuickBooks company file.

Ratio Analysis A tool used to assess a company's financial performance by evaluating relationships between components of the financial statements.

Record A collection of related fields that contain data about a subject or activity.

Report Center A QuickBooks module that allows access to various QuickBooks reports.

Restore File Recreating a company file using QuickBooks. Changing a company file from .QBB (back-up file) to .QBW (working file).

Retained Earnings An equity account that tracks the corporation's income and losses from its inception.

Return on Assets = Net Profit divided by Average Total Assets. It measures the organization's ability to use its assets to generate income.

Return on Equity = Net Profit divided by Average Owner's Equity. It measures the organization's ability to use equity to generate income.

Salvage Value An estimated value of an asset as of the anticipated date of disposal.

Server A computer on a network that services other computers.

Statement of Cash Flows A financial statement that shows a company's cash inflow and outflow over a specific time period.

Statement of Owner's Equity A financial statement that shows the changes in the owner's equity for a given period.

Stock A document that represents a share of ownership in an organization.

Total Profit Margin = Net Profit divided by Sales. It is the percentage of net profit generated from each dollar of sales.

Trial Balance A list of the debit and credit balances of all the accounts in the general ledger. The total of all the debits balances should be equal to the total of all the credit balances.

Vendor Center A QuickBooks module that allows access to vendor information and transactions.

Window A scrollable rectangular display on the screen. Windows can be minimized, maximized, or closed.

Working Capital = Current Assets minus Current Liabilities. It is a measure of an organization's ability to pay its short-term debt.

Index

CUSTOMER NOTE: IF THIS BOOK IS ACCOMPANIED BY SOFTWARE, PLEASE READ THE FOLLOWING BEFORE OPENING THE PACKAGE.

This software contains files to help you utilize the models described in the accompanying book. By opening the package, you are agreeing to be bound by the following agreement:

This software product is protected by copyright and all rights are reserved by the author, John Wiley & Sons, Inc., or their licensors. You are licensed to use this software on a single computer. Copying the software to another medium or format for use on a single computer does not violate the U.S. Copyright Law. Copying the software for any other purpose is a violation of the U.S. Copyright Law.

This software product is sold as is without warranty of any kind, either express or implied, including but not limited to the implied warranty of merchantability and fitness for a particular purpose. Neither Wiley nor its dealers or distributors assumes any liability for any alleged or actual damages arising from the use of or the inability to use this software. (Some states do not allow the exclusion of implied warranties, so the exclusion may not apply to you.)